Final Rounds

FINAL ROUNDS

A Father, A Son,
The Golf Journey of a Lifetime

James Dodson

CENTURY

Published in the United Kingdom in 1997 by
Century

1 3 5 7 9 10 8 6 4 2

Copyright © James Dodson, 1996

The right of James Dodson to be identified as the
author of this work has been asserted by him in accordance
with the Copyright, Designs and Patents Act, 1988.

First published in the United Kingdom in 1997 by Century
Random House UK Ltd
20 Vauxhall Bridge Road, London, SW1V 2SA

Random House Australia (Pty) Limited
20 Alfred Street, Milsons Point, Sydney,
New South Wales 2061, Australia

Random House New Zealand Limited
18 Poland Road, Glenfield
Auckland 10, New Zealand

Random House South Africa (Pty) Limited
Endulini, 5a Jubilee Road, Parktown 2193, South Africa

Random House UK Limited Reg. No. 954009

A CIP catalogue record for this book is available from the British Library

Papers used by Random House UK Limited are natural, recyclable products made
from wood grown in sustainable forests. The manufacturing processes conform to the
environmental regulations of the country of origin.

Printed and bound in Great Britain by
Mackays of Chatham PLC, Chatham, Kent

ISBN 0 71 267741 0

To A. with love.
For our fathers.

A C K N O W L E D G M E N T S

Many people had a hand in creating this book. I owe a tremendous debt of gratitude to Mike Purkey, senior editor at *Golf Magazine*, who first suggested I turn our trip into a book, and Jennifer Hershey at Bantam Books for guiding the project to life. Brian Tart (who really should play more golf) did a masterful job of the final editing and Ginger Barber is a writer's dream agent (too bad she plays only tennis). I must thank others who have rendered cheerful support and enthusiasm along the way. They include Robin McMillan, David Barrett, and Jim Frank of *Golf Magazine*, Gary Walther, editor-in-chief of *Departures Magazine*, Lee Walburn at *Atlanta Magazine*, and the indispensable Tim Clark at *Yankee Magazine*. A special thanks to Bob Sommers, retired editor of *Golf Journal*. I'm grateful to Tony Nickson of Royal Lytham, Norman Crewe of Royal Birkdale, Douglas and Colin Dagleish, and Archie Baird of Muirfield for his spirited generosity and the use of the riding cart. Also, Tony and Julie Gilbert of Carnoustie, Tom and Elizabeth Jessop, and the unsinkable Murdo MacPherson. Thanks to Ms. Randy Jones (my daughter's godmother) and British Airways for helping us go in style. I'm deeply grateful to Edith Hazard, a pal who had the sense to tell me what not to include in the text, and to Kathleen Bennie, my Royal and Ancient mother-in-law, whose wisdom is exceeded only by her remarkably tolerant good humor. I'm grateful to my regular pals—Pat, Terry, and Sid—for bringing me back to the game when I needed it most. Most of all, I thank Opti for giving me the game and much more than I can ever properly repay. I know I still owe him some pocket change.

Thus is the earth at once a desert and a paradise, rich in secret hidden gardens, gardens inaccessible, but to which the craft leads us ever back, one day or another. Life may scatter us and keep us apart; it may even prevent us from thinking very often of one another; but we know that our comrades are somewhere "Out there"—where, one can hardly say—silent, forgotten, but deeply faithful. And when our path crosses theirs, they greet us with such manifest joy, shake us so gaily by the shoulders! Indeed we are accustomed to waiting.

—Antoine de Saint-Exupéry, *Wind, Sand and Stars*

It is nothing new or original to say that golf is played one stroke at a time. But it took me many years to realize it.

—Bobby Jones

A Father's Voice

Toward the end of the afternoon, Tom Watson sits in his office talking to a golf writer. The golf season has just ended. The golf writer is me. We have been talking for almost two hours. There is a thin skin of ice on the pond in the park across the street. Traffic is a muted sigh in the winter shadows of Kansas City. Christmas presents for his children are stacked neatly in a shopping bag at his feet. Watson's wariness of the press is famous, but he has been relaxed and generous, talking about the Ryder Cup team he will soon lead to Britain, about his life, career, children, heroes, even making self-deprecating jokes about his well-publicized putting woes. This pleases me, confirms my best hopes. Watson is forty-three, five years my senior, the best golfer of my generation, now a lion in winter. In my former life as a political journalist, it would have been deemed grossly unprofessional to admit I am my subject's fan. But golf, unlike politics, as Alister Mackenzie is supposed to have once said, is at least an honest game. I am Watson's fan because he played with such honesty and heart during his golden days, and because of how he conducts himself now that the glory has faded and his game seems almost mortal.

Sometimes during these conversations, I find myself unexpectedly wondering with pleasure how I got here. For me, a kid who tagged after his golf heroes and was lucky enough to grow up and be able to sit and talk with them, it's a dream job and a question rooted perhaps as much in philosophy as journalism. All philosophy begins in wonder, and the wonder of what Watson suddenly, intimately reveals of himself in our conversation is both thought-provoking and surprising. I ask if he can identify the worst moment of his career, and he responds by telling me about once rushing out of the locker room at the World Series of Golf, brushing off a boy seeking his autograph. The boy's father followed him and tapped him on the back.

"He looked me straight in the eye and said, 'I just want to tell you, Mr. Watson, what an asshole I think you are. My son was really a fan of yours.'" Watson shakes his head. "I couldn't believe it—how badly I felt, I mean." He falls silent, pursing his lower lip. Somewhere outside the building I can hear Christmas music playing, a slurry rendition of "Jingle Bells" fading away. There are writers around who would love to challenge Tom Watson's sincerity on this, question how such a trivial moment could possibly compare, say, to his heartbreaking loss to Seve Ballesteros at the '84 British Open at St. Andrews. A wayward two-iron shot at the infamous Road Hole cost him a record-tying sixth Open title and made the fiery Spaniard the new darling of the British masses. For a second or two, Watson stares at the running tape recorder, then shakes his head again. "I still feel bad about it," he says simply.

The thing is, I believe him. Watson could not believe what he says he believes—namely, that golf represents the most honorable of games—and feel otherwise. So I flip the coin—best to part on a cheerful note—and ask him for the best moment of his golf life, certain he will either say his famous shot-making duel against Nicklaus at Turnberry in '77 or his "miracle" chip-in at Pebble Beach in '82 to win the U.S. Open. "It's funny," he says, pausing again, "the greatest thrill I had may have been the day my father invited me to join him and a couple of his regular golf buddies at his club. I was so excited, really aching to show him what I could do. I guess I was maybe eleven or twelve." Watson, the former Stanford psychology student, studies me with those eyes that always look as if he's been out walking in a linksland wind. "Even now I think about that. It was a very powerful moment. My father means so much to me. I can always hear his voice in my head, telling me to keep my head still or make a good swing. I don't know if I ever felt that way again, you know?" He smiles somewhat wistfully, revealing the boyish gaps in his teeth. Turning off the tape recorder, I admit that I know what he means because I hear my father's voice, too.

Almost every day of my life.

Opti the Mystic

That Christmas, I sent my father a new set of golf clubs.

I was sure he'd love them. After all, they were ultralight and graphite-shafted, designed to put zip back into a faltering swing, the latest thing in "super senior" equipment technology. My father's Wilson Staffs were almost as old as me, heavy blades meant for a man half his age and twice his strength.

He sent them back to me two weeks later. The box was barely opened but a pleasant note was attached, addressed to Bo, his nickname for me. *"Thanks for your thoughtful gesture, Bo. These are mighty handsome clubs, but I don't think they're for me. I have a good idea, though. Since these are so light and easy to swing, why not keep them for Maggie and Jack to use? I'd be honored to buy them their first clubs. I've enclosed a check. Love, Dad."*

The check was for a thousand dollars. He'd clearly missed the point of my thoughtful gesture. I called my mother to see if perhaps her husband had recently been beaned on the golf course or simply forgotten that his grandchildren were only three and four, respectively, more interested in making music with a purple dinosaur than divots in the yard. When I explained the situation to her, she laughed and said, "Well, sweetie, bear with him. Just between you and me, I think your father may be a little down in the dumps. Although with him, as you know, it's never easy to tell."

She was right. My old man was the original Silver Lining Guy, a man who could have taught the entire Hemlock Society the power of positive thinking. As a teenager I dubbed him, not entirely kindly, Opti the Mystic because of his relentless good cheer, his imperturbable knack of seeing any problem or crisis as "an opportunity for growth," and his embarrassing habits of kissing strange babies in grocery stores, always smiling at strangers, and quoting somebody like Aristotle or Emerson when you least expected it, usually in the presence of my impressionable high school dates.

Among Opti's more unfortunate personality traits, in my view at the time, was that he appeared utterly immune to social embarrassment and almost went out of his way to expose his crazy optimism to strangers. One time he picked me up from a guitar lesson with a startling occupant in his car: a drunk in a Santa suit. He'd found the man wandering aimlessly around the parking lot of his office building with a bottle of wine under a wing, muttering about shooting himself for the holidays.

Only Opti would have rescued a suicidal Santa and attempted to cheer him up. We took the man to the Irving Park Delicatessen, and Dad bought him a hot meal. The man poured out his tale of woe to us—he was dead broke and his wife thought he was a bum and his girlfriend was pregnant again. But after the spiel he calmed down and sobered up and even appeared to feel slightly better for having gotten his problems off his chest. We dropped him off in front of his dingy crackerbox house on the east side of town, and Dad discreetly slipped him a fifty-dollar bill and asked him to buy something nice for his wife.

Perhaps it was a foolish gesture, a hopeless charity. The man's social worker, if he had one, would no doubt have said it was money burned. The guy was just going to go buy more wine and drink himself into oblivion and maybe even shoot himself after all.

I *still* don't know. What I do know is that as he left our car, the man reached over and grabbed the arm of my jacket with a surprisingly firm grip and looked at me with his bloodshot eyes. "Your father's a real southern gentleman, kid," he growled. "I hope you fuckin' *know* that. Merry Christmas."

I knew Opti was a southern gentleman because people told me this my whole life—school chums who thought my old man was cool, girlfriends who thought him amusing and gallant, parents who needlessly reminded me how lucky I was to have a dad like that. In Mrs. Moon's English class I couldn't read Geoff Chaucer's line about the noble knight en route to Canterbury with the other pilgrims—"a gentle, parfit knight"—or hear the voice of Dickens's Old Fezziwig exhorting his employees and neighbors to come join the Christmas dance, without thinking of Opti, my sappy old man.

I knew of plenty of small acts of kindness Opti had quietly perpetrated over the years—funds he sent to crackpot relatives whom the rest of the family ignored, employees he'd helped through hard times, strangers whose cars he'd hauled from ditches, dogs he'd fetched from interstate medians. But on the downside, it sometimes annoyed me to have people think I had such a saint for a dad, a human Hallmark card for a father.

If Opti, after all this time, was now finally "in the dumps" even a little bit, as my mother described it, this qualified as big news. My first thought was that it must be his health. After all, his advertising business was thriving, his golf handicap was holding steady at 22. Pointing out that Cicero learned Greek in his seventies and Socrates took up playing the lyre in his dotage, Dad liked to say he would indeed someday consider retiring, when and if he finally got *old*. But even he had to accept that he couldn't live forever.

It was easy to forget that Dad was pushing eighty and facing, medically speaking, a situation that would have wilted the spirits of a man half his age: a daily injection of insulin and the unpleasant aftereffects of a radical colostomy, now almost a decade old, as well as a poorly done trim job on his prostate that left him wearing a pair of unwieldy collection bags strapped to his thighs the way some undercover cops pack a .38. He also suffered from a deteriorating cataract condition that caused his left eye to drift in and out of focus. His knees were weak, and his hearing was going. Typically, he never even mentioned these problems, and if we mentioned them, he merely laughed off our concerns.

"So what's wrong?" I asked my mother. I was afraid she was going to tell me he'd fallen off the roof while cleaning out the gutters and damaged his excellent shoulder turn. Perhaps he ruined his remaining good eye for lining up putts by blowing up the gas grill in his face.

"He lost his golf group."

I thought about what she said. "You must be joking," I finally replied.

"I wish."

This explained a lot. Dad dearly loved his longtime Saturday morning golf group—Bill, Alex, Richard, and sometimes an old Chapel Hill friend named Bob Tilden. They fussed and squabbled at each other like old married folk and could find more ways to take each other's pocket change than a convention of Times Square pickpockets. But they were clearly addicted to each other's intimate sporting companionship in the best way available to fully grown, heterosexual, registered Republican southern males. I once tried to explain the allure of this mysterious exclusive male phenomenon to my nongolfing Yankee-born spouse, pointing out that its high-minded origins probably date back to ancient Greece, where lonely sports widows used to call it *agape*, an even higher and purer manifestation of the spiritual passion, say, than Arnold feels for Winnie Palmer. My nongolfing spouse only shook her head at the mystery of men.

It turned out that Bill Mims, Dad's best friend and primary golf nemesis, had developed a heart condition that allowed him to play only on warm mornings, and Alex the Scotsman had retired and moved to the south of France with his wife, Andrée. Richard had somehow just "lost interest in playing" when the others gave up the game, which left only Dad, the senior swordsman of the group, to try and soldier along the links on a regular basis.

"He's taken to playing with younger men," Mom reported in a carefully lowered voice, as though Opti might be listening in the other room. "But I honestly don't think he *likes* it."

"*Of course* he doesn't like it!" I shouted back at her, thinking of how desolate I'd feel if my own regular group of buddies and bandits suddenly vanished from my life. "That's why these clubs I sent him are so important. They'll help subdue those dangerous young turks!"

"In that case, maybe you should send them again," she suggested primly. "I'll speak to him."

I mailed the high-tech super senior wonder clubs to North Carolina the next morning, along with the check; he sent the clubs back to Maine the next week. The only people prospering from this long-distance minuet, I began to realize, were the boys in brown from United Parcel Service.

"*Dear Bo,*

Again, many thanks. I just don't think these clubs are right for me. Maybe I'm just too sentimentally attached to my old Wilsons. After all, we've been down a lot of fairways together. *(Ha ha.) I do appreciate you thinking about me, though. When's your next research trip? Any chance you'll be coming this way? I'd enjoy a chance to pin your ears back on the course. Love, Dad."*

Opti the Mystic had spoken. Ha ha.

I donated the clubs to the church's summer auction committee, hoping somebody could find use for them.

The poet Ovid said we give gifts to try and seduce men and the gods.

Seduction was obviously my game. Deep in my heart, I knew that. With those clubs, I wanted to seduce my father into believing he could still compete in the most difficult and fulfilling game of all. I wanted his game to rediscover its vigor and the golf gods to grant us a bit more time on the links together.

We had been golf pals for thirty years, ever since he put the club in my hand at about age ten, showed me the Vardon grip, and introduced me to the complicated splendors of the game he loved most. Like Tom Watson, I can remember the day my father invited me to play with him at his club as if it were yesterday. I was thirteen, the age Mark Twain says boys begin to imitate the best and worst traits of their fathers. I barely broke 100.

Thirteen is the age of manhood in most cultures. My father helped me become a man, and golf showed me the way. But it wasn't easy. I threw a lot of tantrums in those days. I threw a lot of clubs, too. Early on, I cheated, shaved my scores, ignored rules I found stupid or inconvenient. I didn't wish to play golf so much as *conquer* it. As I look back, I don't know how my father tolerated these volcanic outbursts. I was so impatient and in such a rush to reach the future somewhere down the fairway and finally be *good* that he would sometimes place a hand on my shoulder to slow my pace and urge me to "relax and enjoy the round. The game ends far too soon, Bo."

I didn't have a clue what he really meant. He was given to pronouncements like that, an adman with a poet's heart.

Watching me flail at the game, he once observed, "The peculiar thing about this game—any game really, but this game far more than most—is, the more you fight it, the more it eludes you. Everything contains its opposite. By trying to make something magical happen, you create the opposite effect—you drive the magic away. When you worry about finding the way, you lose the path. Someone said the way to heaven is heaven. A little less is a lot more."

He sounded so damn sure about this, I almost hated him for it. Once when I was sulking about a skulled shot, he made me lie down on the golf course. It was so embarrassing—a group of men were back on the tee waiting to hit —but I did it anyway. "What do you feel?" he asked.

"*Really* stupid," I replied, feeling the cool, firm earth beneath my back. It felt good, but I couldn't or wouldn't admit that to him.

"Then tell me what you see."

"Nothing. My eyes are closed."

"Then open them," he suggested. "That way, you'll see everything."

I didn't begin to understand Opti's little exercises, or his words. Not then, at any rate.

It is the fashion these days to speak of golf as a kind of religious experience, a doorway to the spiritual side of man, an egress to the eternal. My father was a man of faith, but I don't think he viewed the golf course as a path to God. He thought golf was a way to celebrate the divinity of life, the here and now, and simply the best way to *play*. He loved healthy competition and was playful to the core. During the Depression, he'd played semipro baseball and helped guide his high school football team to the state finals. Ironically, he'd made money as a caddy in those days but couldn't afford to take up the game seriously until he went away to war and discovered the great golf links of England and Scotland.

For thirty years my father had been the senior southern rep for the world's largest industrial publishing firm. He'd transformed a sleepy advertising backwater into a thriving multimillion-dollar territory, becoming one of his company's legends in the process. Both of us knew he would never give all that up and "officially" retire because he found the daily grind so rewarding and fun. To Opti, hard work was a form of play because work involved solving problems, a life view that fit the philosophy of his favorite game like a glove. Golf was the ultimate playful exercise in problem solving. The real joy of playing, he said more than once, was bound up in the mental process required to create solutions to the riddle of any particular golf shot—an unfair break, a horrendous lie in the rough, and so forth. Golf was the greatest challenge because no two golf shots were ever the same. Every situation was unique, every moment "new and pregnant with possibilities"—another of his favorite phrases. In his view, this explained why the best players were almost always imaginative shot-makers—they could see the problem, create the solution, and seize the pleasure of the moment.

To him, golf was also a character builder that could teach you valuable lessons about yourself, others, and the wide world around you. For that reason, he was a stickler for the rules, a gentle but firm rulebook Elijah. I used to hate this about him, besides all the cornball philosophizing. You marked your ball properly; you fixed dents in the green; you putted in turn; you offered to tend the pin; you congratulated an opponent on a good shot. I sensed he believed these silly courtesies were as *essential* to the game as oxygen, but I suffocated under their constriction.

One day I missed a short putt and slammed my putter into the lush surface of the fifteenth green at Green Valley Golf Club, my father's club. He grew silent, then calmly insisted that I leave the golf course. To add insult to injury, he made me walk straight into the clubhouse, report my crime, and apologize to the head pro. The head pro's name was Aubrey Apple. He was a large man with a smoldering stump of cigar jammed in a corner of his mouth. A profane legend in Carolina golf circles and a teacher who had sent several fine players into the professional rank, Apple called kids like me "Valley Rats." When I'd reported my crime, the pro shifted the smoldering stump to the other corner of his mouth. "You're Brack Dodson's kid, ain't cha?" My father's name was Brax Dodson but it didn't seem like the right moment to correct him. I merely nodded. "Anybody who beats up my golf greens," Apple said, "is a little shit. We don't need any little shits out here." He then summarily banished me from the golf course for two weeks. This verdict was torture, like a death sentence.

Eventually, when I calmed down and grew up, golf became much more than a game between my old man and me. It acted as my personal entry hatch to my father's morally advanced cosmos—a means of seeing who this funky, funny, oddball philosopher really *was*, and who I needed to become. I know no other game that would have permitted us the opportunity to compete so thoroughly, so joyfully, for so long. The golf course—any golf course, anywhere— became our playground and refuge, the place where we sorted things out or escaped them altogether, debated without rancor, found common ground, discovered joy, suspended grief, competed like crazy, and took each other's pocket change.

We played the day Neil Armstrong walked on the moon, and the day Martin Luther King was gunned down in Memphis. We played the day before I got married, and the day after my son Jack was born. We played through rain, wind, heat, birth, death. We played on holidays, birthdays, to celebrate nothing and everything, so many rounds in so many places, I couldn't possibly remember them all. We played some of the best courses in America, and some of the worst cow pastures and goat tracks, too. We discovered that in good company there is no such thing as a bad golf course.

We preferred to play late in the day, following our shadows in the last of the light, the fairway ahead of us robed in hues of red and gold and very often deserted. You could see the contours of the earth so well then, feel the coolness of approaching night, perhaps witness a sliver of moon rising over the creek poplars. Our routine almost never varied. My father would leave work early, I would ride my bike to the club, with my bag swaying on my back. After the round, he would put my bike in the trunk of his car. Sometimes we would grab dinner at the Boar and Castle on the way home, sit eating our Castle steaks in the rustling grapevine arbor while eaves-dropping on the murmurous voices of teenage lovers in the musky foliage around us, or sit in the glowing foxfire of the Buick's radio, listening to the evening news report. There were race riots going on in Memphis and Miami one summer. A full-blown war was raging in Southeast Asia. Poor people marched on Washington, Bobby Kennedy was shot. A tidal wave of so much news—and yet so *far away* from us. A couple times, we stayed out on the golf course to look at stars. My father knew the constellations. He showed me Venus, the evening star, Aries the ram, how to find the North Star if I was ever lost in the woods. I never got lost in the woods, but I loved those times and never even knew it. It's as if I were sleepwalking and he was inviting me to awaken.

This pattern of play, this communion of being, carried us straight through my college years and into my first reporter's job at the same newspaper where he'd begun as a copy runner in the early 1930s. For years we would meet at a golf course somewhere, get in nine, sometimes eighteen before dusk. We walked and carried our bags. Later we took carts, to spare his legs. We did this for years up and down the East Coast, in big cities and small towns. We found this a great time to talk. No topic was out of bounds: sex, women, God, career, money. We argued intensely about Nixon's Cambodian policy, TV evangelists, the fate of the modern novel, orange golf balls. We had epic putting duels on darkened putting greens, in motel rooms, in the lobbies of his business clients.

Jung said children dream their fathers' dreams. In those private moments of play, something ordained my future and sealed my fate. As a boy, I dreamed of being either an actor or a classical guitarist; I grew up instead to become a political journalist, a job I worked hard at for a while before having the good fortune to become a golf writer. More important, at several particularly difficult moments in my life, when I drifted away from the game and even seemed to lose sight of my life's purpose, my old man was always there to shepherd me back to golf, and myself.

Out of the blue he would call up, make a joke, challenge me to a round. He always said he was going to pin my ears back, though he seldom did. He wasn't just my best golf pal, but my best friend.

That's really something. I see that now. As a father of small children myself, I perhaps know some of what he knew, felt, and understood way back then: that we really get only a few precious moments to connect before the magic vanishes. Not surprisingly, I read my children the same storybooks my father read me. The *Just So Stories, Treasure Island, Stuart Little.* Their overwhelming favorite, as it was mine—written by a Scotsman to entertain his niece—is about a boy who lives to duel a notorious pirate in Neverland, a lad who refuses to grow up because life outside that magical realm where no one visibly ages or has to eat their veggies is clearly no fun. Only when Peter Pan fails to believe in happy thoughts does he fail to fly.

The truth is, when my father sent back the new golf clubs, I couldn't bear to think he and I had played our final rounds together. That's why I'd tried to bribe both him and the golf gods.

A child's belief is so strong, an adult's so fragile. At forty, I was *still* my father's child, and I told myself we had unfinished business in Neverland—somewhere out on the golf course. If we believed that, we could still *fly*.

It was not until the next October—far too long to suit my tastes—that we played again. I'd been working hard, traveling a lot, trying to figure out why it was that whenever I was in some glorious, glamorous golf place, I spent so much of my time thinking about home, worrying about my children and my roses, both of which require a lot of hands-on attention.

Two of my colleagues at *Golf Magazine* invited me to join them for a round at Pinehurst Number 2, the marvelous Donald Ross course where Opti and I had played many rounds over the years. The course was one of his favorites. I invited my father to join us, and he agreed.

The day was raw, wet, and cold, and everyone's game was off, but my father's was really desolate. He topped balls and missed putts he could once have made with his eyes shut. At one point I was passing a steep fairway bunker when I heard him sheepishly call my name. I turned and saw him asking me for a hand up. I reached and took his hand. It was trembling ever so slightly. My heart almost broke on the spot.

We attempted to joke off the disaster on the hour drive home. I told Dad those super senior clubs he rejected would have saved his skin, and he said at least nobody died in the train wreck. We rode along for a little while in silence, looking at the slick road and rainy countryside. He seemed as down as I'd ever seen him. Then an idea came to me.

"Let's take a trip," I said.

"What trip?"

"The trip we always talked about. The one we never took."

He glanced at me and steered Old Blue, his ancient barge-sized Cadillac, around a farmer pulling a hay wagon.

"Don't you remember?" I said.

"Of course. But you go there all the time."

"I go there all the time by myself," I corrected him. "I've never been there with you. We've got some unfinished business."

"I suppose so." He managed to conceal his enthusiasm for the idea. I hoped his rotten day on the course accounted for this.

In any event, that's where it really began, the first step in our final golf journey—a trip to the places where he learned to play golf as a sergeant in the Eighth Army Air Corps during the war. "There" was St. Andrews, the birthplace of the game. Thousands of golfers went there every year. But we hadn't. It was now or never and almost that simple.

But nothing is really that simple. I knew not to push my father on the subject. Things were obviously changing fast in his life. Losing his golf pals had merely revealed his mortality. I sensed a powerful urgency in him to tie up loose ends, to finish whatever needed finishing at home and in his life and work.

We didn't speak of it again for months. I got on with my own life, telling myself I'd planted a proper seed. What else could I do? I hoped—I even prayed—it would grow.

Life is weather, someone said. Life is meals—in my case lots of *airplane* meals. Almost before I realized it, summer had come again to Maine, and the routines of my own family's life had nudged thoughts of the trip to the back of my mind. Due to the wet spring, my roses had grown into a tumult of blossoms and thorns that badly needed pruning. But on the plus side, and seemingly overnight, my daughter Maggie had learned to swim in a tea-colored lake, while Jack had taken to stalking around the yard making surprisingly Hoganesque swings at pine cones, half-chewed golf balls, and the occasional sleeping golden retriever, with a cut-down seven-iron he mysteriously called his "outside club."

The mystery resolved itself when I heard him call his cut-down putter his "inside club." *Of course*, I thought. *That's exactly what it is.* During telecasts of golf tournaments, you see, I sometimes practiced my putting on the living-room rug, and the kids, bored with further demolishing their rooms and finger painting the dog, occasionally joined in. Jack never lasted long—the game was obviously too sedate for him. Maggie, on the other hand, displayed signs of becoming a putting prodigy, which perhaps explains why she felt compelled to reveal gleefully to her entire kindergarten class that her father had a job "watching golf on TV." On parents' night, her teacher leaned forward and confided, "My husband would love to have your job. Do you get to play golf with Jack Norman? Ed *adores* him."

"I'm sorry. Who?" I was pretty sure she meant *Greg* Norman.

"The one they call the White Shark."

Unfortunately no, I hated to admit to her. I said Maggie mostly got it right. When I wasn't watching the world's finest golfers perform in person, I was usually watching them on the tube. I left out the uninteresting part about flying forty thousand miles a year, renting the same tired rental cars, and staying in the same tired hotel rooms as I raced either to conduct an interview or to see a golf resort and then raced home.

For some reason many airports are located next to golf courses, and frequently that spring and summer, when I was doing that part of my job, I found myself gazing from a plane window at an unmistakable oasis of green, a familiar patchwork of fairways below, idly wondering if my father had completely forgotten about the golf trip I'd proposed. I heard nothing about it from his end. Hope began to fade. Maybe I would offer to take *Ed* instead.

Stories about the fiftieth anniversary of the Allied invasion of France began to crop up on the news. Reunions were about to happen, old paratroopers were mustering for a jump in Belgium. Clinton went to Normandy. I went off to California to interview a young tour player somebody said would be the next Nicklaus, which usually guarantees nobody will remember him in another ten years.

Then one day in early July, the phone rang. It was Opti. We made our usual lighthearted banter about the state of the world and the decline of civilization as we knew it for a few minutes, then he paused and said:

"Okay. You set the whole thing up, and we'll go. Let's shoot for late summer, after all the D-Day hoopla has settled down."

"Great," I said without hesitation, knowing exactly what he was talking about, trying not to sound *too* pleased. My elation was so strong, I actually felt light-headed and couldn't have been happier if Greg Norman had called up inviting me to play golf *and* borrow his yacht for the weekend.

"I'll give you seven strokes a side on a two-dollar nassau. Two bits for greenies and sandies. Please don't ask for more, though. You're getting the senior citizen discount."

This was our usual game.

"Who's asking for more? I'll take six and pin your ears back, insolent pup."

By early August, everything was set. I'd made plane and hotel reservations, reserved the rental car, and contacted several club secretaries who were enthusiastic about helping out. It read like a grand tour of the British golf establishment: Sunningdale, Royal Birkdale, Royal Lytham, Turnberry, Royal Troon, Carnoustie, possibly Gleneagles and Muirfield, and of course, St. Andrews. I'd been to most of these places on my own but couldn't wait to go back with my old man.

Two weeks before the trip, he called again.

I took the call on our cell phone, standing out behind the perennial garden where I was trying to figure out the best place to build my daughter a playhouse like the one she'd seen in a local theater production of *Peter Pan.*

"I'm afraid the trip will have to be postponed," he said. With a sinking heart, I asked why.

"I had some bleeding. I didn't think it was any big deal, but I guess I was wrong. They did some tests. They want to do some more, starting tomorrow."

The cancer of a decade ago had come back, he said, spreading radically throughout his pelvic region. It had moved into his back, had even invaded his stomach and intestines.

I asked for the official prognosis and will never forget what he told me: *a month, two at most.*

Then he laughed. Only Opti would have laughed at such a verdict. He said he would call back in a couple more days when he knew more.

I hung up the phone and sat down on a wooden bench. My first thought was undeniably selfish: *Christ, we'll never play golf again.* I went through the next few days in a trance. I tried to read stories to my children but kept missing passages. I tried to write my columns and prune my roses but nothing helped. I went to my golf club and played three holes and quit. I picked up the phone to begin canceling reservations but put the receiver down again.

Then my father called back.

"Well, the options are not good," Opti said, sounding eerily like his old self. "They can pump me full of poisons and maybe hook me up to some machines and buy a few more weeks. Who the hell needs that?" He said he planned to let nature take its course.

I told him I admired his courage.

He told me to save my lung power for the golf course.

"I'm planning to whip your tail at Lytham and St. Andrews," he said. "Hope you haven't canceled those reservations or anything."

I said I hadn't.

"Good. Here are my terms," he continued. "No complaints. No long faces. We go to have laughs, hit a few balls, maybe take a bit of the Queen's currency from each other's pockets. But when I say it's time to go home, I go home. No questions asked. I've got plenty of stuff to do. But I do want to pin your ears back for old times' sake—so you'll at least remember me."

I sort of laughed; then agreed.

"Good. See you at the airport in Atlanta," he barked happily, banging down the phone.

Opti the Mystic had spoken again.

I went out and finally pruned my roses, damn near barbering them to the ground.

The Road Hole

As our plane bored through the darkness five miles above the Atlantic, Dad put aside his *Wall Street Journal* and turned to me, smiled, and said, "Know what I'm anxious to see?"

"It's just a wild guess. Either Dean Smith win another national basketball championship, or possibly the Queen Mum in her Calvins?"

"Smart mouth."

"It's my job," I reminded him. This was true. Dad was such a perfect straight man, I always played Bob to his Bing in our thirty-year road show.

His smile widened. "I'm wondering how you'll take the corner when the pressure's on."

I knew exactly what he meant. This was an elliptical code for taking the dogleg corner of the seventeenth hole on the Old Course at St. Andrews, sometimes called the Road Hole, regarded by many as the toughest par-four hole in the world, 475 yards of celebrated Scottish madness that offers the player the difficult choice of firing his ball dangerously over a set of old replicated railway sheds that invade the driving line of the left-to-right dogleg, or the opportunity to play "safe" and face a tough long iron or fairway wood shot to a shallow, unforgivingly firm, slightly elevated green bordered by severe out-of-bounds to the right and an infamous pebble road and wall in back—to say nothing of the murderous pot bunker that lurks in front and has buried the hopes of more ordinary mortals and great players than probably any single patch of sand on earth.

"Same as always," I assured him, sipping my expensive scotch. "Grip it and rip it over the shed to the heart of the fairway. A neat five- or six-iron to the center of the green, followed by two putts. No problem."

"You seem to have it figured out nicely. You've played it that way, have you?"

"Only in my dreams, I'm afraid."

I knew exactly how my father would play the Road Hole, though. His usual short fade off the tee, two more irons to the green, and one good putt for par. That was the ideal approach and how he basically approached every par-four hole—pretty much how he approached life in general, come to think of it, a patient player who accepted the physical limitations of his game and waited for his moments to score. Never gifted with length off the tee, his salvation was his short iron game and his putter.

"How many times did you play the hole?" I asked him.

"Only twice. I took the train to Scotland two times, once in late '43 and again in '44, just before D-Day. Then they sent me off to France."

"So how'd you do on it?"

"I double bogeyed it the first time." He was now fiddling with his earphones, trying to untangle them from his newspaper, preparing to plug into the inflight movie, in which several cars were already exploding. I helped him by taking the newspaper, glancing absently at the date as I did. It was late September, and something gently stirred in me.

"And the second?" I asked.

"I almost hate to say."

"C'mon. I won't tell. A snowman?"

"No. A birdie, I think."

I stared at him. "You *think* you birdied it?"

"Actually, I know I did"—he smiled again, remembering—"because the little gentleman I was playing with was so ecstatic about it, he insisted on buying me supper to celebrate. I have to say, it was one of those crazy shots you couldn't do again if your life depended on it. Basically a fluke. I chipped in from off the green."

"From where exactly?" I was pleased to hear this but shouldn't really have been too surprised. Over the years I'd seen him chip the ball into the cup dozens of times, from the worst kind of lies—out of sand, penal rough, hardpan dirt. Like Paul Runyan, the great short game impresario who used his putting and chipping talents to compensate for his relatively puny game off the tee, Dad seemed to relish any opportunity to extricate himself from Bogeyville with his trusty chipping iron (usually his seven-iron) or bang the ball into the back of the cup from the backside of nowhere with his old Ping putter, crushing his opponent's spirits in the process. I'd been the victim of his great chipping and putting touch far too often to write off his good fortune at the Road Hole, however improbable, merely as a fluke. Still, a *bird* at the Road Hole! I couldn't think of anyone I knew who'd done it. Most professionals never even came close.

Dad was fiddling with the volume knob now, the headphones in place, tuning in to his blow-up adventure movie. He was obviously in no rush to reveal anything more. He sipped his scotch, settled back, then glanced over at me and smiled. "I have a better idea. Why don't I show you when we get there?"

He obviously wanted me to leave him alone for a while. I got up and went to join the after-dinner queue for the toilet.

It's said a great calm descends on you when you begin a long journey.

The road ahead stretches so far, you can think only of what is happening now. The thing was, I didn't have a clue what was really happening at that moment. My father was supposed to be dying, but he didn't appear to be dying, and the idea that he would soon vanish from my life—the worst fear of my childhood—seemed utterly incomprehensible, almost laughable. Opti the Mystic was so alive, so constant, still so *there* despite the direst verdict of medical science. And what's more, we were streaming through a cold black ocean of air, drinking scotch, and getting our digs in as always, finally bound together for the Road Hole. Was it the beginning of a trip, I wondered, or the end of a journey?

As I stood in line for the bathroom, arms braced against the bulkhead, gently swaying with the plane, I stared out a porthole window thinking about that Road Hole birdie and told myself not to put too much expectation on this trip. Opti would have stressed the importance of staying in the moment and not worrying about the outcome.

But living in the moment had always been so difficult for me. So much of my life was spent worrying about things that were going to happen in the future, racing to make plane connections or conduct interviews or make approaching deadlines. Reporters live in the land of tomorrow. So do fathers and gardeners. I was all three. On our hill in Maine, I'd cleared almost two acres of land by hand, propelled by a single vision of how glorious my vast yard and gardens would someday look. Sometimes I worried about the kinds of boys Maggie would bring home or how Jack might fare on his college boards. These events were *only* ten or twelve years in the future.

Through the porthole, I found myself gazing at a star.

The unexpected brilliance of it made me think of my own childhood. Every story my father read my brother and me as children seemed to have two things: a moral and a guiding star. There were legends of Indian warriors crossing wildernesses in search of their destinies, Greek myths of seafaring sons in search of their fathers, Columbus on the prow of the *Santa Maria.* Sojourning man pursued undiscovered worlds by contemplating the stars and the ancient Greeks, for one, believed that men's souls were composed of the same elements as stars. Plato believed a man who lived his life well on earth went to reside happily on a star afterward. He said the soul was pure memory.

Nothing, said Balzac, is insignificant. For me at least, the reason for, if not the soul of, this trip was almost entirely bound up in the memory of hearing about St. Andrews and the Road Hole for the first time.

It was a balmy evening in the 1960s, and my father and I were headed up the eighteenth fairway at Green Valley. A small plane flew overhead. Dad looked up and smiled. "Look at that," he said, with obvious pleasure. "An old J-3 trainer. I flew one just like that before the war."

As we watched, the plane's engine suddenly stopped; the ship seemed to hover dangerously on the evening's air currents, and then the engine refired. "He's practicing stalls at sunset. I used to do the same thing. It's amazing how well you can see everything from up there at this hour. Saint-Exupéry said the airplane revealed the true face of the earth to man."

I looked at him. "You flew an airplane?"

"Sure. Didn't I tell you?"

No, he hadn't. I'd never heard of a saint called Exupéry, either.

That evening a box of old letters and photos came down from the attic. I was surprised to learn my parents had lived another life before my brother Dickie and I were born. Dad had been a pilot, and Mom had won the Miss Western Maryland pageant. They lived on Schley Street in Cumberland, Maryland. Dad wrote an aviation column for the paper, sold advertising space, and flew on weekends. He loved to fly his old Cessna low along river valleys, following the seams of the earth, and he once frightened my mother so badly on a trip down the New River Valley, she refused to fly with him again. She drew the line when he volunteered to fly a plane through a flaming wall at a Jaycee airshow. "I told your father it was that plane or me," she said, sliding him a meaningful look. "For a while," he added with a wink, "it was a toss-up."

Not really, of course. There were all these black-and-white photos from that time. They were both so young, carefree, aping for the camera at the rail of a tramp steamer out of Baltimore harbor or posing in the deep snow outside a handsome white house in a suburb of Chicago—just the kind of cozy little place, my mother explained, where they hoped to raise a family of their own someday. She thought Dad looked like the movie actor Alan Ladd in his tech sergeant's uniform. There were other pictures of him from the war: posing with a bunch of grinning GIs around a big-breasted sculpture of a woman fashioned from the muddy snow outside a Quonset hut in England; sitting astride a white horse at the edge of a forest in France; taking a swing with a golf club on a barren piece of ground with the broken rooflines and church spires of an almost medieval-looking town rising up in the distance. The town turned out to be St. Andrews. The picture went into a frame that sat on my bedroom dresser for years. I used to lie on my bed and gaze at it and think: *I'm going there someday.*

For me, everything seemed to happen that year in the mid-1960s. The Beatles came to America, and I got my first guitar, a Silvertone from Sears. I also got a new set of Northwestern golf clubs for Christmas and a book called *Education of a Golfer* by Sam Snead.

My aunt Polly Tracy lived on the seventeenth hole at Sedgefield Country Club, where the Greater Greensboro Open was played every spring. That April, in 1965, we all went out to the tournament for the first time. Aunt Polly really wasn't my aunt. She was the wife of my father's friend, Bob Tracy. They worked together in advertising and were planning to open their own ad agency soon. The Tracys had a house full of noisy kids—Mimi, Pam, Bobby, Teddy, Paula—people always coming and going, kids carrying on, and meals being served. Mimi's boyfriends were always pulling up in sports cars. Bobby was a golf star on his high school team. Pam had actually drunk house paint and had her stomach pumped out! Teddy was the first girl I ever kissed. Paula was just the tag-along kid.

I wanted to see Sam Snead because he was my father's golf hero. I also wanted to get him to autograph my copy of *Education of a Golfer*. On Saturday afternoon, my father and I followed Snead in the third round. Two months shy of fifty-three, the Slammer was on or near the lead, and the excitement was palpably building in the gallery. I hugged my book and waited for my chance.

We followed him to the eighteenth hole, where the crowds grew very large. I remember laying the book down on a concession table to climb up on a radio broadcast tower to try and see better. My father and I had gotten separated. When I climbed back down, the book was gone. I couldn't believe it. I watched Snead head off, and then I walked back down the fairway toward Aunt Polly's house, furious with myself and blinking back tears.

The next morning, another copy of the book was lying on the breakfast table. "Try and hold on to this one for a while, will you, Bo?" was all my father had to say about the matter, glancing at me over the Sunday funnies.

We drove out to Sedgefield again and watched Snead make history. By winning Greensboro, he became the oldest man in history to capture a regular PGA title. The problem was, his triumph made even getting close impossible. Snead was surrounded by jubilant fans and disappeared into the Sedgefield Inn before I could reach him. My father told me we would get the autograph "next year."

Not long afterward, I told a girl named Kristin Cress that Sam Snead had autographed my book. It was a daring lie, and I don't know why I did it except I desperately wanted her to like me. She was two inches taller and a year ahead of me in school, but we sang in the same youth choir at church. She was very popular and very pretty, a junior high school cheerleader with big brown eyes, shiny black hair, and an unusually fine singing voice. She was the star in school plays, and older boys were always hanging around her.

Kristin didn't seem impressed by my Sam Snead story, and it was another two years before she even seemed to notice me.

By then, I'd invented a secret golf game involving Kristin Cress, which I sometimes played on the putting green at Green Valley. The stakes were always high in these intense fantasy matches. Normally I putted against Jack Nicklaus or Arnold Palmer for the "Championship of the Entire Earth," a cool million dollars, a box of new Titleist golf balls, perhaps a chance to play rhythm guitar with the Beatles, and a new Corvette Stingray I would eventually be old enough to drive.

But this game was different. If I could putt my way completely around the nine-hole putting green in fourteen strokes or less (Kristin was fourteen), it meant Kristin Cress would fall in love with me. I could envision the whole thing. We would marry, have children, maybe move into a big house on a golf course like Aunt Polly's, drive a Stingray, get nice big Christmas cards from Arnie and Jack. But I would have to knock at least four putts into the jar in one stroke and do no worse than two-putt on the remaining five holes. For a while I played this game over and over, after almost every round—you got only one chance per day—for most of my thirteenth summer, trying to make the magic happen. But it never did. Belief ebbed. I pretty much gave up.

Then one day in the autumn, when I was just fooling around, waiting for my father to arrive at the club, stepping up and rapping putts for the heck of it, I realized that all I needed to do in order to complete the sacred Kristin Cress love grail was to finish the ninth hole in one putt.

The putt was a twenty-footer with a one-cup break from left to right. I took a deep breath and set my putter behind the ball. I made a solid stroke and watched the ball roll beautifully to the edge of the cup . . . and stop. I remember looking at the perfect black script—*Titleist.* "Get *in*," I whispered. The ball dropped into the cup. She was *mine*.

It took a while for Kristin Cress to realize this. Four *more* years, in fact. How could I tell the love of my life that I'd won her heart in a cosmic putting match? The answer was, I couldn't. So I admired her from afar, practiced my game, and helpfully grew several inches. Then one day, not long after I'd performed Lennon and McCartney's "Yesterday" in a school assembly, as she and I were walking out of the senior high choir practice room, Kristin turned and asked me for a *ride home.*

As we sat in her parents' driveway, she explained that she'd just broken up with her college boyfriend and out of the blue asked me if I wanted to go with her to the homecoming dance.

I never told her about the cosmic putting match because she thought golf was kind of silly, "Republican religion," as she put it. "That's why so many men worship it on Sunday morning." Her love was drama. Still, after we began dating, she agreed to walk along and watch me play. She picked flowers, wrote in her journal, and studied her lines for *Long Day's Journey into Night* while I took dead aim at the third green with my seven-iron. One afternoon near Christmas, I almost aced the Valley's par-three fifth hole, a steep downhill shot. My ball bounced on the front apron of the green, kicked right, and followed the contour of the putting surface right up to the pin. One more half-rotation, and it would have dropped. I shouted, "Get *in!*" but this time there was no magic. Kristin looked up from her book. She'd missed the brilliant shot entirely. I was incensed. We quarreled, and she left me to finish the round alone. That night I called her to apologize and explained that an ace was every golfer's dream. It was the *perfect* shot in golf.

"If it's supposed to happen," she replied, "it'll happen."

We dated until the beginning of my senior year, at which point Kristin went to a college in the mountains to study drama and I broke off the relationship because I didn't wish to be "tied down." The golf coach invited me to try out for the golf team, but I declined because a music store offered me a better deal teaching guitar for the princely fee of five dollars an hour.

I had a new girlfriend and a new gold Camaro. I played golf matches with my father or my best friend Pat, sang in the school madrigals, earned the musical lead in the Little Theater production of *Spoon River Anthology*, and won the city's short story contest. I gave Kristin Cress no more than a passing thought. At Christmas, she sent me a card with a single star on it. *Have you scored that hole-in-one yet? If not, keep the faith. Everything happens when it should. Miss you, K.* I never wrote back. A year later, I heard she was getting married.

·   ·   ·

"Excuse me," said the man ahead of me in the bathroom line. "I thought I heard you and your friend talking about the Old Course. Y'all must be golfers."

I didn't deny it, which would have been pointless since I was wearing a bright green U.S. Open cap.

"You ever played the Old Course?" he asked.

"A few times," I admitted. "Never very well, I'm afraid. My father, though, says he birdied the Road Hole."

"No foolin'?" He seemed genuinely pleased.

The plane hit an air pocket, and as we bounced together, the man extended his hand. "Name's Bob Tanner." We shook. Bob had an Auburn War Eagle cap on his head. He explained he was with a group of fellow dentists from Birmingham, en route to the golf vacation of a lifetime. "Fourteen days, no wives, and all the single malt whiskey we can legally stash in our golf bags. Two weeks of pure *boy joy*. How 'bout you?"

Without thinking, I explained I was taking my father back to England and Scotland, where he'd learned to play golf as an airman fifty years ago during the war. I realized, too late, I was probably telling Bob a lot more than he cared to know.

"That's great," said Bob enthusiastically. "I wish my old man and I had been like that. We always wanted to murder each other. He used to say there were only two ways in life—his way and no way."

"Sorry to hear it. What did your father do?"

"High school football coach. Real hardass. He was sure I'd be a high school football coach like him."

"You like being a dentist?" I had a picture of Bob going after some poor slob's impacted wisdom tooth the way his old man kicked some lazy lineman's rear end. His hands were massive.

"Sure. I mean, it's okay. I don't think I sat around as a kid thinking, 'Hey, Bob, you oughta be a dentist when you grow up,' but it's kinda fun. Pays good. I get to play a lot of golf." He gave a dopey grin. "That's the important thing, isn't it? How 'bout you?"

I admitted I got to play a lot of golf, too.

He asked what I did for a living. I considered telling him I sold coffins. A curmudgeonly golf editor I knew sometimes did this to prevent people from asking him for swing tips or wanting to know what Jack Nicklaus was really like. I worked for the same magazine as Jack Nicklaus, had watched him play in person dozens of times over thirty years, and had even spoken to him a couple times on the telephone, but I basically had no clue what Jack Nicklaus was *really like*. As for swing tips, in my book it was better to receive than give them. Still, I enjoyed being a golf writer immensely—getting paid to watch golf on TV, as it were—and usually had no problem admitting it. I got to travel to a lot of swell places, test new equipment, hang out with tour players and meet the game's living legends, eat free meals, sometimes even get free golf stuff. Who wouldn't like that? One of my regular golf pals in Maine liked to say he couldn't wait to see what kind of a *real* job I got when I finally grew up.

"I'm a golf writer."

"I'll be dogged." Bob was impressed. "How do you get a job like that?"

I'd known he was going to ask me this. Unfortunately, I didn't know quite what to say. The answer was either very complicated or pretty simple, either destiny or dumb luck. So I said what I always say.

"You know, Bob, I'm still trying to figure that one out."

Bob the dentist laughed, and I laughed. The bathroom door opened. The plane bumped again. I guess he thought I was joking.

Dad was snoozing when I got back to my seat. I took the scotch glass out of his hand, removed his earphones and spectacles, lifted *The Wall Street Journal* from his chest and covered him with the blanket, then turned off his overhead light. I leaned forward and gazed out the window. The brilliant star was still there, guiding our little odyssey.

I sat back and stared at the front page of the *Journal* but didn't really see what was written there. Kristin had been on my mind a lot lately, a bittersweet apparition that always seemed to come calling around the middle part of autumn. Some years the hauntings, as I thought of them, were worse than others. This year they were worse than most. Why was that? Had the stark reality of my father's approaching date with death triggered an unexpected flood of thoughts and feelings about Kristin I thought I'd kept safely bottled up for years? It was possible. My father and Kristin had been so much alike in many ways. I'd lost one. Now I was losing the other.

Was that it? As passengers around me settled down under blankets to sleep, I tugged my father's own blanket up to his chin and sat there wondering why the past is such a maze we never seem to escape. My mind slipped into that dangerous maze to try and find an answer.

I'd almost finished my English degree and decided to take extra semesters of religion and drama classes to kill time and figure out what I was supposed to do with my life. The problem, in some ways, was having too many options. I'd been offered a reporter's job at the *Greensboro Daily News,* and the English teaching assistant's position I'd applied for at a Virginia university looked as if it might pan out. To complicate matters, a drama professor had urged me to consider seriously graduate studies in theater up North, while somewhere in the back of my mind I even thought of going to a music conservatory to study classical guitar. Heck, maybe even striking off for Nashville.

Predictably, my father was elusive as fairway fog on the subject, of no help whatsoever in the parental advice department. My best friends, Pat and Frank, by stark comparison, had fathers who had no difficulty whatsoever rendering advice—in their case, *proper assembly instructions* was more like it—about what they should do with their lives. Frank was going to Duke graduate school and make a zillion bucks in finance, Pat was someday going to take over his old man's thriving electrical supply company after he cut his hair, quit talking about impeaching Richard Nixon, and stopped dating the rock-and-roll singer (whom he eventually married).

When I posed some of these same questions, my old man merely smiled and came back with one of his maddeningly Socratic evasions: "What do *you* really want to do, Bo?" His response put the whole thing ridiculously back on my young shoulders. Finally, one afternoon when decision deadlines were looming and we were playing together at Green Valley, the subject came up again, and I snapped at him that all I *really* wanted to do was talk to Kristin Cress.

"Why don't you call her up," he said, as if that were all there was to it.

"Yeah, right, Dad. In case you forgot, she's married."

"So? Doesn't mean she won't be pleased to hear from you."

I took his advice and called her up. Kristin's marriage had ended, and she was living in a small house on the outskirts of Hickory, a town in the Smoky Mountains, working as a social worker and part-time steakhouse hostess, and acting with a highly respected Equity rep company at a mountain playhouse on weekends. She invited me up to visit.

We stayed up all night, that first night, talking and catching up. In the morning we went out to watch the sun come up over a quarry lake. There was a high rock where Kristin went on Sunday mornings. She called it Sabbath Rock because she no longer believed in "any one church." Her interest was in the religions of the East, Buddhism and Hinduism mainly. I learned she'd done a play off-Broadway and was saving money for a long trip to India. Meanwhile, she was rehearsing for a Bertolt Brecht play called *The Good Woman of Szechwan* and working with a black woman named Elsie who was trying to raise her three grandchildren in a shack near the ice plant.

We took Elsie's kids bowling at the college, then for chili dogs at Tastee Freeze. Kristin, the only vegetarian steakhouse hostess in America, had to work later, so I went back to her house and put on a Chopin record and started making bouillabaisse for a midnight supper. I practiced my guitar, talked to her cat Omar, then browsed her bookshelf—a translation of *Tao Te Ching*, Kapleau's *Three Pillars of Zen*, *The Collected Poems of Rainer Maria Rilke*, a modern translation of *The Upanishads*.

When my head was sufficiently full of this mystical soup, I went outside and practiced sand-wedge shots over her gorgeous rosebeds, causing an old lady across the street to visit her porch and glare at me. It was a balmy evening in late September, but Kristin's red roses still had blossoms as large as grapefruits, and I was suddenly incalculably, almost unbelievably happy.

I went back to see her four weekends in a row, a five-hour haul down the interstate each way, falling more under the spell of my first love, I believed, each time. I gave her my spare classical guitar and taught her beginner chords. We sat on Sabbath Rock and read books or sometimes said nothing until I couldn't stand the meaningful silence any longer and started cracking jokes. She told me I should learn to meditate because silence "quieted the soul" and made true speech possible. I told her she should learn to play golf because reaching a par-five in two was a religious experience. She said golf and music might be my *yanas*—rafts to enlightened consciousness. I wondered if you had to pay green fees when you got to Heaven.

"The great spiritual teachers of almost every tradition say that Heaven is right here and now, all around us, every second. We only have to wake up to that fact in order to see it," she said. "The only sin is ignorance of that awareness."

I asked why she was so hot to go to India, and she said spiritual journeys always revealed things—not always pleasant but true realities. I said this might explain why I'd always wanted to go visit St. Andrews. Been dreaming of it since I was a kid, I admitted. Every man has his India. Mine just came with caddies, tee boxes, and yellow flags.

She looked at me and, smiling, shook her head. She said I would probably never grow up. Unfortunately, as I shot back at her, growing up was precisely the problem. Her remark gave me the perfect opening to ask her what she thought I should do with my life. Take the reporter's job? Go to drama school? Study classical guitar? Jump off this cliff?

Like my father, Kristin maddeningly resisted giving a straight answer. She said I would find my *dharma*—life's purpose—when I quit searching for it. I told her she sounded just like Opti the Mystic, my old man and his famous *less is more* spiel.

"Your dad's always been very cool," she said, "for a Republican and a golfer."

She suggested that we meditate. I asked if this meant we were going to take our clothes off, but she only smiled. We put our legs in the lotus position, tilted our faces to the blue sky. I felt incredibly self-conscious, like the time my father had made me lie down on the golf course, wondering if some hiker across the pond was laughing his hindquarters off at us. I closed my eyes and began to snore, making my usual mockery of her daily ritual.

Two days later, Kristin was dead.

My father drove down to school to break the news to me. On the Tuesday after we parted, she'd gone to work at the steakhouse, and three young men had strolled in to clean out the cash register.

One of them put a gun to the pretty hostess's head, and terrified patrons later recounted to authorities that they heard her speaking consolingly to the guy, reassuring him. He pulled the trigger anyway. The killer had just turned seventeen, a baby robber.

I drove home to Greensboro in silence with my father, numb to the bone. I told him I couldn't bear to visit the funeral home, or see Kristin's family, or face any of my friends, or even attend the funeral. He said he understood these feelings but thought I should make myself go anyway. Addled with grief, seething with anger, I said nothing. I'd finally shut up.

"I have an idea," said my old man. "Let's play a straight-up match. No strokes given either way. If you win, you choose whether to go or not. If I win, you go whether you want to or not. And I'll go with you."

I looked at him as if he were crazy, searching his pale gray eyes for the reason he was pushing me on this. It was so unlike Opti. Didn't he understand what the hell I was going through? Hadn't he ever felt so goddamned miserable, all he wanted to do was find a hole to crawl in and hide? Public grieving, I said emphatically, wasn't my style. Besides, if I went to that funeral, people who knew what Kristin meant to me might sit there and feel sorry for me. I didn't want or need their damned pity. Even worse, I might sit there and feel sorry for myself. And who wanted that? Feeling sorry, I insisted, wouldn't do anybody any good, and most of all it wouldn't bring Kristin back.

"No," he agreed, "but a long time ago I learned it may help you go on."

I looked at him. We were sitting in his office off Battleground Avenue near the end of the workday. I remember hearing a clock ticking faintly in the outer office and the sigh of Friday afternoon traffic outside.

"What are you talking about?"

He shrugged, slowly turning a paper clip in his fingers, and smiled a bit. "Something that happened long before you were born, Sport. A little girl I knew died. I probably should have gone to her funeral, but I didn't. I regretted it later. It's what stays with you." He fell silent. Then: "Shall we get our spikes?"

"You don't have a chance," I snorted. My handicap was probably nine strokes better than his.

"We'll see."

He had me dormy by the sixteenth hole, shut-out one hole later.

"You knew you'd win," I said to him as we climbed the eighteenth fairway toward our second shots. The hike had done me good. My mind felt clearer, my troubled soul a bit more at ease. At least the entire world was no longer lining up against me.

"No," he replied. "But I knew you'd go."

I sent roses and a small note to Kristin's parents that said, *She gave to all and showed us how to give.* I don't know why I wrote those words. I also didn't know until many years later—because I never went back to her grave—that Abe and Alice Cress had those words engraved on their youngest daughter's headstone.

All I knew for sure at that moment was that Kristin had given me something powerful and nurturing, and some kid with a handgun had taken it away from me forever.

The church was packed—her old cheerleader pals, kids we'd known from catechism class and choir, lots of her professors and acting mates from college. Even her ex-husband showed up, taking a seat somewhere at the back. It was very possibly Greensboro's saddest public occasion that year. I sat through the service without uttering a peep, my father's hand resting helpfully on my left shoulder throughout.

·   ·   ·

Out the window of the plane, I realized, the sun was coming up. A new dawn was on the horizon. Patches of green below the swirling mass of clouds would be Ireland or maybe even Scotland itself. Our descent, our trip, was finally beginning.

My father was still sleeping, mouth open, snoring lightly. I unfolded his *Wall Street Journal* and tried to read a story about a bank megamerger deal, hoping to chase away the phantoms of that terrible far-off autumn.

That's when it came to me: It was now twenty years since Kristin died.

We stand against fate, Emerson said, as a child stands against the wall of his father's house, notching his growth year by year. A biblical generation had passed since my first love's incomprehensible death. I'd grown up entirely since that sorrowful autumn, moved south and then north, got on with things nicely, found a career I loved, started a new life, married a wonderful woman, became a father, and planted roses of my own. Like a mature rosebush, I had plenty of visible notches of growth to show. Yet apparently I hadn't entirely outrun every demon of anger and grief. Once upon a time Opti had simply asked me to grieve. And I'd done the best I could, and then I'd gotten on with living my life. Wasn't that *enough*?

Wishing to think no more of these things, I leaned forward to see if our guide star was still loitering around. As fortune would have it, it was—shining like the Morning Star. But in the new light of day, I realized something pretty funny. This whole time I'd been meditating on the plane's wing navigation light, a regular Telemachus in Topsiders.

Another time, I might have laughed out loud.

A Sunday in London

I opened *The Sunday Times* and settled into one of the Hotel Berkeley's overstuffed reading chairs, hoping the four aspirin I'd swallowed would soon do their job. The combination of too much scotch and too much thinking and too little sleeping had given me a doozy of a headache.

Dad was in the suite's spacious bathroom, preparing to shower. We'd been in London only four hours. The suite had lovely fruitwood paneling. I was already bored and still worried, which is why I hoped to distract myself with somebody else's problems.

According to the *Times*, John Major's declared war on Yob Culture was a miserable failure, and London's tourist sites were crumbling into the Thames. A sign of how bad things were in Britain these days was the fact that the Queen was reduced to digging for oil beneath Windsor Castle, prompting one Fleet Street wag to rename the place South Fork-on-Thames.

I heard the bathroom water start and stop and my father swear softly. I got up and walked to the door and knocked softly.

"You okay in there?"

"Yup. Just trying to remember how to work fine British plumbing."

"It can be a challenge. May I help?"

"Uh . . . sure."

I opened the door and went in. He was stripped naked, wrapped in a large white terry towel, standing uncomfortably by the sink. Against the harsh afternoon light, he looked pale, vulnerable, and old. He felt embarrassed, and I did, too. His shaving kit was open on the marble vanity; there were various rubber bags, frightening straps, and unopened packages of syringes lying about. I tried not to look at this medical paraphernalia, but I could smell his menthol shaving cream and see his old-style blade razor lying on a fresh towel, where he'd just laid it aside to dry. As a boy, I'd loved to watch my father shave. He shaved so slowly, standing before the mirror and lathering his face with meticulous care, making a little ritual out of each pass with the razor. He told me civilized men always shaved this way. In college I started shaving with a disposable razor in the shower and never broke the habit.

I fiddled with the ornate knobs on the shower, remarking, "Isn't it strange that the same English brains who invented golf, the Magna Carta, and Page Three girls almost in the same year can't seem to produce two showers that function the same way."

"At least they have showers in hotel rooms now," he replied. "I doubt Kate Bennie would appreciate you giving credit to the English for inventing golf, Sport."

He was right about that. Kathleen (popularly known as Kate) Bennie was my Scottish mother-in-law, a no-nonsense daughter of

Glasgow's Netherlee neighborhood, a proud school principal, devoted grandma, and something of a one-woman Royal and Ancient rules committee whom I could reliably count upon always to take the opposing view in any discussion about God, politics, or the future of organized field sport. Scots are naturally contrary, the way Germans are naturally humorless or Russians giftedly morose.

As it so happened, at that very moment Kate was up visiting her Scottish homeland, making her annual tour of the premises just to ensure that everything was being properly looked after. We planned to try and hook up for a haggis lunch and perhaps a quick, invigorating debate of some sort in the days ahead.

"You're quite right," I agreed, stepping back out of the shower. "Better strike that heresy from the record." The bath pipes were singing lustily now, the water beginning to steam invitingly. I backed away giving a butlerlike wave of the hand. "Your shower awaits, m'lord," I said.

"Your cockney accent needs work."

"True. So does my short game. I'll work on both while we're here. Meanwhile, I was thinking of ordering a sandwich. Would you like one?"

"Make mine ham and cheese. Now scram."

I went back to my comfy chair by the window and dialed room service. At well over three hundred dollars a day, the venerable Berkeley, one of London's premier society hotels, had been specifically chosen by me as our starting point because fifty years ago my father's first night on English soil had been spent hunkering under a military poncho in the November rain.

He'd come over with three thousand other GIs on the *Queen Elizabeth* but had had it better than most. Having been picked by the brass to serve as a military liaison to the ship's head purser, he was given the run of the ship, an actual cabin bunk, a dry wool blanket, as much bad coffee as he cared to consume, and at least one hot meal a day. Many of his friends slept either in the *QE*'s congested hall-ways, on the passenger decks, or in the empty swimming pool and had to live off cold rations or marmalade sandwiches, which the *QE*'s crew sold for the extortionate price of three dollars apiece.

Dad's job, as a de facto peacemaker and policeman, was to make sure nobody got thrown overboard during the inevitable disputes that arose from negotiations in the thriving marmalade black market, as well as help the crew keep a sharp eye posted at the stern for lethal U-boats. Because of severe military food shortages on land, his first three meals on British soil had been vanilla ice cream.

A Jeremy Irons impersonator answered the Berkeley's room ser-vice phone. I told him I wished to place an order for two ham-and-cheese sandwiches, lightly toasted, with a dollop of real English mustard and perhaps a splash of mayo, two large Cokes, chips if available, and perhaps a nice sturdy dill gherkin or two.

"I'm terribly sorry," said Jeremy. "The hotel kitchen is closed for the afternoon."

This surprised me. A world-class hotel kitchen shut down on a Sunday afternoon? Jeremy didn't sound the least bit sorry, though. He sounded as if I'd thoughtlessly interrupted the annual reading of *Brideshead Revisited* to the housekeeping staff. I explained that my fa-ther and I had been up most of the night flying in from Atlanta, gotten lost taking the shortcut I knew like the back of my hand from the airport to the hotel, and missed both lunch and a scheduled teetime at Sunningdale Golf Club. Jeremy was unfazed by this tragic summary of our day thus far.

He explained that the kitchen staff of the Berkeley had been given the day off because they were recovering from a big debutante party in the hotel the previous week. London's social season had just wound up, he explained, a tradition "that dates all the way back to the restoration of the monarchy." Sniff, sniff.

"We don't require a whole lot," I reassured him. "How about a nice nutty cheese log, or just some baloney and cheese wedged between some bread? A nice pot of real British tea would help take the chill off."

"I don't believe we have any . . . cheese logs or *baloney*, sir. But I'll see . . . what can be done." Jeremy softly recradled his phone. I pictured him shaking his head, picking up his Waugh, and clearing his throat.

I went back to our sitting room and turned on the telly, hoping to get the weather for Royal Lytham, our first stop the next morning. Instead, as usual, championship snooker was on because it's on at any hour of the day I come to Britain. Championship snooker is about as thrilling as watching your neighbor wash his Buick. Next to televised soccer—which Brits call football—and possibly cricket, a game named for an insect that can take weeks to play, championship snooker is the world's greatest cure for insomnia. I know how Philistine this sounds because Kate Bennie constantly reminded me what an uncultured boob I was for saying soccer is an appalling waste of good fairway grass. "British football is so boring," I once told her, to no noticeable effect, "the fans have to kill each other in order not to fall asleep."

There was no weather report, but I did find a spellbinding football match. The Middlesex Morons were tied one-to-one with the Shropshire Sheep Worriers. I turned the channel again and found two men in clerical shirts having a heated theological argument on a stage. I knew they were arguing because one man's eyebrow was arched indignantly. "The problem with England, Bishop," said the man in the gray dog collar, "is we're a nation of churches where polls show no one goes to church anymore. It's a worrisome trend, you see."

I switched off the TV and looked at my watch. It was now approaching early Sunday afternoon in London. Too late for golf, too early for dinner. Dad was bushed, the Berkeley had no baloney, and all my fabulous plans—a round at Sunningdale, perhaps a motor-carriage tour through the city, followed by dinner at the Savoy River Grille—seemed to be trickling hopelessly down the tubes with the bathwater.

Just then, Dad appeared, washed down and redolent of the House of Aramis, dressed in fresh golf duds. I was happy to see him wearing the green Ashworth shirt I'd sent along with the new golf clubs two Christmases ago. At least he'd kept the shirt.

"Any luck with the grub?"

"Yes. It's being prepared by a man who believes in no baloney, even as we speak."

"Good. Maybe I'll scoot in the bedroom and give your mom a little wake-up call." I saw him consult his watch, mentally trying to figure the time back in Carolina.

He disappeared into the bedroom to call my mother, and minutes later I could hear him avidly describing seeing St. Paul's Cathedral for the first time in half a century (". . . can you imagine something that big, Jan, and the Gerries just couldn't hit it! The bombs just bounced off the roof, actually . . . it was made of lead, you see, the roof I mean . . .") and other landmarks on our way into the city. A few minutes later, I heard someone start up a small chainsaw in the bedroom and went to look. My father was flat on his back on the bed, gently snoozing. Out for the count.

I settled back in my chair and switched to the *Sunday Telegraph*, which was reporting that there was a pesky hole leaking water into the Chunnel, the recently opened $10 billion wonder tunnel linking England to France, the people they most love to detest. Maybe more interesting, a secretary from Luton had caused a major row in Parliament by having her breasts lifted on the National Health Service, and the Ministry of Health was reporting that there were now approximately two rats for every man, woman, and child residing in Britain.

Restlessly, I set the paper aside and stared out the window at the street below, where a young man and a pretty dark-haired woman of about twenty had just emerged from a black London taxi. They were laughing and holding hands. I tried to imagine their names.

Suddenly, my autumn ghosts had returned, and I found myself thinking: *Good lord, I've been here before.*

The two years following Kristin's murder were difficult for me.

I finished my undergraduate studies, passed on the teaching assistant's job, stalled a very patient newspaper editor indefinitely, and took a three-month job selling advertising space for my father. I told myself I needed time to "cool out" and play some golf and make no formal plans.

I sold one pathetically small ad to a man in Atlanta who made industrial cloth belts. He had an office window that overlooked the state prison and a murky blown-up photograph of St. Andrews on his cheaply paneled office wall. I remember sitting in his wardenlike office one gray winter afternoon listening to him drone on about the exciting advances in synthetic belt-binding technology, unable to keep my eyes from drifting back to the garish photo of St. Andrews. He caught me eyeing it. "I took that myself," he said proudly, shifting the toothpick slowly between his lips. "That's St. Andrews. The birthplace of golf. Ever been there?"

I admitted I hadn't.

"You play golf?"

Used to, I said.

He snorted gently and signed the ad order, and I walked out to my Chevy Monza in my new Palm Beach suit wondering what the hell I was doing there.

Something weird was happening to me. I'd lost interest in playing the classical guitar, and little by little, I could feel even my desire to play golf leaking away, too. A short time later, I sold my guitar for a fraction of its value to a former student and discovered that every time I went to Green Valley my game seemed to get worse, my scores ballooning. It was as if I were forgetting the game or the game forgetting me. People kept telling me how well I was "handling" Kristin's death, but beneath the skin I felt like a walking triple bogey—so angry I wanted to beat somebody to a pulp. But whom? A seventeen-year-old kid? I honestly wondered if this might not be the early stages of madness.

I got it into my head that going to the Episcopal seminary would calm me down. I did the necessary paperwork, gathered the necessary recommendations, and got admitted—only to abruptly back out. I went out to the Greater Greensboro Open that spring at Sedgefield, thinking I'd clear my head by maybe latching on to a caddy job and spend a year hanging around the PGA Tour. Unfortunately, I learned, PGA players had their own professional caddies, but I was assigned to carry the bag of a marginal star from a bad television sitcom in the tournament's celebrity pro-am, an obese comic who had a spectacular talent for loudly passing gas after he four-putted. The comic tipped me two dollars for my work and informed me his mother could have read Sedgefield's greens better than me. She'd been dead for *years*. Ta-dump. He nearly doubled over laughing. It seemed like an omen of sorts.

When the nice lady editor at the *Greensboro Daily News* called a few weeks later to make one final job offer, I accepted the reporter's job. My father, after all, had begun there as a copy runner, and I'd been the wireboy at the *News* the night Richard Nixon resigned. It seemed to be a family tradition and the work I was destined if not happily determined to do. Three months into the job, though, haunted by something I couldn't quite place a name to, I walked into the lady editor's office and resigned, saying I had to go to Scotland. She asked me what was so all-important in Scotland.

"I don't know," I said, then added: "Golf courses."

Nobody except my father believed it was the right thing to do. Colleagues told me it was career suicide, indicating mental flakiness. Dad drove me to the airport and gave me an extra thousand dollars. "Emergency money," he called it. I remember how we sat in the empty airport lounge having Budweisers and not saying much, and then he gave me a new blue Seiko watch. Instead of graciously accepting the watch, a belated graduation gift, I asked my father if he would hold on to it for me until I got home from Europe. I explained that I didn't want to risk losing it. The truth was, I thought it was the ugliest watch I'd ever seen, the kind of gaudy timepiece a car salesman would wear.

If my father's feelings were hurt, he didn't show it. He tucked the watch back into the box and put the box into his pocket. We stood, embraced, and I went off to Europe. It was almost exactly two years to the day since Kristin died.

I roamed around the continent for nearly three weeks, riding trains from Luxembourg to Germany, down to the south of France and back up to Paris, ludicrously dragging my unused golf bag with me the whole time. I read Graham Greene novels and slept in cheap hotels filled with hungry-looking East European students and sometimes went to museums or just hung out in cafés drinking strong black coffee and reading Greene on rainy days. My rough idea was to make St. Andrews the grand finale of this strangely rudderless pilgrimage, but on a train from the Gare du Nord to the Normandy coast, my golf bag got swiped and I found myself arriving in London short of funds and golf clubs. I stayed with a friend's friend in Clapham for a week, then caught the *Flying Scotsman* to Edinburgh, where I rented a car and drove across the Firth of Forth and down the little peninsula of the Kingdom of Fife into the cathedral town of St. Andrews.

It was raining lightly, but the Old Grey Toon, as it's called, looked pretty much like my old man's picture of it, dark, windswept, oddly majestic. I stood on a knoll beside the Road Hole and watched several groups of golfers play through, the October sea wind penetrating my skin. It was too late in the day to find rental clubs, and most of the shops along the Links road were closing, so I wandered up around the town until I found a small hotel. I checked in and went back out and found a crowded pub in the basement of a hotel not far from the eighteenth fairway of the Old Course, and drank enough ale to make sure I felt it in the morning.

I remember wobbling home through the quaint streets thinking how strange it was that I'd finally reached the birthplace of golf but felt none of the magic I'd grown up believing was there. I'd finally seen the famous Old Course, but to me it looked just like any other golf course in the rain, and I felt no real desire even to play it. What was the big deal? My little pilgrimage, I decided, was a bust because I was still as sad as the day I'd left home. I remember wanting to weep, but I couldn't even be bothered to do that.

It felt like my childhood was over.

There was a soft knock at the door. I opened it and found a pleasant young waiter pushing silver service on a rolling table.

He asked me if I was having a nice afternoon at the Berkeley. I told him if London got any more thrilling that afternoon, I'd probably soon require a respirator. He laughed and said, "You should see if there's a football match on, mate."

Under one ornate silver hood was a crustless sandwich with a thin swipe of fish paste and a sprig or two of parsley, what Brits call gents' relish. It was basically inedible by anyone who hails from below Richmond, Virginia. Under hood number two was a toasted cheese sandwich hard enough to use as a drapery sashweight. There was no pickle or chips. It was a lunch fit for a title by Conan

Doyle—"The Curious Case of Jeremy's Revenge." At least the tea was delightful. So I sat by the window drinking the tea, listening to my stomach growl, and watching traffic pass through the late sunny afternoon, alternately wishing we were playing golf and wondering if I hadn't made an enormous mistake dragging my dying father to Britain.

On that first pilgrimage twenty years ago, I'd set off to Europe with my old Hogan golf clubs, my dad's "emergency money," and a lot of impossibly high expectations that a journey to the birthplace of golf would somehow clarify my thinking and rekindle my zest for the game of my youth. In the process, it would repair whatever was deeply broken in me, cure cancer, and bring about lasting world peace. Was that too much to ask for one four-week trip abroad?

Apparently so. The Old Course had been a dud, and just the opposite had happened: I returned home and abandoned golf, took a reporter's job in Atlanta, and spent the next seven years interviewing convicted murderers and traipsing after presidential hopefuls, never playing golf once inside the city that produced Bobby Jones, the greatest player in the game's history. During my self-imposed "exile from the game," as I preferred to think, I played Green Valley exactly twice, on Christmas Day sometime in the late 1970s, and another time when I stopped over on my way home from Washington, where I'd just interviewed Jimmy Carter's media guru. Jimmy Carter was having a difficult summer. The press was murdering him. The age of pack journalism had arrived, and my sights were already set on working in Washington. I was sure I wanted to be one of the pack.

Now, a biblical generation later, was this trip I was dragging my dying father on simply an eerie shadow play of that former failed odyssey and its doomed expectations—some foolish and vain attempt to finally get things right? Was there *still* something missing I hoped to find or reclaim or perhaps simply exhume by dint of another trip to the sacred turf of the Old Course? If so, what? I'd been to the Old Course many times and grown to love it and even understand a little bit of its brilliant subtle contours; I knew people in the town and even counted a couple local players as golf buddies.

That first trip was simply a bad memory, I told myself. Though I was once again heading to the Old Grey Toon with a lot of high expectations, *this* trip had a different set of dynamics, problems, and challenges, not least of which was the fact that my mother was sitting at home six thousand miles away worrying her brains out about what calamity might befall her husband.

Days before we left she called me to say my father had just bought a new rain suit because, he had informed her, we would be walking several golf courses in Britain as few places had motorized golf carts. She said this surprised and worried her. I explained that it was merely one of the timeless charms of British golf—you *had* to walk, and as a result, you could play in just about any kind of weather. "That may be," she observed feistily, "but I don't think your father's legs are up to walking *any* golf courses, especially in the rain. He won't tell you that, but I will."

She gave me her list of worries about the trip: Dad would probably skip taking the various pills designed to ease his pain or reduce the swelling in his legs and ankles; he might drink too much alcohol for a man under such medication; he might suffer a stroke or simply collapse under the strain of such travel. Someone in her church circle told her the health services in Britain were "appalling." The doctors were all underpaid socialists. True, Dad's (overpaid capitalist) physician had "tanked" him up with several fresh pints of blood before we left, but what if his bleeding returned?

I tried to assuage my mother's worries, explaining that since the days of Maggie Thatcher, all the doctors had become strict Conservative monetarists with bulging offshore accounts in Jersey. "This isn't a joking matter," she replied, unmoved by my speech. She said she hated to think of us driving along all those "scary little roads where people drive on the wrong side." I told her not to worry because most of the roads in Scotland were so damned narrow it didn't matter which side you drove on. I assured her we would be fine. I would monitor everything Dad did. I wouldn't take any chances. I would drive *slowly* on the wrong side of the road.

"I hope so, darling. Your itinerary sounds ambitious."

The itinerary I'd finally settled upon was a bit ambitious: The day after we arrived in London, we would drive three hours north to Royal Lytham, then dip south to Royal Birkdale before heading up the west coast of Scotland to Turnberry, Prestwick, Royal Troon, Muirfield, Carnoustie, and St. Andrews. If Dad's strength was holding up after that, we might drive up through the Highlands and angle back to catch a commuter flight to Islay—where Kate Bennie's father's ashes were scattered near a golf course—then grab a flight down to France, finishing up in Paris and driving out to Compiègne, where Dad ran a prisoner-of-war camp briefly after the liberation of France. In the beech forest next to Napoleon's old summer palace at Compiègne, my father had carved his and my mother's initials in a tree. I had this crazy idea we might search for the tree, assuming a shopping mall hadn't been built on the spot.

"Call me an old romantic," I'd said, after explaining the whole thing to my mother.

"I'll call you a lot worse than that if anything happens to your father," she said.

Now, while my father slept, I sat by the window in the deeply upholstered silence of the Berkeley, brooding on these matters and feeling the first genuine pangs of worry creep in as I recalled our first day's minor catalog of delayed arrivals, wrong turns, canceled rounds, and general miscues—to say nothing of the bad sandwiches and the fitful showers that undoubtedly awaited us down the road. Perhaps I hadn't fully appreciated the magnitude of what I had promised my mother until I saw my father stripped down and vulnerable in the Berkeley's bathroom. He looked so frail and thin—not at all like a man who was expected to walk seven or eight golf courses in the autumn elements.

Once again, I was dangerously traveling with a golf bag full of hope. But hope for whom? This trip was my dream, but was it my father's as well? I knew in my heart there were things I wanted to say to Opti, but I couldn't think what they were. There were things I also hoped to hear from him, though I couldn't at that moment imagine what.

Being from good Southern Baptist stock, I sometimes conjured up a "Dixiefied" Greek chorus of my long-gone Carolina kin, who helpfully gathered upon my summons, à la Marley's ghost, to give me the benefit of their collective wisdom from the Great Church Supper Beyond. Considering they were a bunch of no-nonsense, Scripture-quoting pinewood teetotalers, they were usually a surprisingly friendly and supportive bunch, often telling me exactly what I needed or wanted to hear. The group I conjured up now from the Berkeley's rarefied ether, though, gave me only a strong whispered rebuke: *Take no more, let this good man go home and die in peace. You have no more claim on his precious time.*

For a few minutes, I honestly sat there in a panicky little sweat trying to figure out what the hell to do—proceed into the scary unknown or cancel yet another of my dumb little pilgrimages before my mother's worst fears came to pass.

Luckily, there were sudden footfalls on the carpet outside the door, followed by a woman's stifled laugh. A late-rising deb and her beau were no doubt fleeing. The sounds receded. The Greek chorus packed up and vanished. My panic eased off a bit.

I suddenly realized why we were there. We were *there*, by God—and maybe even by the grace of God—to play golf. To have a few laughs, to see some old familiar sights in each other's company, to take each other's pocket change. That had been Opti's own list of terms. And whatever unexpected difficulties faced us, that was good enough for me.

I got up and walked to the bedroom, paused, and peeked in at my father. He was lying perfectly still on his back, his face a serene pale mask, with his hands perfectly crossed over his chest like a Westminster poet laureate in repose.

For a second or two, I thought I'd already lost him.

Then he cracked open an eye and smiled up at me.

"How about a nice little putting match?" he proposed, already beginning to rise. "Loser buys supper."

Putt Like a Kid

The unshaven attendant at Hyde Park looked up from his book. He was a good-looking kid of about twenty with a lime-colored streak of green running through his hair and one perfect small gold earring piercing the flange of his left nostril, a heartthrob yob. I wondered if he might be John Major's son. He was reading a book called *How We Die*.

"That seems to be a pretty popular book," said my ever-cheerful *père*. "I've seen it around a lot of places. How do you like it?"

Major minor offered an indifferent shrug. "Kinda technical and dull, like, to be honest."

Dad smiled. "Dull? Death? Wasn't it Saint-Exupéry who said death is a thing of grandeur because it rearranges the world?"

"Please don't give away the ending," I insisted. "I always like to wait for the movie version myself."

The clerk stared at us as if we were a pair of escaped lunatics, two Yanks armed with putters and dressed as if we were on the first tee at La Costa Country Club instead of a windblown corner of Hyde Park. The edge of his mouth tilted up slightly. When faced with potentially dangerous foreigners, his employment manual perhaps read, always *humor* the rotters.

"Right, gents. One pound fifty. Each."

We paid our fee and walked out to the first tee. It wasn't much of a tee. In fact, it wasn't much of a putting course—a woefully neglected collection of putting greens set down by some cricket fields, just off Rotten Row near the Alexandra Gate.

I reminded my father that people no longer read Antoine de Saint-Exupéry, the author of *The Little Prince* and the best books ever written on flying.

"I know. That's too bad," he said, dropping a Top-Flite ball. "I carried *Wind, Sand and Stars* all over Europe with me when I was here. I think that book was one reason I was so anxious to become a flier. I even gave it to my mother one Christmas. She kept it right beside her Bible for a long time. She was crazy about flying, which is pretty funny when you realize she was a woman who came east on a flatbed wagon from the plains of Texas the year they captured Geronimo in Arizona."

I remembered how my father's mother, Beatrice, had loved to fly; how after my grandfather Walter's death she'd come to live with us and was always flying off to visit one of my father's younger brothers at the drop of her pillbox hat. She always insisted on having a window seat in an emergency exit row, so she could look out the windows and have more leg room. I did the same when I flew. Like pioneer woman, like grandson.

Dad pulled out a pound coin, to flip for honors.

"How'd she get the flying bug, anyway?" I asked him.

"One year when I was about twelve or thirteen, we rented a farm out by the Greensboro airport—just an airstrip in those days. Amelia Earhart came through town, doing exhibition flights. I believe she might have had a Ford Trimotor plane. At any rate, your grandmother won some kind of drawing and got to go up with her for a short spin. Amelia Earhart was just about the most famous woman in the world at the time. I think that was the beginning of it, really. Mom used to joke that she never got to fly again until she was an old lady. We were pretty poor in those days."

"What a great story," I said, pleased that the trip had already yielded one juicy morsel of unknown family history. "I just saw a documentary on public TV that said Amelia Earhart was a terrible flier who never bothered to learn Morse code."

"Really?" Dad thoughtfully wiped a speck of mud from his putter face with his thumb and shrugged. "Well, she was a hell of a heroine to your grandmother. Frankly, I don't know why people are so anxious now to tear down historical figures like Amelia Earhart. The people who complain the loudest that kids don't have role models anymore seem to be the worst offenders."

I agreed with him, saying at least we had Arnold Palmer. The day public TV did a documentary trying to smear the King, I said, was the day I either hung up my clubs or destroyed my TV with a golf club.

"I agree," my father said. "Shall we play?"

We flipped the coin, and Dad won. He always seemed to win our coin tosses. For that matter, he always seemed to win our putting matches, too.

He dropped his ball and putted. Watching his ball scamper along the sparce turf, my eyes were drawn to a man and two small children ahead of us on the putting course. The man was about my age, and the children—presumably his, a boy and a girl—were about my own children's ages.

It pleased me to think that nothing about my father's putting stroke really ever changed. He was a deadly putter, wasted precious little time over the ball, and used the kind of gently stabbing wristy style that modern instruction gurus deplore. Bobby Locke, Billy Casper, and Gary Player putted this way in their prime; as did Arnold Palmer, to some extent, the blade almost always passing his wrists at impact in the old films of his early career. The modern player who perhaps comes closest to this technique is John Daly, who slightly bends his wrist during the takeaway portion of his stroke. The vast majority of modern players, good amateurs and pros alike, work hard to remove any trace of "wrist" from their putting strokes.

Like his famous contemporaries, though, my father's putting stroke was always his salvation. Over the years I'd seen him make some awesome putts, but the one that still stood out in my mind was one he made just a few years before, during a small Atlantic gale on the Ocean Course at Kiawah Island. We were playing a par-five on the closing nine with an assistant pro and my old pal/nemesis Patrick McDaid. Pat had just wedged up a shot within five feet of the hole, to lie three. As was his custom, he immediately began harassing me about my wayward wedge shot, which flew the green and took my hopes for a tie with it. The pro was also in decent range of birdie—a birdie that would seal the match in their favor. Dad had limped his *fourth* shot to the front of the green but faced an impossible eighty-footer uphill for par. As near as I could figure, his ball would have to pass through several small swales and break at least three different directions.

"C'mon, Brax," Pat needled him. "Let's see you make one of those patented giant killers of yours."

"You really want me to?" Dad calmly gave it back to him.

Pat smiled. "Sure. Otherwise you guys are dead. We need to keep this match *interesting*." I saw him give his partner the pro a confident wink. Then he stuck out his nasty little tongue at me.

"Very well, then." Dad stepped up to the ball, looked at the hole, and popped it with his wristy stroke. The ball seemed to take *forever* rising and crossing the green. It turned left, then right, and then seemed to gather speed as it came off the slope and raced toward the hole. The ball thumped the back of the cup and dropped in. After everybody stopped laughing, both Pat and the pro missed their birdie putts. We halved the hole and went to the eighteenth still one hole down and there lost the hole and the match, but Dad's brilliant putting had once again made it *interesting*.

Now in Hyde Park, though, his putt was poor. He would have called it a Little Mildred. It bounced weakly along the sorry turf and plunked into a little sand trap fifteen feet short of the hole.

"Tough break."

"I'm just getting warmed up, Sport."

I dropped my ball and lined it up. Putting is the weakest aspect of my game. Basically I am a longball striker who can slug the ball to the next zip code, occasionally even the correct one. Like lots of Americans, I grew up admiring the social grace of Arnold Palmer but copying the playing style of Jack Nicklaus, whose power fade, according to John Jacobs, the famous British teacher, turned America into a nation of slicers. The main difference between me and Jack Nicklaus, I sometimes tell myself—aside from the fact that he is (a) rich, (b) famous, and (c) the most successful golfer who ever lived— is the fact that, unlike me, the Golden Bruin can really putt.

This time my ball rolled past my father's ball and dropped into the hole, proving golf really is a riddle wrapped in a conundrum.

I announced: "I think maybe we'll go to Rules, for bitter and steak with onions."

"Don't order your steak and kidney pie just yet, sonny boy."

After just nine holes, I was already two down—our usual depressing pattern. It was yet to be determined if my father could walk an entire golf course, but he undoubtedly could still *putt* one. In a few minutes, we caught up to the father and his two children. The father's name was Tom Neek. He was an actor, with a face like a pugilist beneath a flat wool cap, a natural Iago. Tom was reading a newspaper as his children, Sarah and Andrew, took turns slugging balls at the cup. I wondered if they were named in honor of Britain's second most famous battling royal couple.

"Daddy," complained Sarah, in her shiny yellow rain slicker, "Andy keeps knocking my ball away. Tell him it's not fair, please." I liked the way she said Daddy: *Dod-day.*

"Andrew, that's not fair. Let your sister putt unhindered, please."

Andrew said, "She's a sack of hammers."

"Daddy, please tell Andrew not to call me a sack of hammers." *Dod-day.*

"Andrew, please don't call your sister a sack of hammers."

"Tell her to putt, then."

"Sarah, *dah-ling.* Please putt."

Tom glanced at us. "I'm afraid it's American TV, where they get that sort of thing," he explained, a bit defensively I thought. "Rather a silly little game, don't you think? Knocking little balls in holes and such."

"Probably true," agreed Dad. "But that's why we love it so much."

I saw my father smiling goofily at Sarah. He sometimes went goofy around small children, especially little girls. Perhaps this was the result of having had two sons. When my daughter Maggie was born, he insisted on calling her "Magic," and I never heard a recitation of Mark 10:14—the bit where Jesus says "Suffer the little children to come unto me, for of such is the kingdom of God"— without thinking of my father's goofiness around small children. Kids turned him into a cartoon character.

Tom Neek and his children stepped aside and allowed us to play through. "You remind me of my granddaughter," Dad said to Sarah, mussing her hair gently as we passed; I saw Sarah slide Andrew a look and roll her eyes. *What a sack of hammers, eh, Andy?*

By the end of our first eighteen, I'd managed to climb back to within one hole of squaring the match. Dad suggested another circuit, so we started again.

I reminded him that my first golf lesson had been on a putting green with him when I was about six or seven. I couldn't remember where the lesson had taken place, but I could recall some of what my father had told me because he told me the same thing for a year. "First get your balance, because golf is a game of balance. Then try and keep your head still. Lead with your left hand, and PLK."

"What?"

"PLK. That stands for *putt like a kid*. That's what you told me. 'Remember,' you'd say, 'lead with the left hand, and *putt like a kid.*' "

He smiled. "I think I remember saying something like that. God knows where I picked it up."

"Actually, I think you were on to something. I never knew what you meant, but I think I do now."

"What do you think I meant?"

"Kids are fearless putters. Just watch 'em. They're about as unmechanical as you can get. They set up, aim, and pull the trigger without a lot of second-guessing and body tension." I told him about Maggie's emerging putting prowess. She seemed to think the object was to *move* the hole back a foot or two. "She's not the least bit shy about it. Loves to bang it at the hole. Leads with the left, putts like a kid. Wish I could putt half as well as her," I admitted.

"Interesting theory. I wasn't aware you're afraid of putting."

"Utterly terrified," I said, lining up a three-footer for my twopar. "In my little golf group, it's the running gag. They'd rather see me three feet than thirty feet from the hole."

"Hold it right there," Dad said. "Step back."

I stopped, looking up at him. "What?"

"Let's see you set up again, and this time"—a smile crept across his face—"let's see you lead with your left and putt like Maggie."

I told him I didn't think I could do it. For one thing, I'd have to have a mouth full of bubble gum. For another, I'd spent years trying to banish the "wrist" from my stroke and learn to putt like a machine.

"Are you a putting machine?"

"More of a putting fool."

"Why not try to putt like a kid, then."

I shrugged and took a deep breath. I walked away from the ball and came back, got my balance, set up, took one look at the hole. I putted with the wristy old style of my childhood. The ball clattered into the cup.

"How 'bout that," Dad said with a grin.

"Even I get lucky."

He shut me out at the thirty-second hole, five up with four to play, the usual rout. Tom Neek and his kids were long gone. The sun was going home from Hyde Park, too, and the guy with the nose ring and strange reading tastes was padlocking up his booth.

We walked to Alexandra Gate to hail a taxi.

"Well, you won," I said. "I'm buying dinner. Where shall we go?"

"How about Rules?" Dad proposed as a black taxi separated from the sea of whizzing cars and pulled over. "I haven't been there in at least half a century."

I was glad he chose Rules. Rules of Covent Garden, London's oldest restaurant, had significance to us both. On leave during the war, my father thought he saw novelist Graham Greene dining with friends at Rules and almost asked him for his autograph.

He told me this story again as we settled over beers at the bar. It was still early at Rules, and waiters were setting up for the dinner trade. The restaurant has a cozy Victorian feel, lots of brass fixtures, signed photos of famous patrons on the wall, and small linen-clothed tables pushed tightly together. We were early, the only dinner customers in the place as yet.

"Thank God I didn't go over and disturb the man. I wasn't even certain it was Graham Greene. Someone only said that it was him because he always ate at Rules. I think Greene had been in Sierra Leone prior to 1943, but I guess it could have been him."

"Why didn't you go find out?" I knew the answer to the question, but considering the setting, I wanted to hear the tale all over again. I sipped the yeasty head off my Old Peculiar.

"My group was, how shall I put it—a bit rambunctious."

"Drunken?" I helped him.

"And a bit disorderly. That's what happens, I'm afraid, when you give five American sergeants real English folding money and a week's leave and point them generally in the direction of a large city."

"How skunked were you?"

"Still sober enough not to want to make a horse's ass of myself in case it wasn't him—or maybe worse, really was him. American GIs weren't all that popular in some places in Britain, for good reason. I knew guys who did nothing but gripe about English food or the weather or the toilets. I'm no prude, but the language could get really raw from these idiots. They didn't disguise the fact that they thought Britons were damned lucky to have the American cavalry saving their skins."

"How'd you pick Rules? Had you read Graham Greene?"

"Nope. I wasn't that literary, I'm afraid. Some fella selling newspapers at Victoria Station told us the classy good-looking girls went to Rules. A big Dutchman named Culp came back from the bar and said a man seated at a table in the back was Graham Greene. Culp was a big ape from Pennsylvania. He was always trying to get me into trouble. He said as the only college boy in the crowd, I ought to go over and introduce myself to the famous novelist. I was tempted to do it, but luckily I thought better of it. Hell, I'd never even read one of Greene's books."

"Did you ever?" I asked.

"Just the one I gave you."

The book he gave me in 1969 was *Travels with My Aunt,* one of Greene's later novels and perhaps his most charming tale. In it, a stodgy unmarried bank manager named Henry Pulling is yanked by fate from his humdrum dahlia-growing existence by his bawdy Aunt Augusta and dragged on the adventure of a lifetime. A typical Greenesque transformation of the character occurs: While racing from one exotic setting to another (from Paris to Istanbul to Paraguay), Pulling, confronted by a cast of rogues and dangers both imaginary and real, is forced to confront the ghosts of his own past. In the process, he discovers for the first time what it means to really be alive. *A long life is not a question of years,* Aunt Augusta lectures her reluctant traveling companion at one point. *A man without memories might reach the age of a hundred and feel that his life had been a very brief one.*

My father had had a long life, no doubt, because he had the kind of rich memories Aunt Augusta would have found appealing and necessary for a rewarding passage. I had memories, too. By the time I arrived in London on my strange nongolfing golf pilgrimage after Kristin's death, I'd read every book Graham Greene had written. His romantically sad protagonists—drunken priests, lonely foreign diplomats, businessmen reluctantly made spies in service to Queen and country—and his theme of redemptive loss greatly interested me. I didn't want to know Graham Greene so much as *be* him. Absurdly, I'd even written him a fan letter—my first and last—addressed via the *Times* where Greene had worked *thirty* years before as a subeditor. I suppose I hoped some kindly soul would pass the letter along and the great man would agree to see me.

On one of my first nights in London, I set out to try and find him. I knew, thanks to my father, that the writer was a habitué of Rules. The most seductive love scene in all literature, in my view, takes place at Rules in Greene's book *The End of the Affair*, his famous précis on the eternal war between *agape* and *eros*, when Bendrix, the world-weary writer, falls for Sarah, his friend's wife, over a plate of steak and onions—a scene that apparently gave British censors a few sleepless nights when it first appeared in the mid-1950s.

Fortunately for Graham Greene, he wasn't at Rules the night I went there looking for him. He probably hadn't been in the place for years. But I certainly wouldn't have hesitated to ask him for his autograph—finishing what my father had started thirty years before.

I told my father this sad little story as we had our beers, and he made me feel better by smiling. "I don't think you were really look- ing for Graham Greene," he said. "I think you were really looking for *yourself*." He paused, then added: "That was a pretty difficult time you were going through. I can see why you found Graham Greene so appealing."

I turned my pint slowly on the cardboard coaster, noting how the condensation made a perfect circle on it. After he accompanied me to Kristin's funeral, we never talked about her death again.

"Did you know it's been twenty years since Kristin died?" I said. "It occurred to me on the flight over."

"Good heavens. Has it been that long? I had no idea." He fell silent.

"The strange thing is, it doesn't feel that long ago. It feels like it happened . . . I don't know . . ."

"She was a marvelous girl," he said.

"Funny how we never talked about it afterward," I reminded him.

"I thought if you wanted to talk, we would talk."

"I wouldn't have known what I wanted to say."

"Do you now?"

I looked at my father and smiled slightly. "I don't know. I guess life doesn't seem to make any more sense than a Graham Greene novel. Life is probably much tougher than art."

"It certainly separates us—life, I mean."

"The way I separated you from a thousand dollars."

"How's that?"

"That was the emergency money you gave me at the airport," I reminded him. "I used it to come over here and mope my way through the glorious capitals of Europe like a poster child for post-Woodstock depression. I hung out with Bulgarian exchange students who reeked of garlic, and lost my favorite golf bag—that was the trip's only major highlight. Somewhere in France right this minute is the kid of a reformed train thief using a very nice old Byron Nelson MacGregor driver to dispatch woodchucks in his papa's vineyard. I loved that club. Talk about a waste."

"With all due respect, Sport, I disagree."

I searched his eyes, waiting for him to explain.

"I don't think it was a waste at all. On the contrary, I think you learned something very valuable."

"Right. I learned I wasn't Graham Greene. He seemed to go out of his way in a country of just forty million people to avoid me. I guess I can't really blame him. I made his characters look downright jolly."

Dad ignored me. "Grief is powerful stuff. Especially when you don't let it go. I forget who said the dead are the lucky ones because they don't have to grieve. It may even have been your friend Mr. Greene."

Before I could say more about this, a waiter appeared. He led us in to dinner, seating us at a table by the window. We ordered fresh beers and game hens, and my father excused himself to go phone my mother, to remind her, he said, that tomorrow was garbage collection day.

My parents had been married fifty-three years and were obviously devoted to each other. My father took care of most of the external duties of domestic life. He earned the money, paid the bills, kept the house in good working order, saw to the yard maintenance, even did the lion's share of the grocery shopping and some of the weekday cooking. My mother handled the social duties and the decorating, kept up on neighborhood gossip and both their complicated medical routines, talked on the phone, volunteered at the church soup kitchen, and occasionally produced very good meals.

I knew he worried about her a great deal. She suffered from a painful lung condition that caused her to be hooked up to a lung medicating device for an hour or so each day. Though otherwise fit and even pretty agile for an aging beauty queen knocking toward the end of her eighth decade, the mental image of her seated at the den counter doing her "treatments" while *The Young and The Restless* blared mindlessly from the television set was the governing, and most troubling, image in my mind. I sometimes wondered how she would possibly cope with the exigencies of life when my father was gone. I knew he had recently been teaching her how to properly keep up with the checkbook, pay bills, and replace blown fuses. Other seminars on car maintenance, Social Security, insurance, and income taxes were apparently scheduled soon to follow.

My father came back with a little smile on his face.

"Everything okay back at Camp Jan?"

"Fine." He took a seat, tucking the napkin over his knees again. "It's just your mother never ceases to amaze me. She can get worked up over the smallest things."

I asked what she was worked up over this time. Last time I spoke with her, she was worked up over me taking my father to Britain.

"Well, she was over at the shopping center a couple weeks ago, and a woman came up to her and told her something about her husband being in jail and her needing to borrow some money in order to get to Florida. Your mother drove her to the bank and took out some money, then drove her to the bus station. She never heard from the woman again, and the Greensboro police just told her she was the fourth person that week to be hit by the scam. She feels pretty bad."

"How much money was it?"

"Ten thousand dollars."

I pretended to strangle on my beer, wiped my mouth, and said, "I'd feel bad, too."

"Why?"

"*Why?* Give me a moment, and I'll give you ten thousand reasons why. She was basically robbed."

"I suppose that's true. Another way of looking at it, though, is that the woman, whoever she is, may actually be on the level and planning to return the money, and even if she isn't, well, at least your mother wasn't injured. That's the important thing. Besides, maybe the woman will do something good with the money. Who knows? I told your mother to forget it, just to let it go. But you know your mother. She can't."

"I frankly don't think I could, either."

"That doesn't come as a particular shock to me."

"Really?"

"You're like her in many ways. She's feisty and so are you. She's also the most generous person I ever knew. It didn't bother her to give that woman ten grand—only that she might have stolen it."

"It didn't bother her to try and make me date the daughters of her friends, either," I pointed out. "I remember one who bore an uncanny resemblance to Charles de Gaulle. She was a congressman's daughter. Even had the funny little moustache."

Dad laughed. "You were her baby. She only wanted somebody nice for you."

"I had Kristin. And I eventually found Alison—all by myself."

He nodded. "That's right. You did. We all loved Kristin. I'm glad you found Alison."

I asked him to finish what he'd started to say at the bar—the bit about my learning something important from that bootless trip to Britain twenty years ago.

He chewed the last piece of his game hen slowly. I could see him thinking this over. Perhaps he was thinking that his answer was important because our first time discussing the subject would also probably be our last.

"You learned your mother and I loved you enough to let you go, and enough to welcome you back. That's something even more powerful than grief. Everyone needs second chances, new starts, whatever you want to call them. I sometimes think that's why we like golf so much—every round is like a second chance to finally get it right."

"I must have been driving you and Mom nuts," I said.

He laid aside his silverware. A waiter moved toward us with a water pitcher. "As you're discovering, the hardest job on earth is being a parent. Every child has to grow up. You'll have to let Maggie and Jack go and trust them to do what is right. That's the hard part. I think Francis Bacon said a parent's joys and sorrows are secret—they won't speak of one, they can't speak of the other."

I remained silent, thinking about this. There was a sudden burst of raucous laughter from a table in the back of Rules. London's oldest restaurant was congested and buzzing now. The check came, and before I could pay it, Dad had signed the credit card slip and we were walking outside with our coats, angling up the darkened narrow street toward a Covent Garden taxi stand. You could smell the river mud of the Thames drifting on the chill evening air, a sad end-of-summer fragrance. My father stumbled a little bit on the street's cobblestones. I took his arm.

I started to admit to him that I'd come dangerously close to canceling our golf trip that afternoon, what with all the obstacles facing us and to say nothing of my mother's immutable fears and my own pesky Greek chorus. But then I remembered once again why we were here, and why we would go on for as long as possible—the golf. My father was already one up on the putting greens, with the real fairways yet to come. Where I and others saw trouble, Opti the Mystic saw only another challenge, a chance to play and solve the problem.

Our dinner conversation reminded me of one last little-known Graham Greene story. It involved the great man's brief encounter with golf. The end of that affair came quickly.

"Greene, you know, tried to play golf at Balliol College," I explained to my Dad. "He beaned his caddy on the first swing, and that was all it took. His companion shot his ball through the open window of a passing bus and nearly killed the driver. They threw their clubs down and ran like hell."

"I've had days just like that," Dad said with a robust laugh. "Unfortunately, not all of them were on the golf course."

The Road to Lytham

Our little Omega was flying through the rain along the M6 motorway early the next morning, angling toward the Lancashire coast, dodging lorries and motor coaches. The plummy-voiced weather girl on the BBC Radio advised us there would be *"periods of heavy downpours in the south and west portions of England this morning, followed by showery breaks this afternoon and more heavy rains this evening."* It wasn't the golfer's forecast I'd been hoping for. A suicidal Hungarian composer's orchestral tribute to mental illness came on. I yawned and switched the station to someone who couldn't sing who was shouting rock lyrics I couldn't understand to an audience that probably couldn't care less. I shut off the radio.

"We need a road game," I said. "Something to keep me from falling asleep at the wheel and driving into the rear end of that bus."

"What's the funniest thing you ever saw on a golf course?" my father responded, sitting up. He'd been lightly snoozing because the passing landscape might have been Ohio in a fogbank for all you could see of it.

I thought about it for a moment. "That would have to be a Norwegian golf writer named Olaf who got a telephone call in his golf bag."

"Really?"

Olaf and I had been playing in the same foursome during an international golf writers' tournament in France. He had just putted out when his golf bag rang. He unzipped the side pouch and took out a cell phone with a picture of the red Norwegian flag on it.

"He turned out to work for the North Atlantic Treaty Organization," I explained.

"I thought you said he was a golf writer."

"He was. Norway is apparently such a small hard-working country everybody does *two* jobs. Olaf was the country's top golf writer *and* chief of security to the King of Norway. Heck of a nice guy. Always joking around. Had a grip like a polar bear. When I asked him if I could call Henry Kissinger on his golf bag telephone, he laughed and slapped me on the back hard enough to loosen a crown."

"I don't think I can top that," Dad said.

"Sure you can. I see you top balls all the time."

He took a shot at it anyway, reminding me of the time I was so eager to reach a ball in the fairway, I sped off and accidentally tossed my mother out of a golf cart, breaking her right forearm—which, we figured upon reflection, wasn't really *all* that funny—and fondly recalled another time I rolled a cart over on the side of a steep hill, sending two sets of clubs and half a million balls racing down the hill onto a busy state highway, causing brief automotive mayhem but luckily no loss of life.

"I think your mother was always a little worried about the state granting you a driver's license," he said.

"I've got a better one," I said.

I reminded him of the time we were playing a famous resort course in Florida behind a trio of slow-moving ladies, and he, in a rare display of impatience, decided to prod them along with a tactful approach shot to a short par-five; he'd picked out the biggest target in the group, a large lady in red plus fours, and breezily joked about "tattooing Titleist on her bottom unless she gets a move on." The ball, a magnificent three-wood shot, bounced once on the front of the green and scored a bull's-eye. My father nearly fainted from embarrassment. "I remember how you jumped in the cart and raced up to apologize. I've never seen you so rattled. You were even redder than her britches. Now *that* was funny."

"That wasn't even remotely funny."

"You're right. It was hilarious. But a brilliant shot."

"Thanks." He shook his head in mock horror. "Did I ever tell you about the time Bob Tilden nearly killed himself with a tee shot?"

"Gosh no."

Bob was one of my father's oldest chums, a charming but taciturn man who almost never said a word on the golf course. "It was the usual suspects, Bill Mims, Bob, Alex, and me," my father began. "We were playing down at the university course in Chapel Hill, and Bob had won a couple holes and was really feeling his oats when we came to a big par-five. He said to us, 'Boys, when I hit this drive, you're gonna say to yourselves, "Goddamn, Bob, we've never seen *anybody* hit a golf shot like that." ' His drive hit a tree and flew straight back and hit him on the forehead and the three of us shouted at him, *'Goddamn, Bob, we've never seen anybody hit a shot like that!!'* "

"Was he hurt?"

"Only his dignity. We remind him of it every time he has the honors."

A sign to Preston suddenly appeared, and we veered off and began twisting through a series of turns that led to a stretch of potholed road that seemed designed to deter us from ever wishing to live in the city of Preston. We passed a lot of vacant warehouses and garbage-littered lots, followed by more warehouses and empty lots. We finally crossed a small bridge, and my father cheerfully piped up, "That's the River Ribble. We're getting close." A McDonald's appeared, followed by another empty lot strewn with garbage. *Oh, good,* I thought. *Elizabeth, New Jersey.* It wasn't the romantic view of England I'd hoped for.

A few minutes later, though, we were driving along a better dual carriageway, and even the inky sky was brightening above us, allowing glimpses of a widening river estuary through forest trees to the left.

"I used to ride a bicycle along this road," my father mused, looking closely for familiar landmarks. "All the way from Freckleton to Preston."

"To meet girls at McDonald's?"

"No, wise mouth. To go to the movies. Come to think of it, there were always these English girls waiting around the movie house looking for an American date. Their boyfriends and husbands were in North Africa or the Pacific. They'd spot your uniform and stroll up and say, 'Hello, Yank. Care to have some fun tonight?' "

"Going to the movies in Preston must have been fun. Ever manage to see any movies?"

"A few," he said, looking out the window with a smile.

Between November 1943 and December 1944, my father served as one of four chief parachute inspectors at Warton Base Army Depot Number Two, the sprawling Eighth Air Force maintenance facility on the Ribble Estuary and the Irish Sea, just on the outskirts of a village called Freckleton, where ten thousand Americans lived and worked, primarily repairing, testing, and building B-24s and other Allied aircraft. Freckleton during those years was called "Little America," and it was my father's home for thirteen months prior to being sent to northern France.

A few miles north of Warton's front gates lay Royal Lytham and St. Annes Golf Club, sometimes simply called Royal Lytham, where Bobby Jones captured the British Open in 1926 and Seve Ballesteros became a hero to the British people by winning the Open twice, in 1979 and 1988. The British Open was going to return to Lytham in 1996, but more important to me, it was where my father used to play golf on his days off fifty years ago. The first round of our last trip was going to be here.

I slowed the Omega as we rolled into Freckleton's picturesque village center—now *this* was the postcard England I wanted to see!— past a collection of tidy chemist and chips shops and a large dark brick Anglican chuch where the standard read "Harvest Festival this Sunday. Everyone welcome." I saw my father staring at the church, then his eyes abruptly shifted to a group of schoolkids fooling around on the corner. Naturally, he smiled.

We'd left London early enough so that it was now the school hour in Freckleton. Children in dark blazers jostled along the wet sidewalks where the sun, in stiff defiance of the BBC weather lady, bravely broke through dense ragged clouds. Many were in pairs or alone, a few accompanied by their mums. Watching them, my father said, "We had kids just like that hanging around the base. A lot of them were evacuees from London and Birmingham. We'd give 'em candy and magazines."

"You could get twenty years for that today," I said.

He ignored my joke. "One of my jobs was to put together the daily information briefing for the base colonel. I carried around an old camera and took photos of a lot of the kids from Freckleton. We had one wall at the PX covered with nothing but snapshots of local kids."

We drove straight through Lytham's bustling town center and on into the outskirts of adjoining St. Annes. The golf club was several blocks off the main drag, and amazingly, my father remembered the way. There was one car in the car park, and we found Eddie Birchenough, Royal Lytham's popular head professional, sitting in his cozy office in the pro shop. He shook my father's hand vigorously, welcomed him back on behalf of the club, and explained, "I'd hoped to scour up a couple members to play with you this morning, but the truth is, I think the dirty weather kept them all in the hutch. You gentlemen are welcome to play at your leisure, though. Maybe I'll join you for a bit of lunch or a coffee afterward."

I explained that Tony Nickson, a former club captain and Lytham's historian, was meeting us that afternoon for a tour of the premises.

"Ah, well, you're already in the best of hands then."

Birchenough refused to accept a visitors' green fee from either of us, so I purchased a wool sweater vest with the Royal Lytham seal on it. We thanked him and collected our bags and deposited them on pull carts, what the Brits call trolleys. A few minutes later, zippered into windbreakers, we were standing on the first tee.

Dad's eyes roved slowly across Royal Lytham's flat green landscape, taking in the course and the prim-roofed town beyond. He pivoted slowly, almost making a full circumnavigation, studying the ivy-wreathed Victorian redbrick clubhouse, the sedate white dormy house, the nearby empty putting green, and finally the small white pro shop, where Birchenough had burrowed back into his own hutch. The sun was welcomingly bobbing in and out, but the light breeze had a chilly bite.

"So how does the place look to you?" I asked.

"Very nice indeed. What's Auden's line about being unable to repeat the past but also leave it behind?"

I admitted I didn't know the quote and patted him on the back. Only my old man would have been thinking about Auden at such a moment. I asked him how many times he reckoned he'd played Lytham in the thirteen months he was here.

"Hard to say. Quite a lot. I used to ride my bike up here at least one afternoon a week. What I liked was, they always welcomed American servicemen, and you could always scrounge up a match. The British love to play matches. We Americans spend all our time worrying who has the lowest score."

"Who do you think is right?"

"Oh, I think the soul of golf resides in a golf match," he said without hesitation. "Maybe that's something I just picked up here, but the idea of competing against the field seems rather shallow to me. The joy of going with a fellow and playing him head to head, regardless of the score at the end—that's special. Let the pros keep medal play if they want."

I agreed with him on this. A growing number of the world's best players seemed to hold similar sentiments, witnessed by the explosive popularity of the Ryder Cup, golf's greatest match-play event. If you asked them their goals for any particular year, the Davis Loves and Nick Faldos would invariably answer: "To make the Ryder Cup."

I asked my father how in his view Lytham compared to Royal Birkdale, its Open rota neighbor twenty or so miles down the Lancashire coast.

He said: "Some of the other guys used to like to catch the train down to Birkdale—I did, too, once or twice—but I always thought this place was somehow more special. There was a simple honesty about Lytham, its old clubhouse and little pro shop, that appealed to me. And the course is deceptive, a lot tougher than it looks. At least it was back then."

"I know why you liked this place so much," I said.

He looked at me, arching a brow beneath his St. Andrews cap.

"It resembles Green Valley. Think about it. Simple and straight-forward. Set down right in the middle of the town. But the grass is lovely, and it probably is capable of ruining your scorecard fast."

"Nice theory," Dad replied. "Only one problem. The chronology is all wrong. I never played Green Valley before I came over here. It wasn't even built, in fact. I'd caddied at Sedgefield, but I never really got to play until I reached this place."

"So much for theory. Shall we play?"

I pulled out one of the Queen's pound coins and flipped it. Dad naturally won again.

Some say Royal Lytham lacks the physical charm and visual majesty of the other great British linkslands because its contours are fairly subtle and the course is hemmed in by a coastal road and suburban neighborhoods on all sides. It doesn't have the magnificent dunes of Birkdale, the eccentric double greens of St. Andrews, the thatched-roof aristocracy of Royal St. George's, or the soulful ocean vistas of Turnberry. What it has, though, is extraordinary grass, and a glorious history of beating up the world's best golfers. Did I mention the 190 lethal sand bunkers?

Bernard Darwin, the great British golf writer of the early century, once wrote of Lytham: "It has beautiful turf but not much else of beauty. It is a beast but a just beast." When a young Tom Watson came here in 1979, he was no fan of British links golf, but Lytham helped convert him to the *less is more* theology of links golf. Recently, Davis Love III had told me that if he could win only one major, it would be the British Open at Royal Lytham because his father had briefly led the British Amateur there when he was a little kid.

The first hole is certainly a Darwinian little brute, a 206-yard par-three guarded by a series of sand traps. I watched my father tee up his Top-Flite. His takeaway was clean, quick, and self-assured.

Tom Watson had this same kind of uncomplicated swing, which appears so natural, you simply must be born with it. Dad sent his ball scampering along Darwin's beautiful turf, throwing up a fantail of water. He'd topped his Top-Flite.

"Take a mulligan purely for old times' sake," I suggested.

A brisk shake of the head. "No, thanks. I'll play that." A mulligan here perhaps would have been a sacrilege to him. He'd suddenly grown reflective. The old golfing sergeant had come home.

We played the hole in silence, recording double bogeys. It was a poor start. As we stood on the second tee, a commuter train whizzed past just beyond the trees to the right. We stood and watched it pass, tons of rocketing steel blasting through the air. I saw a whitish blur of faces. Commuters. Because of its location on the Ribble Estuary, Lytham was known as far back as the days of the Magna Carta, and was even mentioned in the Domesday Book, but as recently as 1875 its neighbor St. Annes hadn't even existed. It grew up as a vacation town for cotton managers from Manchester, a sort of Victorian version of Hilton Head Island, while nearby Blackpool attracted the working-class hordes.

Our second tee shots were much better. I was again thinking about whether my father could make a complete round on foot. The limp I'd noticed in his gait on the first hole, however, began to disappear as we walked. He lofted a beautiful three-iron shot to the front of the second green, and before I knew it, he was toddling off down memory lane again.

"I remember there was this friendly pro here in those days named Fergie or Furman or something like that. Real nice fella. A club-maker. That's how pros in those days made their money. He always wanted to make me a custom set of clubs. I was never in any hurry because I used the clubs of a member who was away in the war. They were good clubs. Handmade also. I took good care of them."

"Did you take any lessons?"

He smiled. "No. But I had some help with my swing from an unusual source—the pro's daughter. Her name was Nickie. She was about seventeen and had this mass of red hair and really knew her stuff. She liked to caddy for me. She used to tell me to keep my head down and get my bum into the shot. *Head down and bum into the shot, love.*" He laughed. "I haven't thought about that in years."

"So you're telling me my golf swing is descended from a girl?"

"Something like that. A sturdy redhead. Very lively lass."

We played two more holes more or less with our bums down and no chatter, the long (457-yard, par-four) third, which neither of us reached in two swats, and the somewhat tamer-looking fourth, which had far too many bunkers around the green for my liking. Lytham's long par-fours are difficult critters and hold the key to scoring well. By the end of the fourth hole, alas, I'd already toured *three* of Lytham's famous bunkers, and my scorecard was beginning to hemorrhage. With fourteen holes to play, I'd already shot *half* my handicap.

On the plus side, Dad showed no indication of fatigue whatsoever. There was even a discernible lilt in his step. At the frighteningly bunkered par-three fifth, he made a beautiful swing with his Big Bertha three-wood and caught an awful break—his ball striking the front of the green and kicking off into the right front trap. Mine reached the green, my first shot to reach in regulation. He followed next with an exquisite sand shot that left him a mere tap-in for par, his first par. I holed a ten-footer for par to prove I hadn't only just taken up playing the game. The day was getting better in several respects.

"Did you wear your uniform when you played?" I asked him as we walked off toward six.

"Of course. Every time. We all did. It was wartime."

I could picture him swinging in his staff sergeant's uniform, all necktie and peaked cap, handing his mashie niblick to a wartime Fanny Sunneson. I once wrote a column in which I helpfully suggested that modern tour players wear neckties and wool Norfolk jackets in order to make the game more colorful and challenging. A friend from the PGA Tour suggested I quit writing advice columns.

"How many matches did you win?"

"None that I remember. I wasn't very good."

"Probably forgot to keep your bum down, you bum."

I managed to birdie the par-five seventh hole, and Dad was nearly up to his old magic at eight, just missing a chip-in from the fringe for bogey. Soon we were standing on the ninth tee, which ends the course's outward march toward the sea. The ninth is the shortest hole on the course, a tidy par-three of just 164 yards. An easy six for me, a firm three- or four-iron for my father. I saw him take out a six also.

"Don't you want to reconsider?" I said, pointing out that the wind was diagonally in our faces from right to left. There appeared to be half a million little bunkers set into Darwin's "beautiful turf" around the ninth green, each one whispering my name like a sea siren. The pin was back. A six probably wasn't even enough for me, either. I put the club back and pulled out a five.

Dad went back to a five, also. It wasn't going to be enough, but I wasn't going to give him any more advice.

I said: "I've never had a hole-in-one. Wouldn't this be a perfect spot?"

"Any place would be a perfect spot for a hole-in-one," he said.

"Here goes," I announced, then proceeded to fire my ball into the depths of the huge yawning bunker in front. "What I meant was, this would be the perfect spot to make two from the bunker." Dad looped his five-iron shot to the grass just in front of the green, chipped on, missed the putt, and made bogey. I made double, saving my ace for another day.

We sat down to rest on the grass at the tenth tee.

"Our scores are awful," I said, adding up the damage.

"Ah, well. No matter." He yawned. "This is so delightful. Look at those birds."

I glanced up at several white seabirds darting over the roof of the train station and the peaked red rooftops of St. Annes. Our halfway scores were lousy, but the sun was now sprinkling late September warmth over the Irish Sea (wherever it was), and the moment really was delightful, proving, as someone who probably never broke 80 once said, that golf is mostly about whom you choose to play with.

"People were very decent to soldiers here," my father, still in reminiscent mode, observed as we sat there resting our legs. I noticed him gently massaging his left leg, reminding me what an effort this hike really was for him. Thank God, I thought, for Lytham's gentle old terrain. I noticed, as well, that one of his collection bags was leaking, staining the front of his trousers. He hadn't noticed, though, so I kept quiet.

"We were basically a bunch of smart-aleck kids a long way from home, and they made us feel welcome. That may strike you as just an old soldier's sentimental memory," he said to me, "but there was such civility in the way we were treated here. You don't forget kindness like that. The world could use some civility like that."

Watching the birds soar and plunge to earth, I agreed.

We carded a 42 and 53 respectively on the outward march. They weren't good scores, but if the trip had ended right there, it probably would have been just fine.

The back nine at Royal Lytham is loaded with danger and history. Bobby Jones played heroically down this stretch to capture the first of his three Open championships in the first year, as it happened, that golf fans actually paid gate admission to watch a golf championship—an attempt aimed at controlling crowds rather than making money. In those days the Open concluded on a Friday, with a thirty-six-hole final, and ten thousand spectators paid half a crown for the privilege of watching the two best players in the world compete. Both were Americans but might have hailed from different galaxies: Walter Hagen and Bobby Jones.

Jones and Hagen were symbols of golf's past and future, playing the game for entirely different reasons. Jones was the ultimate amateur in an age when *amateur* meant something good. He entered twenty-seven majors in his relatively short career and won thirteen of them, including four U.S. Opens and three of the four British Open championships he entered. At twenty-eight, in 1930, a mere stripling by today's standards, he hung up his clubs and called it quits "to avoid getting myself into a position where I would have to keep on playing." He noted that he intended to "keep golf in perspective" by using it as "a means of obtaining recreation and enjoyment."

Hagen was something quite different: brash, flamboyant, money-loving, a failed Philadelphia Phillies prospect and drinking pal of Babe Ruth's who took the golf world by storm and became the game's first touring professional and slickest "mental" player.

Beginning in 1914, Hagen won a pair of U.S. Opens, four British Opens, the Canadian and French Opens, and five PGA titles, four of them in a row. Opponents claimed Hagen intentionally mismarked his clubs to throw them off—a charge he took pains never to deny—and the British press ripped him for his cheeky off-course extravagance, which only endeared him to the masses. He chartered airplanes to fly to tournament sites and dined on champagne and lobster in clubhouse parking lots. For the 1920 British Open, he booked a room at the Ritz in London and appeared at the golf course in an Austro-Daimler limousine with a footman. He often departed a tournament site by bouncing balls to kids. His golf philosophy was "Never hurry and don't worry."

Pursued by ex-wives and creditors, consorting with British royalty and Gatsby rogues, Sir Walter became the game's first true glamour boy. "Into this gaudy period," Charles Price once wrote of him, "stepped the Haig, as he was called, with the sangfroid of a Valentino, his black hair pomaded to an iridescence, his handsome features browned by the sun and the wind until they had the hue of briarwood."

Jones played his way to Lytham in 1926 by firing 66/68 at Sunningdale, in Berkshire, near London, to easily qualify for the Open. Because his first round was a model of symmetry—requiring thirty-three putts and thirty-three shots with irons and woods—his Sunningdale performance became popularly known as the "perfect round of golf." Bernard Darwin simply summed it up as "incredible and indecent."

By the third round of the Open at Lytham, though, neither Jones nor Hagen was on the lead. That belonged to a Detroit club pro named Al Watrous, who held a two-stroke lead at 215. Since they were paired for the final round, Jones suggested the two competitors retire to his hotel for a quiet lunch and a bit of rest before the final that afternoon. When they returned to the players' entrance at the course, the guard refused to readmit Jones, who had left his player's badge on the dresser at his hotel. The guard could not be persuaded he was one of the competitors, and Jones finally trotted to the main entrance and paid admission to reenter—the only player to ever pay his way into his own major championship title.

As Dad and I began the long walk home to the clubhouse from the tenth tee, we talked about Jones and how his love of sportsmanship really set golf apart from every other sport.

"Jones, you know, came here during the war."

"You mean to Lytham?" I said.

"Right. He did a Red Cross exhibition match here in the summer of '44. Unfortunately, I didn't get to see him. I don't remember why—probably because it was just after D-Day and we were working double shifts at the base. Some of the guys from the base saw him, though. They said he was as nice a gentleman as you'd ever wish to meet." He added with a chuckle, "Of course, they were sergeants. Jones was a lieutenant colonel."

We played the next four holes more or less in silence. Trying to concentrate on my game, I didn't feel any need to speak, and Dad seemed to be lost in a pleasant reverie or two of his own. I noticed that we'd slowed our pace even more; he was limping slightly again. *Oh well,* I thought. *Never hurry and never worry.*

Lytham holes eleven, twelve, and thirteen strike some connoisseurs as a trifle dull, but hole fourteen begins a final stretch of long par-fours that can wipe out anybody's score. The grassy dunes, as they are somewhat ambitiously called, begin to rise a bit as you approach the critical closing holes, and the greens themselves seem to hide behind the swelling land as if to signify impending high drama.

During the final round of the Open in 1926, Jones came alive at Lytham's daunting fifteenth, a 463-yard par-four some say is rivaled in difficulty only by St. Andrews' Road Hole. He birdied it to catch Watrous. The players were still even at the seventeenth, a 462-yard par-four that bends slightly to the left and where a player's drive must be played to the right so he can have an open approach to the green. In Jones's day a frightful sand waste area stretched down the left side of the fairway, and that was unfortunately where he pulled his tee shot. Unable to see the green, and with Watrous's ball already on the putting surface, Jones fired one of the most miraculous shots in golf, ripping a flawless four-iron over the dunes. His ball came to rest on the green closer to the flagstick than Watrous's ball. Shaken, Al Watrous three-putted to oblivion. Jones got down in two.

Fittingly, there was really only one man left on the course with a chance to catch Bobby Jones, the new leader in the clubhouse. That was Sir Walter the showman. Playing almost two hours behind Jones,

Hagen came to the final hole at Lytham two strokes behind Jones, needing to hole out from the fairway to tie. The cause was basically hopeless. It was an impossible shot. But gifted entertainer that he was, Hagen walked slowly to the green and asked his caddy to please hold the pin. Sir Walter's theory on performing for the masses was to *make the hard shots look easy and the easy shots look hard.* He walked back to his ball and took aim. His pitch nearly struck the pin before trickling off the back side of the green.

Jones had his first Open championship. But the Haig once again sent the masses home smiling.

My father soldiered along Lytham's rugged back nine with his usual collection of bogeys and doubles and only one triple, but my game, despite better concentration, came seriously unglued. I made the hard shots look hard and the easy shots look *harder*. At sixteen, where Seve Ballesteros had intentionally missed the fairway and driven his ball into the temporary car park at the 1979 Open, then got up and down with a brilliant sand-wedge shot, I could barely manage double bogey and wondered why my game was foundering so badly. Was it the distraction of the emotions I was struggling to keep at bay? Perhaps. Perhaps not. Perhaps my golf game simply reeked that day. Golf is like that, as fickle as any BBC weather forecast.

At seventeen, the hole where Jones struck his brilliant recovery shot, I found the little marker that commemorates the blast. I was lying *two* in the same sandy spot. I used my six-iron to advance my ball approximately ten yards. Then I chili-dipped, followed by a miserable shank, which preceded an angry skull. I eventually found my ball buried in a thick tuft of grass behind the green and scowled over at my father. À la Sir Walter Hagen, he was busy chatting up two elderly ladies who were playing along the nearby second fairway, blissfully unconcerned for my fate. He strolled back just in time to hear me mutter a murderous oath about the game.

I finished the hole with an *eight*, ballooning my score to 88.

Dad bogeyed the eighteenth. I escaped with a par. His 102 was respectable enough, considering his age and the fact that he hadn't *walked* an entire golf course in over a decade. My 92 was one of the *worst* golf scores I could just about remember. I don't know which of us looked more exhausted.

Tony Nickson was waiting for us.

Nickson was a former club captain and treasurer of Royal Lytham, a dapper seventy-six-year-old semiretired chartered accountant in a blue blazer and club tie who had recently authored the club's comprehensive history, *The Lytham Century*. He gave us a delightful walking tour of the large Victorian clubhouse, which is one of those great drafty places that seem to be all ancient paneling, cut-glass doors, and wide quiet corridors.

Nickson showed us pictures of Lytham's distinguished line of Open champs, including Bobby Locke (1952), Peter Thomson (1958), Bob Charles (1963), Tony Jacklin (1969), Gary Player (1974), and Ballesteros (1979 and 1988). As he described each of these players' conquest of the claret jug, I was struck by the pivotal role Royal Lytham played in each man's career.

Locke and Thomson were at the peaks of their careers when they won at Lytham, and Charles became the only left-hander to ever capture an Open, confirming the belief that the best courses bring out the finest in the best players. Jacklin's win made him the first native son to win in twenty years and transformed him into nothing short of a national hero. Gary Player's third Open win in 1974 would be his last, effectively a coda ushering in a new generation of champions named Watson and Miller. Nobody outside of Britain knew much about a twenty-two-year-old called Severiano Ballesteros when he came to Royal Lytham in 1979. Three years before, the young Spaniard had tied Nicklaus and nearly beaten eventual winner Johnny Miller at Birkdale with brilliant iron play. He was dark, broodingly handsome, and spoke terrible English. But he played with such breathtaking passion and creativity—as his car-park recovery shot in the final round at Lytham in 1979 proved (the wayward shot, Seve later insisted, was intentional, designed to give him a better angle at the green)—Europe's most glamorous golf star was born on the spot.

Seve's follow-up act at the Open, his win over Nick Price at Lytham in 1988, was merely the crowning touch of Ballesteros magic—but it also set Nick Price up, Price will tell you, to earn his claret jug at Turnberry six years later. "In order to win the Open," Price told me, "you have to first get close to winning. That helps you believe it's possible. Lytham is special to me because it's where I first got close. Playing there convinced me that winning the British Open, my childhood dream, was within my reach."

As Tony Nickson emphasized, though, one name transcends the rest at Royal Lytham—Bobby Jones. He led us into the empty club room, with its high ceiling and vast polished wooden floor, and showed us what amounted to a shrine to Bobby Jones, various memorabilia including the famous original J.A.A. Berrie oil portrait of Jones and copies of his original cards for all four rounds in 1926. There are also photos of Jones in the heat of competition and being presented the Open trophy afterward. The mashie club he used to strike his famous shot from the sand at seventeen is hung just below Berrie's famous painting.

We had a drink in the men's bar, and Tony invited us to step out onto the small private porch off the bar, which overlooks the eighteenth green, explaining slyly, "During the Open, of course, access to this spot has to be fiercely monitored due to its proximity to the eighteenth green. Certain members, emboldened by spirits, have been known to issue a few untimely remarks over the years."

I left the two gents to warm themselves in the sun and went back inside to snoop around some more. Drafty old clubhouses—as opposed to sleek, swank new ones—reek dignity and character and greatly attract me, and I was eager to spend a few minutes alone to try and decipher the crime I'd perpetrated on such a fine golf course. I went back in the club room, pausing to pay my respects to Jones, then went out and looked again at the wall of Lytham champions. There were several photos of Seve in action. In every one of them, the Spaniard looked seriously annoyed. In those days, whenever Seve looked seriously annoyed, the rest of the field usually booked the next train out of town.

I heard a phone ringing somewhere in the recesses of the old building. I heard footsteps echoing, a door open and close, and suddenly in this great place where I'd never been but felt such warmth and kinship, I once again found myself marveling that my father and I were finally *here.*

All this talk of Bobby Jones had opened up a host of my own memories. Bobby Jones had brought me here, in a sense. But it wasn't the Bobby Jones my father and Tony Nickson were chatting about out there on the members' porch.

It was the female version of the greatest player who ever lived.

One day in 1983, after years of hard work and no golf, I called my father from an unlikely place—the office of the Vice President of the United States. I was in Washington for a long-hoped-for interview at *The Washington Post,* and the editor I'd spoken to was encouraging about my prospects. At dinner the night before, a friend named Rudy Maxa, who'd worked for years on the paper's award-winning Style section, urged me to pursue my ambition to work at the paper of Woodward and Bernstein but quipped that I would need two things if I came to the greatest newspaper in America—a good literary agent and a *great* psychotherapist.

Rudy was just being funny. The competition, he meant, was awesome—you'd need to commit *everything* to making a name for yourself there. But his joke deflated something in me. I felt a sudden unaccountable fatigue and sadness. Why was that? It didn't add up or make sense. Wasn't this why I'd worked so hard, skipped vacations, even given up my golf game? I wanted to be the next Woodward and Bernstein, or at least the next Rudy Maxa.

On my way out of town, thinking it would make me feel better, I stopped by Vice President George Bush's office to say hello to some of the staffers I'd spent several weeks with on the campaign trail in 1980. I suppose I foolishly hoped I might even get to say hello to Bush. Several times over the weeks I spent with him on the campaign trail, we talked about our mutual love of golf. Bush, at least, still *played.* The staff was all new, and Bush was out of town. The secretary was kind enough to let me use a phone. I called Opti.

"I think I don't want to be a reporter anymore," I told him flat out.

"Really?" He sounded surprised. "Maybe you're just tired. When was the last time you played golf?"

"Let's put it this way. Carter's polls were still good."

He suggested that I change my plane ticket and meet him in Raleigh. He picked me up there the next morning, and we drove to Pinehurst. He had my brother's Wilson clubs with him. (I never bothered replacing my Hogans after they were stolen on that train in France.) We played Pinehurst Number 2 with a vacationing real-estate couple in matching designer warm-up suits, the Rizzos. They were from somewhere in New Jersey—"The really *nice* part of the state," Doris Rizzo kept assuring us. Dad played his usual game and finished in the respectable mid-80s. My drives, on the other hand, kept screaming off into the surrounding pine woods, prompting Rizzo the real estate baron to ask me, "Is your natural shot a duck hook or a peeled banana?"

Afterward, Dad and I sat drinking iced teas beneath a slowly turning ceiling fan in the club's Donald Ross grill room.

"So why are you tired of being a reporter?" he asked.

I shrugged. "I don't know. Journalism is supposed to make democracy work. Mostly it's making me feel creepy."

He asked if I had any clue why that was.

I replied that I used to like writing about crime because it provided a nice little window on the human psyche—murderers and extortionists, the theory goes, actually do things the rest of us only vaguely *think* about—while writing about politics was just plain fun. Like covering a war without bloodshed, to paraphrase Chairman Mao.

"Maybe you're tired of the battle."

I thought about this, conceding he might be right. Politicians and their assorted handlers, regardless of party stripe, were all beginning to sound eerily the same to me, and every time I wrote a crime story, I admitted, I increasingly felt like I was earning my rent on the back of somebody else's problems. The problem was, as I explained, all my hard work and no play had finally begun to yield some tangible rewards—the prospect of a job at the *Post* and a couple enticing book possibilities. Two editors had recently made inquiries. One wanted me to consider writing a book about America's fascination with serial killers. The other had a bio of my home state's arch-conservative senior senator in mind. Both projects would come with respectable advances.

"You must be flattered. You've gone far in your journalism career for such a young buck." He smiled.

"I guess so. But here's the deal breaker. I can't see spending the next two years of my life living, eating, and dreaming about serial killers—or hanging around Jesse Helms, for that matter."

"Then don't do it," my father said. "Other opportunities will come along. Maybe you're just writing about the wrong subject. What would you *like* to write about?"

I sighed and glanced around at the photos on the walls. My eyes fell on several great golfers in their prime. Nicklaus. Snead. Hogan. Nelson. Palmer. Floyd. They'd all been through Pinehurst; through my own life, too, in a sense.

"In a perfect world?"

" 'Fraid there's no such thing, Bo."

"I dunno. You'll laugh."

"Try me."

"Golf, maybe."

My father didn't laugh. He took a thoughtful sip of his tea.

"In that case, maybe you should become a golf writer."

I laughed at his suggestion, pointing out that I didn't know a soul in the golf world, didn't even belong to a club, didn't even *own clubs*, wouldn't know how to begin to crack into the fraternity of golf hacks, hadn't played in years, and couldn't keep my balls out of the woods in any case. It would be easier, I said, to start a career as an astronaut.

"If you believe that, it probably won't happen. On the other hand, I've found that anytime I followed my heart, good things almost always happened. It may not be what you think will happen, or even what you think *should* happen. But the heart can open doors. I really believe that. Thing is, you'll have to walk through them on your own. You may be surprised at the possibilities."

I smiled at him, choosing not to think too much about what he'd just told me. So often his words took time to sink in.

"Thanks, Opti."

That's how we left it, as simple and direct as always. He drove me to the airport in Raleigh, and we said good-bye. I remember looking out the window at a golf course as my plane lifted into the sky and thinking that at least I could finally play golf again. It was almost as if some kind of *permission* had been given from on high. I still had a journalism career to try and untangle and a life's direction to figure out—not to mention a new set of clubs to buy—but I felt a lot better.

A short while later, against the advice of several colleagues, I took a job at an old established New England magazine called *Yankee*, telling myself, rather self-importantly, that I was granting myself a working hiatus from the "serious" journalism of the Beltway press corps, a year to "cool out" before I got on with my career. (Besides, it was an off-year election.) A critical shift in the axis of my world had already taken place, though, and in my heart I knew I would never go back to that world of cynical press pools and candidate image-makers and antacid-eating homicide cops.

I moved to a small solar house on a river in Vermont, got a retriever pup, took up fly fishing, and chiseled down my golf handicap to a respectable double digit at an old club where Rudyard Kipling was supposed to have once chased the pill while finishing *The Jungle Book*. My pieces for *Yankee Magazine* still occasionally canted toward the criminal and politic, but mostly they had a "kinder and gentler" tone to them, as one of my better-known profile subjects might have said.

One day Tim Clark, the magazine's managing editor, who knew of my revived ardor for golf, came to me and asked if I'd ever heard of someone named Glenna Collett Vare. "Sure," I said. "She was called the female Bobby Jones. Won something like five or six national championships. Died several years ago."

"Somebody evidently forgot to tell her," he deadpanned with

perfect timing, handing me a small clip from a Rhode Island news-paper. Glenna Vare was not only alive but about to play in her sixty-second Point Judith Invitational. He wondered if there was a nice little story in that.

I drove down to the town of Narragansett on a sunny morning and walked across an immaculate lawn to a huge shingled ark of a house. No one appeared to be about, but I heard a strange thumping sound. I knocked on the screen door and was commanded by a stern voice within to enter. I pushed open the screen and eventually discovered, up on the second floor, a stocky, heavily sun-tanned and wrinkled elderly woman up a stepladder, giving the ceiling sturdy cracks with an ancient brassie club.

"Have you ever had raccoon piddle on your ceiling?" she demanded.

I admitted I hadn't. "I've got a whole family of raccoons vacationing in my rafters," she explained. "I'm trying to urge them to *leave* before I have to call some dreary man who will come with a gun." Eventually, she came down from the ladder and we shook hands. At eighty-one, Glenna Vare still had a grip.

"So what is it you want, young man?" she asked testily. "I was about to make some soup."

I explained that I'd come to talk with her about winning six U.S. Women's National Amateur Opens. The LPGA's Vare Trophy, handed out annually to the player with the lowest scoring average, bore Glenna's name.

"Oh, nuts. Nobody cares about that," she said, dismissing me with a wave of her hand, marching down the stairs and tossing her brassie into an umbrella stand that held, among other things, an intriguing collection of vintage wooden cleeks and spoons. She rambled toward her kitchen with her small dog Jimmy frowning at me from her heels, and snapped over her shoulder that nobody had written about her "in at least twenty years." I got the sense that the female Bobby Jones felt rather forgotten by the golf world, but perhaps thought that's how it should be.

I followed her into the huge sunny kitchen and tried to explain the point of doing a story on her. She instructed me to "pipe down" and chop some carrots. I chopped carrots and then onions. She poured me a glass of sherry while the soup cooked, then told me that since I'd helped make the soup, I'd better eat a bowl of it.

We ate soup at a small table on Glenna's big porch overlooking Narragansett Bay, and I asked if she would permit me to caddy for her at the Point Judith. "Absolutely *not*," she replied quickly. "Nobody should watch an old bird like me play golf now if they don't have to." My penance for making this ludicrous request was not terribly severe: She made me get on the stepladder and whack the ceiling with the golf club while she went to change into her "driving shoes." She invited me to ride with her into town to "start the mail delivery," which I did, holding Jimmy on my lap, as she gunned her Cadillac through the thickening tourist traffic.

We talked about contract bridge, her grown children Ned and Glenny, the nuisance of summer tourists (she was one, too, though I didn't point that out), Gene Sarazen's shoes ("That man always had the spiffiest shoes"), shooting skeet (Glenna was a former champ back in Philly), the new generation of LPGA stars ("some most attractive young women, though some of them could do with a bit of makeup"), and other things that got lost in the roar of the Caddy's engine and Glenna's gently muttered oaths as we ran a gauntlet of luggage-loaded station wagons and sunburned pedestrians. When I finally had the nerve to nudge the conversation back around to golf, Glenna made me swear I wouldn't show up to watch her in the Point Judith. She let me off beside my car, smiled sweetly, and said, "You're a nice young man. You should get married. Come back sometime, and we'll have soup again."

The next day, I sneaked out and watched her play from a safe distance in Point Judith's thick yew bushes, and I was gratified by what I witnessed. Her driving touch turned out to be as solid as her grip. I went back to have lunch with Glenna, as she preferred me to call her, every spring upon her annual return from Florida for the next four or five years, until her death in 1989. We became friends and exchanged Christmas notes, and she took me for several nerve-wracking spins in her Cadillac, but she never agreed to let me watch her play golf. She said her golf game was "dead." She was happy to learn I was getting married. "It's about time you did that," she said. "Who's the lovely but unfortunate victim?"

I explained her name was Alison. She was an editorial assistant at my magazine. Her parents were real Scots. She'd gone to Harvard. She looked like the actress Ali McGraw.

"Does she play golf?" Glenna demanded.

"No."

"Probably just as well. Too much in common, you know, can kill a marriage. Always leave some mystery."

The story I wrote for *Yankee Magazine,* about making soup with Glenna, was read by the editor of *Golf Journal,* the periodical of the United States Golf Association, who purchased it for his magazine. The editor of one of Britain's top golf magazines read it there and mentioned it to an editor at *Golf Magazine,* who called me up exactly eight months after I'd met Glenna. He asked if I would care to write a profile of a promising young player named Davis Love III.

Just like *that,* the door my father had talked about that day at Pinehurst had unexpectedly opened. I effectively stepped through to a brand-new world, a place I felt comfortably at home.

The golf gods giveth. They taketh away, too.

A week after I met Davis, my father called to tell me Green Valley Golf Club was closing its doors. A parkway and medical arts complex were soon going to occupy the spot. It was stunning news. I immediately flew home with my fiancée and dragged her out to the club for the final day.

There was a festive wake going on, lots of old stags and their wives wandering about the clubhouse with Dixie cups of Jim Beam. Groups of men and women were headed out onto the course in boisterous *sevensomes* to abuse the turf one last time. I found Aubrey Apple in the sadly empty pro shop, pleasantly yelling at somebody, with the same old stogie jammed in the corner of his mouth. I introduced myself and asked if he remembered me.

"Hell, yes!" he bellowed. "You're old Brack Dobson's boy. How the hell is old Brack?" Nobody ever seemed to pronounce my father's name correctly, least of all Aubrey Apple.

I said Dad was fine and asked if we might take a cart and play a few holes for old times' sake. I wanted to show Alison hole number three, my favorite par-five in the world, the place I'd made my first birdie.

"Damn right." Aubrey smiled at Alison. "Your boyfriend, honey, used to be a Valley Rat. That's what we called all the snot-nosed kids that hung around this place."

Apple asked me what the hell I was doing now to stay out of jail. I told him I'd just written a story for one of the big golf magazines.

"No joke? Well, how 'bout *that*." He took the stogie out of his mouth and aimed it at the bridge of my nose. "I got a great story for you, by God. You ought to write about the time you beat the crap outta one of my greens with your putter and I kicked your little fanny off the course for a solid month."

"It was just two weeks. It only felt like a month."

"Helluva story," Apple assured me, plugging the stogie back into its socket.

·   ·   ·

To

Jim

with all our love

May and Chloe

I walked back to the members' porch and found Dad and Tony Nickson flipping through a large scrapbook filled with black-and-white photos from Lytham's war years. As Tony slowly turned the pages, I saw lots of photos of American servicemen, muscular American faces, lopsided farmboy grins, master sergeants and staff sergeants. Golfing sergeants.

"You seem to have attracted a lot of sergeants here in those days," I said, searching for a face that could have been my father's.

"Yes, it seems so," said Nickson. "No one knows why that was, exactly. But we certainly had lots of American sergeants round the area. See that fellow posing with the sergeants in the picture? That's Tom Fernie, our pro here then. Absolutely marvelous chap, Tom."

"Fernie," Dad murmured, nodding. "I knew him. He wanted to make me a set of clubs, but I was very fond of a set that belonged to a member who was away."

"My goodness. Perhaps you used my clubs." Tony Nickson blushed at the possibility. "I was away exactly then, you know. The infantry in Burma."

I was still scanning the book for a staff sergeant who looked like a young Alan Ladd, but I couldn't find him.

"Whosever clubs they were, I tried to take good care of them," said my father. "I remember they were very fine clubs."

"Yes," Nickson said, "I do hope you enjoyed them."

"Very much. Thank you. Wouldn't it be funny if they were really yours?"

"A lovely coincidence," Tony said with a broad smile.

Lady Sunshine

In the morning, while Dad rested his legs, I took another shot at Royal Lytham. I wore my best khaki pants, a white polo shirt, and my new Lytham sweater vest, and just to be on the safe side, I carried my lucky Pebble Beach ball in my left rear pocket.

I tell myself I'm not really superstitious on the golf course. But most golfers really are. Were it not for the indisputable fact that I always play better when I wear my lucky khakis and a white polo, use an odd-numbered Titleist balata ball, make sure I have only *white* golf tees in my left pocket, wear my lucky Footjoy teaching shoes, eat a Granny Smith apple on the way to the golf course, and carry my lucky Pebble Beach golf ball (a time-ravaged Spalding Dot, circa 1950, that I plucked from a hedge on Pebble's fifth tee, shortly before miraculously going par-birdie-birdie-par)—if it were not for these field-*proven* aids to scoring, I would probably be the first to tell anybody who is *genuinely* superstitious on a golf course that they have, à la Glenna Vare, raccoons in their rafters.

My luck at Lytham, not surprisingly, was better this time. I shot a respectable 82, playing alone until the back nine on a somewhat raw and windy morning, which gave me time to work out my swing flaws and reflect on events of the preceding afternoon. Our golf scores hadn't been pretty, but everything else had worked out so beautifully, and it was possible to take the suddenly improved mood of the trip as a sign of good things to come. Dad had thoroughly enjoyed his roast beef and Yorkshire pudding feast at a local pub afterward and was sleeping like a babe by ten that night. All in all, a perfect reunion. A nearly perfect day as well, flawed only by my sorry 92.

At Lytham's intriguing short ninth, the par-three where I'd brazenly predicted my first hole-in-one but taken five, I watched an elderly man tidy up his putting business on the green, pick up his ball from the cup, and stroll off. Pausing to watch me play, he waved stiffly, and I waved back, trying to convey the message that I was in no hurry to play. He waited, so I played.

This time, for a change, I wasn't thinking about making an ace. Perhaps since that day on the seventh tee at Green Valley with Kristin, I quietly obsessed about making golf's perfect score, no doubt in part because everybody I knew seemed to have at least *one* ace. The list included my regular golf pals, other golf writers, and every other stranger I hooked up with at a golf resort. The elderly mother of one of my best friends, for Pete's sake, had *four* of them! She'd taken up golf at sixty. Sometimes I comforted myself with the knowledge that Ben Hogan, maybe the best ball-striker who ever lived, scored only one ace in his competitive career, but then I'd sit down on a plane next to some three-hundred-pound guy named Chuck with forearms like Hormel hams, and the conversation would inexorably drift toward golf and the touchy subject of holes-in-one. Chuck, flagging down the flight attendant for more peanuts, would casually mention that he'd just aced the island hole at Sawgrass or Cypress Point sixteen or some other murderous par-three gem on the PGA Tour. "That makes eleven aces," he'd grunt, tossing a handful of nuts down the little red lane, then sliding a sidelong glance over at me—"You?"—seemingly under the impression I was a member of life's roving freemasonry of acers. "None," I'd say modestly, offering a strained little smile. An embarrassed silence would follow, followed by me asking Chuck his handicap. "Hell, I don't know," Chuck would chortle, waving for more nuts. "Last time I had the nerve to look, it was *twenty-five!*"

Every now and then, I toyed with the idea of starting up a grassroots organization for ace-challenged golfers like me, a place where good-intentioned, fate-wounded, mid-to-low-handicap golfers could turn for a little comfort and understanding in a world overrun by insensitive ace-makers. I would call it the Hole-in-None Society, and we would share horror stories of lipped-out seven-irons or balls that traitorously struck the hole in flight and popped out. We would work through our collective angst over the patent unfairness of a game that permitted the undeserving Chucks of this world to skull shots that raced through ravines or ricocheted off lake surfaces and somehow wound up in the hole, whose balls caromed off trap rakes or the sides of golf carts and indecently came to rest in the cup. If nothing else, we would count our blessings that *we* would never stoop to bragging about a lucky ace, that *we* had never had to go broke buying the entire Nineteenth Hole drinks after a round in which an ace was foolishly scored. Any member of the society who was caught making a hole-in-one would immediately be required to tender his membership card and forfeit all society benefits.

For the second day in a row, I failed to score an ace at Lytham's ninth. (Surprised, huh?) My ball flew toward the pin but landed on the front of the green and stayed there, leaving me 15 yards shy of expulsion from my own society. As I walked up to the green, the elderly gentleman was still watching from a few yards off the back of the putting surface. "Quite an unlucky break," he commented. "You seemed to be headed to the flag nicely."

I thanked him. He invited me to join him for the march home. His name was Alex Gordon, a Lytham member playing a quick eighteen before his wife picked him up for the dentist. Alex proved to be a lively conversationalist, and I asked him how the club's members viewed hosting the Open championship—as an honor or as a bit of a nuisance? I qualified my question by explaining that a man I'd met at a famous club that hosted the U.S. Open every dozen or so years confided to me that having the Open drove the members into a collective state of despair—their course was essentially taken hostage for more than a month by the superintendent and tournament officials, TV crews, and other invaders.

"It's quite the contrary here, I should think," Alex said. "Oh, a few will no doubt grumble here and there about being kept off, but most of the members rather enjoy having all the attention." He went along a few steps, then added as an afterthought: "Golf seems to have grown rather *frightful* in the States, hasn't it? I mean, all that fancy equipment and all those big tournaments and whatnot. I must say, some of the courses, like Augusta National, appear to be positively flawless."

"They are flawless," I said. "That's why Americans can't seem to win your Open anymore. A writer named Herb Graffis was once asked to name the most important technological advance in golf. He said it was the lawn mower."

Alex Gordon laughed. This observation seemed to deeply please him. As we finished the rugged seventeenth (which I parred, thank you *very* much) and headed toward the next tee, I asked if he'd ever heard of a red-haired girl named Nickie who might have caddied at

Lytham during the war years and would probably be a woman in her early seventies now. "That name doesn't sound familiar, I'm afraid," he said, shaking his head. "Good caddy, was she?"

"Apparently. I might owe my golf swing to her."

Alex smiled at that. He introduced me to his wife, who was waiting for him when we came off the course.

My father was already at the Taps, a low-beamed tavern on the small street just behind the Clifton Arms Hotel, the drafty four-star hotel where a lot of the American players billet during Lytham-hosted Opens.

We'd planned to rendezvous there at four in the afternoon, but I was a half hour late and found my father in the midst of a lively group of locals enjoying an afternoon snog, a few steps from a crackling fire. He waved me over, ordered me a bitter, and asked if twice proved a charm at Royal Lytham. I said it had indeed and showed him my much-improved card.

"Stick around," he said, "and you may get to like the place."

"I already do."

Dad was in excellent spirits. I asked how his day had been. He said great. He'd risen late, soaked in the tub, phoned home to check up on things, and taken a leisurely breakfast in the dining room, then put on his sneakers and gone for a walk around the town. He'd bought my niece Rebecca a little silver bracelet and gone to the library to read *The Times.* While having lunch at the Ship and Royal, a pub up on the main drag, he'd met a couple of retired local school-teachers who spent an hour filling him in on some of the town's changes over the decades. The cars had gotten too big, the gist of their narrative went, while the streets remained too small, kids didn't respect their mums and dads, and nobody in Lytham was really as neighborly as they used to be. New people seemed to come and go.

British Aerospace was maybe going to lay off more workers. The pubs were full, the churches empty.

After that, he'd taken the wheel of the Omega and cruised up to Blackpool to see if it was still as "delightfully honky-tonk" as he remembered it being.

"I hope you remembered to drive on the left," I said. "Was Blackpool everything you hoped for?"

"Worse, I'm afraid," he said, chuckling. "I think I saw it during the good years."

Someone slapped me vigorously on the back, and I turned around to see who'd hit me with a tree limb. My assailant was a little old man, a short, white-haired gent, with a weather-beaten face and alert red-rimmed eyes. He squinted at me like a troll in a fairy book, offering a hard grin.

"This is Jimmy," my father said expansively. "We've been talking about Bill Clinton."

"I hate the bloody bugger," Jimmy explained with a heavy Irish growl.

"Jimmy comes from Ireland."

"Yer the golf writer son, are ye?" Jimmy said, still squinting at me with one eye. The other eye seemed to be roving off roughly in the direction of Portugal.

Since I was still standing beneath my U.S. Open lid, I didn't try and deny it.

"Come to sample our fine local courses, have ye?"

"My dad was in the army here during the war. We're playing our way up to Scotland."

"Good for ye. That's a proper son, to take old Da aboot. If it was me, though, sonny boy, I'd go to Ireland instead. That's where the *fookin'* best golf courses in the world are, ye know. Not a bit of dispute about that fact." He placed his thick lips on the edge of his pint and lowered the tide of stout in the glass about five inches.

"So what's your favorite Irish course?" It seemed the logical question.

Jimmy wiped his mouth and sniffed. "I don't care for the game, myself. Seems a wee bit dull for my purposes, all that cracking aboot." He fixed his dark round troll eyes on me and demanded, "Yer da tells me ye used to write aboot politics, too. So what do ye make of President Flintstone?"

"Who?"

"He means Bill Clinton," Dad explained unnecessarily, giving me a look.

I nodded and sipped my own beer. Talking politics in bars with angry drunks was no longer one of my semi-tax-deductible favorite pastimes. I'd much rather have talked about golf courses in Ireland or the revenge I'd surgically exacted on Lytham's dreaded seventeenth, or the Hole-in-None Society, whose official bylaws I would soon write up, or why there is no cure for golf hat hair. Where was my thick-skinned Clinton-loving Scottish mother-in-law when I needed her most?

"Seems like he's trying hard," I replied. "I gather you don't agree."

"He's a *fookin'* disgrace, him and that crazy wife o' his. She's the one wears the britches in dot family. Dot's what I *really tink*."

Dad smiled sympathetically at my predicament and excused himself for the gents, encouraging Jimmy to rant on for a while about Gerry Adams and a speech my president had supposedly made on a podium with German Chancellor Helmut Kohl, in which he'd reportedly said, among other *fookin' crazy tings*, that Americans were closer to Germans than to Britons. Jimmy, shifting closer, as if a swift cuff about the ears could follow for an incorrect answer, demanded to know if I thought this was true. I replied that in my opinion it wasn't true. I said I personally considered everyone in

Britain a potential golf pal, and if it helped, the only German I knew
was Bernhard Langer.

We were drawing a little audience. A man named Jeff leaned in
to inquire if Dad and I were planning to stay in the area awhile, and
his wife Rachel wanted to know if we had attended the recent
D-Day reunion at the former Freckleton base, now the property of
British Aerospace. I could have kissed them both for interrupting. I
said we had missed the reunion and were unfortunately only planning to stay in the area a day or two because we had to meet my
Scottish mother-in-law for lunch in Glasgow.

"She's *Scottish*, is she?" Jimmy barked.

"Very much so."

"Sounds like a fine woman to me."

"Glad you think so. She thinks the world of Bill Clinton." I
broke it gently to him, sending his snout plunging back into his pint.

"Lots of Americans came to the reunion," Rachel said. "And
there was apparently quite a memorial service up at the church, you
know, because of the bomber."

My father came back and climbed onto his stool. He picked up
his beer, took a sip, and tuned in to the conversation.

"What bomber?" I said.

"Why, the bomber that crashed," Rachel replied. She glanced
from me to my father and then back at me. "It was such a heartbreaking thing, wasn't it? All those lovely babies gone. People round
here never quite got over it."

I glanced at Dad and saw he was staring at Rachel. He said
nothing.

I shrugged and admitted, "I don't know anything about a
bomber crash."

"Dot's crazy," the ever-helpful Jimmy growled. "Everybody
knows aboot da bomber."

I looked at my father again. "Do you know the bomber they're talking about?" He nodded almost imperceptibly. His high spirits were gone. His complexion had turned pale.

"Yes."

Jimmy scowled at him. "Ye mean to say ye never tol' yer own son aboot dot ting? Jesus Christ, man, dot damned ting *wiped out* half da bloody *fookin'* village."

Dad's voice was scarcely more than a whisper.

"It was . . . very bad."

I could see ripples of tension coursing through his jawline, indicating this was a discussion he wanted no part of. His eyes shifted to the burning fire. What the hell, I wondered, was going on? Rachel apparently saw the same thing and gently touched my arm. "Your dad tells me you have two little ones at home. A boy and girl. How brilliant. I own a children's shop over on the promenade. You must come into the shop tomorrow and let me show you some things."

Absently, I promised I would. My mind was groping to find an explanation for my father's sudden mood shift. I'd never seen anything like it. What did the crash of a bomber have to do with him? I knew most of my old man's war stories, and there was nothing in them about a plane crash. His sudden, stricken withdrawal made me queasy.

The Taps was growing hot and loud with men rowdily arguing over soccer standings. Jeff and Rachel finished their drinks and left. When Jimmy mercifully staggered off to hunt for the loo, I leaned over and asked my father if he was all right.

"No," he said, looking at me with a startling intensity. He took a final sip of his beer, then pushed it aside and got up.

"Come with me," he said. "There's something I have to show you."

·   ·   ·

Despite all the stories I knew, there were things about my father's war years I didn't understand. Back home in Maine, there was an accordion file with various documents that amounted to a paper trail of his activities between the years 1942 and 1945. In late 1942, married to my mother and working in the ad department of the *Cumberland News*, he'd enlisted in the Army Air Corps and been offered a chance to go to officer candidate school, where he hoped to become a combat or glider pilot. Simultaneously, though, he'd learned that his "home" draft board in High Point, North Carolina, had already mailed him a draft notice assigning him to the technical training school at Chanute Field, Chicago, so he went there instead. At Chanute, he scored in the top five percent of his class and was offered a second opportunity to attend OCS, this time with the personal recommendation of General Hap Arnold.

He declined the recommendation and stayed at Chanute for six months as a life-raft and parachute inspector. In early '43 he was shipped off to San Antonio, where he was made a staff sergeant and continued teaching but once again turned down OCS. In November of that year, he was sent to the war in Europe to fill a chief inspector slot at Warton Air Base in Freckleton, which the Air Force called Base Army Depot Two. There he stayed for thirteen months, assigned to a "casual" pool, which granted him an unusual amount of freedom of movement—hence his two golf trips to Scotland. Twice more during that period of time, the top brass recommended him for OCS—and twice more he declined.

Why was this?

On our first night in Lytham, over that feast of summer's last green peas and a perfectly sculpted Yorkshire pudding, in the afterglow of our great day at Royal Lytham, I'd put the question directly to him. His quietly rendered answer had taken me by surprise.

"When I joined the army, I was a pretty cocky young guy. I had a beautiful wife, a good civilian job, and a zippy comeback for everything—not unlike you, come to think of it. I suppose part of that was an intellectual arrogance. I'd read a lot of books, been a few places. I thought I knew more than most other guys, including the colonels and generals. That somehow made me different, maybe even a bit better than them. Coming here taught me otherwise."

I'd asked how so.

"Oh," he answered vaguely, "just something that happened. I'd really rather not go into it. The point is, smart guys like me grow up thinking we've got it all figured out. We think we're fully in control of everything that happens. The truth is, the control we think we have is really an illusion. Shadows. The only thing life really promises us is pain. It's up to us to create the joy."

I'd asked what happened to change his thinking in this way.

He'd taken a bite of peas and chewed them for a minute, then looked at me and said two words.

"The war."

We drove, in the fading light, after leaving the Taps, toward the village of Freckleton. I now knew that the answer to my question the evening before had something to do with a bomber that crashed. But that's all I knew because Dad was stone silent, looking out of the Omega as we went along with his hands folded on his lap.

A few school kids were still straggling home in their plaid jumpers and navy blazers. I saw a little yellow-haired girl walking with a chubby black-haired companion who reminded me of my daughter and her best friend Eileen. Their heads were bent together as if they were whispering, the larger girl dragging her overcoat on the pavement behind them.

"Stop the car here," Dad suddenly said.

We were in the center of Freckleton, near Trinity Church, just off the Preston Road. There was a post office, a small market, a fish-and-chips parlor, and the handsome redbrick church. In the breezy late afternoon light, Freckleton looked even more like a postcard of tranquil English village life. Pansies were still blooming in window boxes.

He opened his door and got out. I followed him in silence across the street toward Holy Trinity. He stopped on the sidewalk and stared at the residential close of private dwellings next door. He seemed to be trying to orient himself. Without speaking a word, he walked purposefully toward a small pedestrian lane that ran between the close and a small button shop.

The lane led to a gated burying ground at the rear of the church. On the far side of the graveyard was a public park of some sort, with a rose garden at its center. Dad opened the iron gate and proceeded along the stone pathways of the graveyard, eyeing the headstones. I followed him to a large polished granite cross positioned near the rear of the cemetery. It was a common grave. Wreaths and wild-flowers had recently been placed there, but the chill nights had turned them rusty, bundles of asters and poppies and chrysanthe-mums. I read some of the names inscribed on the stone border: *Gillian and June Parkinson. George Preston. Michael Probert. Kenneth Boocock. Lillian Waite. Silvia Whybrow. Judith Garner. Annie Harrington . . .*

The names went on, thirty-eight in all. A mass grave.

"How did these folks die?" I asked.

"They weren't folks," he replied softly. "They were children."

The words didn't sink in at first. We stood there for a few seconds staring at the names.

"Children?" I repeated finally.

He nodded. "Four- and five-year-olds. Maggie's and Jack's ages.

They went to the infants' school here at the church. One of our bombers crashed into the school. The airfield was just over there." He lifted his head, solemnly, to indicate where.

I didn't have a clue what to say. I'd never heard of anything so awful. So for a change, I said nothing.

We stood in silence for a few minutes more before he spoke again. He shut his eyes and opened them. I wondered if he was praying or just reliving scenes I couldn't begin to imagine.

He spoke evenly. "It was about ten in the morning. A large thunderstorm had just come up. We had our parachute crews working double shifts because this was six or seven weeks after D-Day. I'd just stretched out on my cot in our Nissen hut to steal some shut-eye when I heard a big roar overhead, followed by an explosion. The whole hut just shook. *Jesus,* it shook. . . . I knew it was one of our birds. The hut I was in was probably the closest one to the school here. One of the other guys jumped up and ran out, and I ran after him. It was raining like hell, but I saw fire down at the school and started running. We were all running."

Dad cleared his throat. He was shaking a bit. I placed my hand on his arm. He continued:

"I guess I was one of the first to reach the school, though others got there quickly. God . . . what a sight. The plane had gone right through the school and struck a café where lots of our guys and R.A.F. personnel used to hang out. It set half the town on fire. Burning fuel was running down the street. I just remember . . . starting to pull away pieces of things . . . pieces of the plane, you know, also bricks and mortar . . . and all these precious little kids inside . . . buried alive or killed by the explosion. I remember the sound of a child weeping. I couldn't seem to find her. We pulled out several of the children. They were dead or badly injured. You didn't have time to think. You just kept digging."

His voice stopped. I saw tears gathering in his eyes for only the second time in my life. The first time had been when we buried my nephew Richard, one summer day in 1987. Richard, his first grandchild, had been gamely battling a rare nervous system disorder when he died in his sleep. Richard was nine.

I slipped my arm around my father.

We stood that way for several more minutes. He cleared his throat again and said, in a stronger voice: "I knew a lot of these kids, Jim. As I told you, they were always hanging around the base. The guys loved them. We each had our favorites. There was one little girl in particular I loved. She was always laughing, like your Maggie. I called her Lady Sunshine. I used to tell her I hoped I had a daughter like her someday. She was one of those killed."

Good lord, I thought.

"A week or so after the crash, after the funeral and all of that, I found a note attached to the bulletin board from that little girl's parents. They wondered if anybody had taken a photograph of their daughter. Can you imagine? They didn't even have a picture of their only daughter. I took them all I had. They were so grateful. We sat there in their little front parlor and just cried. I don't think I ever experienced anything quite so sad."

"Were you okay?"

My father gave me an anguished look. *Dumb* question, I realized.

"*Hell, no!*" he snapped. "How could anybody be okay after something like that?"

"I'm sorry. I guess I meant physically. Were you injured . . ."

"Yes . . . no . . . my hands were burned a bit. Wore bandages for a while. No big deal. I was fine . . . but I didn't feel up to going to the funeral. They brought Bing Crosby in to sing to the people of Freckleton. I couldn't even stand to go hear him sing. I think I went somewhere and tried to play golf. Burned hands and all. I just wanted to be alone."

"Do you remember the little girl's name?"

Dad, better now, considered the names on the grave.

"Harrington. Maybe it was Annie Harrington." He took out a handkerchief and blew his nose. "Lady Sunshine," he murmured.

I took my father's arm, and we left the burying ground, slowly closing the iron gate behind us. Two boys on bikes were pedaling furiously up the alley and swerved to avoid hitting us. One of them turned his head and gave us a dirty look. My father, rubbing his eyes, didn't see it. The air was cold. The moon was already out. It was going to be a beautiful night.

"I'm surprised you never told me this story," I said when we reached the car.

He paused and looked back at the church, a looming shape in the early shade of evening now. I saw a single small light burning somewhere inside.

"The war ended for me right here," he said. "I promised myself I would never speak about it again."

Sometime in the early morning hours at the Clifton Arms Hotel, I woke to the sound of my father's voice barking angrily from the twin bed just beside me.

"I want you men to get *back*. Get *back* now! We need help here. Can't you see that? Get going now. On the double . . ."

He was having a bad dream.

"Dad?" I said quietly, reaching over to touch his arm. He was rigid as a board. "You okay?"

There was silence, then he calmly answered, "Yes, Jim. I was just . . . go to sleep now, son."

I waited till his breathing told me he was asleep again. He slept peacefully, but I lay there for a long time watching the moon over the Irish Sea, trying to decide if I felt better or worse about having exhumed this devastating event from my father's past.

My father's world had forever changed one rainy August morning fifty years ago, and in thinking about this unspeakable sadness, I could no more believe God had caused a tempest to hurl a B-24 fully loaded with a ton of petrol fuel into the ground killing ten American servicemen, four sergeants from the R.A.F., thirty-eight children, and nine citizens of Freckleton—darkening the soul of a town and an incalculable number of innocent lives—any more than he had made my golf game fall apart that first round at Royal Lytham. It was just something that happened, probably for a variety of reasons no one could ever comprehend.

It's strange how clear some things seem at the bottom of the night. Suddenly, I now fully understood why my father had been so adamant about me attending Kristin's funeral—willing to wager everything on the outcome of a silly golf match.

It wasn't, as I'd first believed, a gesture intended to simply honor Kristin's memory and lend support to her grieving family. It was a way of prying open a door to liberate something deep in me. In the years that followed Freckleton, he'd obviously learned the importance of surrendering everything to grief, even though his strongest impulse after the bomber crash had been exactly the same as mine: to run away and hide.

Listening to my father's calmer breathing, another powerful insight came to me: Had the cocky young sergeant died in the wreckage at Freckleton and Opti the Mystic been born right then and there? That would explain so much—why he seemingly never let life knock him off stride and went about afterward spreading good cheer like some self-appointed Appleseed of joy. *Life promises us sorrow,* he'd said the night before. *It's up to us to create the joy.* Mims, Opti's oldest golf pal, once said to me, "No matter what he shoots, your old man never seems to have a bad day on the golf course." Perhaps a bad day period—after Freckleton.

I thought about these complicated things for a while, lying on my side watching the moon spilling its light over the tranquil sea. I thought about my own young children somewhere on the other side of that light, preparing to go to bed about now, perhaps saying their own prayers.

They were growing up in a world full of shadows, a place where children like Lady Sunshine vanished too soon and for no acceptable reason. My own Christian tradition held that God's greatest gift was hope. As I lay there in the untouchable moonshine, I told myself it was enough for me to *hope* that my own children would someday find God, whoever and wherever God was, or that God at least would simply somehow find them.

I hoped they'd never knew the kind of pain my father had known at Freckleton and I'd known with Kristin—or maybe, if they must, that the pain would simply serve to pry open their hearts and wake them up to become Appleseeds of joy. My own prayer was simple: Please make them little Optis.

I don't even remember falling asleep.

Return of the Slammer

A few years ago, I spent a day with Sam Snead. We met at the Greenbrier in West Virginia, where he'd just returned to serve as Pro Emeritus, and teed off to do a playing interview on the Old White Course, where he'd once given Dwight Eisenhower golf lessons.

In his inimitable fashion, Snead regaled me with tales about playing golf with hacker movie stars and pigeon millionaires and presidents he'd known (and in Richard Nixon's case, caught cheating—moving his ball in the rough), and somewhere in this movable jamboree of memories, I asked Snead if he fully comprehended what he'd done for golf—not only won more tournaments than anybody else (81 by the PGA Tour's count, 86 by the Slammer's own) but also been the first true media "star" of the postwar generation that produced the biggest popular golf boom in the history of the game. Snead, Ben Hogan, and Byron Nelson had set the stage for the grand

entrance of Arnold Palmer, who paved the way to superstardom for
Jack Nicklaus, who handed the mantle to Tom Watson, who presented it to Greg Norman and Nick Price.

"Yeah, I've thought about that from time to time," Sam admitted, giving me a sly granddaddy-catfish smile. "That's not bad, I
reckon, for an ole country boy who taught himself to play with a
stick in a cow pasture."

I suggested we play a match, but Snead declined, explaining that
he never wagered on a match "until I see a man play." So we played
along, content to chase the pill and have a friendly chat. At eighty,
Snead's butter-smooth swing was still a marvel to behold. Both of us
hooked drives deep into the oak trees on the first tee, and my host
suggested we take mulligans. We tied the first hole with bogeys.
Snead went out in 35, while I managed 38. On the tenth tee, he
spotted a problem with my setup and gave me the same advice he'd
once given Ike. "Stand up straighter, and stick your butt out more."
He noted how that would promote a better shoulder turn and a
straighter shot.

I asked the Slammer how the commander-in-chief had responded to being told to stick his butt out more.

"He kind of laughed—I reckon he wasn't used to people talkin'
to him that way. Nice fella, though. Real serious about his golf.
Wanted like hell to be good. Ike's real handicap, you know, was a
state secret," Snead explained. "They didn't want the public to know
because if he was bad, they might wonder why he was bad, and if he
was good, they might think all he did was play golf all day."

This begged the logical question from an old political dog like
me: How good was Ike?

"Not that bad, 'bout a ten or twelve handicap, I reckon, at his
best. Never seen a fella more crazy about a game, though."

Off Old White's sixteenth tee, Snead showed me where he often
hunted four-leaf clovers. As luck would have it, I was one stroke up

on him for the back nine. Snead birdied seventeen, and we arrived at Old White's eighteenth dead even on the home nine. "How 'bout a little match?" my host said, grinning again like a granddaddy catfish. "Let's say the winner buys lunch."

From the rear tees the eighteenth, an unusual finishing par-three hole, played just 165 yards. My host had the honors but invited me to shoot first. Just then a golf cart with two old leathery-faced geezers rolled up, and one of the men drawled, "How much money's that crook taken from your wallet, son?"

"Y'all shut up and clear off," Snead growled at them, winking at me.

They turned out to be two of Snead's regular victims, a couple local men who'd known him since he was pounding drives onto 350-yard greens as the young head pro at the Greenbrier fifty years before. One of them proposed joining us for the final hole, and Snead asked me if that would be all right. I sensed a setup. We agreed to play the hole straight up for ten bucks a man. I invited the two newcomers to shoot first. The first man's ball flew to the rough behind the green. The second, with a quick stab, plopped his ball on the steep bank just below the green. I made a decent swing with my six-iron and landed my ball 15 feet to the right of the pin, certainly within range for a birdie.

Snead teed up his ball and took his stance.

"How many times you reckon you've aced this damn hole, Sam?" one of the geezers needled him, obviously trying to break the Slammer's concentration. The man bit his tongue, grinning.

"I'm gonna send you boys back to your naps," Snead said, then swung.

His ball landed a foot above the hole and spun back a bit. No chance of an ace, but Snead turned, looked at him, and said, "Almost one more."

The geezers picked up. I conceded the five-inch putt to Snead.

He watched me take my position over the ball, a smile playing faintly at his lips. I was tempted to ask him for a read but decided against it. My nerves were taut, and the resulting stroke was poor. The ball leaked two feet left of the hole.

"Let's go have lunch," Snead declared, picking up my ball and tossing it underhand to me. He finished with a one-over 73, while I cobbled together a quite respectable 76. I watched the great man collect a tenner from each of his pigeons, and then we walked into the Greenbrier's clubhouse grill, taking a seat at a rear table away from the glare of the windows. He refused to let me pay for lunch.

Snead ordered a chocolate ice cream and a whiskey and asked me, with a suspicious squint, for the second time that day, if I was sure old Linwood Dodson wasn't my *deddy.* "That ole boy used to hustle the pants off me," he remembered, shaking his head at the memory. He said my golf swing reminded him a little of that sorry sumbitch Dodson.

I assured him there was no connection. I said my father was an adman from Greensboro who'd taught himself to play golf with a stick in a pasture.

"Well, I'll be damned," Snead said with a genuine smile. "Greensboro was always special to me. It's where I won my last regular tour event. Won that sucker eight times, y'know." I said I knew. "That last time made me the oldest man to ever win a regular tour event."

I said I knew that, too, because I was there.

I explained how my father had taken me to the Greensboro Open in 1965, the year I was twelve. I explained about Aunt Polly living on Sedgefield's seventeenth hole, and how I'd carried around a copy of Snead's memoir, *Education of a Golfer,* hoping to get his autograph, for the entire weekend.

"Did I sign it?" he wanted to know, shoveling a spoonful of ice cream into his mouth.

"No. I lost the book. By the time I got another, you were busy making history. I couldn't get close."

Snead found this story amusing. He asked me if my father was "still kicking around." I said he was indeed, still working and still occasionally lightening the pockets of his own regular golf pals at his new golf club just outside of Greensboro.

"Good for him," Snead said. "Tell 'im ole Sam Snead says hello. Us country boys, ya know, stick together."

At that moment, ironically enough, a waitress came up to the table and asked if Snead would mind signing an autograph for a little boy. He told her to have the boy come over. The boy's father walked him over. The boy was eight or nine. He had no clue who Sam Snead was. The father smiled nervously as Snead signed the boy's napkin and patted the kid affectionately on the head. "You love to play golf?" he asked the boy. "No," the boy said. "I like soccer." The father grinned sheepishly.

When they were gone, I pulled out my beaten-up copy of *Education of a Golfer*, which I'd brought with me in anticipation of this meeting, and asked him to autograph it. "Aren't you going to ask me if I love to play golf?" I said as he flipped through the pages.

"Hell, no," Snead snapped. He wrote in my book, *To my good friend, Jim. Always, Sam Snead*. He handed it back with a lopsided grin.

"I still think you must be related to ole Linwood Dodson. Man oh *man*, that sucker used to rob me blind."

Dad and I drove down the Lancashire coast to Southport, the next morning, hoping for a chance to play Royal Birkdale, the course where Arnold Palmer revived the languishing British Open by winning during a week of tumultuous winds and rains in 1961—establishing himself as the dominant player of his day and ensuring the best American players would always come to Britain thereafter.

Birkdale, with its rugged high dunes and penal bunkers, came late to the ranks of Open championships (the first one to be hosted there was in 1954, won by Peter Thomson), but in the past thirty years no British club has hosted more major events. The pros like it because its fairways are essentially flat valleys between high dunes, producing fewer of the quirky and unpredictable bounces than at most seaside courses. With roughs that can be freakishly difficult due to thick native grasses, buckthorn and willow scrub, Birkdale rewards the straight driver.

The rearing sand hills also make Birkdale an ideal venue for spectator viewing, and several of the Opens there were ones I would have loved to witness in person. Peter Thomson's and Tom Watson's victories here (in 1965 and 1983 respectively) marked the climax of two outstanding careers, and Lee Trevino (1971) and Johnny Miller (1976) played the golf of their lives in order to subdue the field at mighty Birkdale Opens. For the likable Aussie Ian Baker-Finch, who won after a sensational finish in 1991, Birkdale remained the site of personal glory that must now have felt as distant as the moon. For reasons no one could clearly fathom, including himself, Baker-Finch's splendid game had fallen to pieces after his brilliant Birkdale Open. He'd made only a handful of cuts in the five years since that moment. It was the kind of precipitous fall-off all tour players fear, and the kind of abyss from which few players ever reemerge.

Unfortunately, as our Omega rolled into town, the rains that had kindly held off at Lytham roared back with a gusty vengeance in Southport, which calls itself "Sunny Southport" and "Montpelier of the North." With a forecast calling for even heavier weather by midafternoon, we decided our best hope for playing Birkdale would be to make a beeline straight to the course and save checking into the Prince of Wales Hotel, our planned stop for the night, for later.

I drove slowly along Lord Street, Southport's normally bustling main drag, allowing Dad the opportunity to reacquaint himself with a town where fifty years ago he had come to play golf on nearby linkslands (Formby, Southport, and Ainsdale are both close) and to listen to live big band orchestras in the famous seaside hotel ballrooms. Unfortunately, Sunny Southport was wearing a gloomy face that morning and looked like any other slightly down-at-the-heels holiday town at the end of the season in the rain. The arcades along the beachfront were gated and padlocked, and the few people who were out hurried along Lord Street's ornately canopied sidewalks with somber urgency, fighting gusts of winds with their umbrellas.

"Good thing you bought that new rain suit," I commented, and then thought about my mother's worries in this regard. The temperatures were supposed to reach only the high fifties at best. The weather was what my grandmother used to call "pneumonia weather." "Sure you're up to a hike in this mess?" I asked.

"I am if you are," he replied, as we passed through the town proper and started toward the southern outskirts, where Birkdale's stark white art deco clubhouse sits dramatically among the sandhills.

At the pro shop there was a bit of a snafu. Norman Crewe, Birkdale's hospitable club secretary, whom I'd written to in advance and later spoken to by phone, was off for the day and had apparently left no instructions for the young assistant pro on duty. This was too bad. I'd hoped we might have a proper visit with the secretary, following our round. The assistant, who didn't look any older than my daughter's baby-sitter, said he would attempt to call the secretary at his home, but my father intervened, saying that wasn't necessary— we'd better play on before the weather got worse. The young man collected our fifty-pound green fees and explained that another group of Americans had just gone off ahead of us.

Dad deposited his bag on a trolley and I slung mine on my back and, sure enough, we found a trio of Americans who'd brought their own caddies—their teenage sons. "We've come this far," a paint contractor from Pennsylvania assured us with a stoic grin, "damned if we're going to let a little liquid sunshine ruin it for us."

The rain was slanting sideways, coming off the ocean at a pretty good clip.

We watched the fathers hit their drives, all three missing the first fairway by wide margins. Their caddy sons exchanged smiles. "C'mon, Dad," a tall one in a Cornell cap with a prominent Adam's apple encouraged his father, "when the breeze blows, nice and slow."

"Right," the paint contractor said. "Remember that so I don't have to remind you tomorrow." He teed up and hit a provisional ball even farther wide of the fairway and, smiling sheepishly, explained that tomorrow the roles would be reversed: fathers would be caddies.

We said good-bye, and wished them luck, and watched them make their way down the dune-bordered fairway into the gloom. As we stood there waiting to hit, getting colder and wetter by the minute, I asked my father what his father had thought of him caddying at Sedgefield when he was thirteen.

"He thought golf was a game for rich playboys. But basically he didn't object too much. Golf was entirely beyond his ken. The Depression had just hit. The money in caddying was pretty good. My regular customer, old man Sapp, paid me thirty cents a round plus a dime tip—that was what John D. Rockefeller regularly tipped on the golf course."

Old man Sapp was a prominent Greensboro attorney named O. L. Sapp. My father liked to say his best customer's initials really stood for *Oh Lookout* because he was wild and impatient off the tee, prone to terrorize slow-footed groups ahead of him. It was Sapp, however, who gave my father his first iron, a hickory-shafted seven-iron, which he practiced with in a pasture next to the farmhouse they rented west of town.

I knew my grandfather only as a kind old man in paint-flecked rumpled pants who smoked King Edward cigars and seldom spoke much except to comment about the weather or what chicanery the Republicans were up to in Washington. He'd had no more than a rudimentary education and had done odd jobs most of his life, including tobacco sharecropping, driving a milk truck, and making kitchen cabinets. He'd also worked on crews that raised the first steel electric towers across the South and helped wire the Jefferson-Standard Building in Greensboro, North Carolina's first "sky-scrapper." His name was Walter, which was my middle name. He taught me to saw a board properly in a straight line and took me fishing in his flat-bottomed skiff in the bayous of central Florida.

I forget who told me my father's father lacked "gumption"— possibly my crazy maiden aunt Lily, Walter's older sister, who lived with us for a time when I was in third grade. By *gumption*, she meant ambition. When I asked my father if this was true, he smiled and explained that if his father lacked ambition, it was a trait he'd inherited honestly from his own father, Uncle Jimmy Dodson, a prominent Orange County landowner who prided himself, as Dad put it, "on never letting work interfere with the pleasures of life."

Uncle Jimmy kept a north pasture full of cows and a south pasture full of horses. A family story held that during "the War for Southern Independence," he creatively sold horses to the invading Yankees and then had them stolen back at night. He was a dapper rogue who wore a white handlebar moustache and a blue felt bowler. A tintype photograph of him, taken on his seventy-seventh birthday, looking as pleased as if he'd just swiped a few Yankee horses, sits on a shelf in my house in Maine.

Uncle Jimmy, I knew, was a revered figure to my father. Dad spent most of his childhood summers at Uncle Jimmy's farm near Chapel Hill, and long before he was earning Oh Lookout Sapp's premium wages by looping at Sedgefield, Uncle Jimmy paid him a buffalo-head nickel for finding a lost horse chain in the pasture. Some men remember the first dollar they earned. My father remembered his first nickel from Uncle Jimmy.

Thinking of these things as we stood in the dreary rain on Birkdale's first tee, I asked my father what Uncle Jimmy thought of golf. He seemed to have had the perfect disposition for the auld game.

"To tell the truth, I don't know that he'd ever heard of golf. Uncle Jimmy was pretty much a man of the last century. But what a delightful old codger," Dad remembered, smiling. "He thought of himself as something of a backwoods philosopher, and he used to say to me, 'Braxton, remember it's always better to laugh than to cry. You just remember that, son, next time you feel like cryin'.' You know what? I did, too."

It seemed like useful advice—especially for Birkdale in the rain.

"We came here for some laughs," I said, staring impatiently at the group ahead of us. They seemed to be playing Birkdale's first hole in slow motion. "The problem is, I'm about to start crying."

"It doesn't seem very promising," Dad agreed.

I glanced around. I didn't see another soul anywhere out in those famous dunes and fairways.

"Come on," I said, consulting a damp course-routing card. I picked up my bag and grabbed his hand trolley.

"Where are we going?" he asked.

"To the spot where Arnold Palmer saved the British Open."

We hiked down the eighteenth fairway and crossed through some heavily grassed dunes, wandered confusedly around for a bit, then finally came out near Birkdale's fifteenth tee. A pair of four- and five-pars constituted Birkdale's home stretch, which was where almost all the history of the place was made, much of it by Americans.

As I hoped, the fairway ahead, and the par-three fourteenth just behind (where Hale Irwin carelessly tried to execute a one-hand tap-in for par in 1983, missed the ball, and was forced to penalize himself one stroke—then lost the Open by a stroke to Tom Watson), were empty.

"Let's play a four-hole match," I proposed. "I'll give you two strokes a hole due to the regrettable playing conditions."

"Don't dig yourself too deep a hole, laddie. You're feeling your oats this morning."

"Must be all the porridge we've been eating."

Dad teed up and swatted a little fading drive that was boosted by the wind, which was beating over our right shoulders more or less in the direction of the green. I teed up and made a swing that was much too quick, producing one of my patented power fades that usually finishes with the sound of breaking glass and a voice shouting in alarm. I saw my ball vanish far into the dunes on the right.

"Just like Arnie," I remarked as we walked off the tee.

"Really?" Dad sounded amused. "How's that?"

I explained that when Arnold Palmer, battling for the lead in 1961, arrived at Birkdale's fifteenth hole during the Open's last round, he lost his tee shot to the right. His ball dived into trouble at the base of a grassy bank. There was supposed to be a plaque on the ground somewhere near the spot where he struck one of the most wondrous shots in Open history. His blast with a six-iron dropped the ball on the green and left him an easy two-putt for par. He went on to win the championship, and many felt his victory and personal magnetism revived American public interest in the British Open.

"It's doubtful there was a man present at Birkdale who wanted Palmer to lose," Henry Longhurst wrote of the tournament when it was over. "It's impossible to overpraise the tact and charm with which this American has conducted himself on his two visits to Britain. He has no fancy airs or graces; he wears no fancy clothes; he makes no fancy speeches. He simply says and does exactly the right thing at the right time, and that is enough."

Unfortunately, I couldn't find the plaque commemorating the blessed event. Maybe worse, I couldn't find my ball. I tromped around in the wet knee-high grass while my father struck his second shot, then I looked at the hole and realized something odd. The fifteenth was a par-five of 540 yards. How could Palmer's second shot have reached the green? Not even the King could wallop a six-iron 300 yards.

"Are you going to play or daydream?" my father called out. He was standing out in the fairway looking at me. The rain was picking up pace. The hood of his rain suit obscured his face. I dropped a ball at the fairway's edge and smacked a three-wood, catching it cleanly. It wasn't enough. With the penalty and two poor chips that came afterward, I managed a double bogey—just tying Dad. He was one up.

We went to sixteen, a par-four that doglegged slightly to the right. The rain was hammering us now. "I think we'd better forget this," I said.

"We'll play in fast," Dad said, teeing up his ball. He struck a nice little drive. I put mine in play, too, and we walked off the tee with our hoods lowered, keeping to ourselves.

Watson's dramatic finish here in 1983 was an important little milestone to me. I'd sat in my little solar house on the banks of the Green River in Vermont watching my favorite player win his fifth Open championship. My television set barely received the Boston station's signal, and the championship faded out entirely into electronic snow by the end. I had to call up my dad in North Carolina to make sure Watson had won.

Considering the awful weather, we played Birkdale's sixteenth pretty well. Dad slapped a beautiful third shot off the soggy turf and managed a bogey. I reached the green in two and parred. But with the strokes I'd given him factored in, he was now two up with two left. The course turns back toward Birkdale's distinctive clubhouse, which is supposed to resemble a ship at sea, after sixteen. Unfortunately, this meant we were now hitting directly into the teeth of the gale. The hole is a long par-five, which played monstrously long in the wind.

"Are we laughing or crying?" I said to Dad, having to remove my glasses because water was trickling down my cheeks.

"I think laughing," Dad said, wiping his own face. He smiled at me. "I hope so, at any rate." He teed up and drove his ball about a hundred yards.

"At this pace I should get there about Thursday," he quipped.

I teed up and set my Big Bertha driver behind the ball. A gust rocked me gently, and my club nudged the ball off the peg.

"That's one," Dad said cheekily. "I always heard you were straight but short off the tee."

"Very funny. Please leave the low humor to a professional," I urged him.

I reteed and hit a nice drive that flew about as far as I normally hit my seven-iron. We resumed our silent march to the clubhouse.

My father had the sweet disposition of his father (and his father's father), but he also had plenty of gumption, a gift no doubt from his mother's side of the ledger, the Taylors. The Taylors were from north of Raleigh, an ambitious and upthrusting tribe of good-natured Baptists. They had a lot of natural gumption in them, and my father had a lot of my grandmother, Beatrice Taylor, in him. A native of the plains of West Texas and a distant relation of Zachary

Taylor, she was a firm believer in the powers of Holy Scripture, good biscuit-making, and "book education."

Her advice to my father, dispensed about the time he was caddying for Oh Lookout Sapp at Sedgefield, was that the Lord liked a boy who wore clean underwear, worked hard, and steadily improved his mind, an injunction he clearly took to heart. At fifteen, he played semipro baseball and sold *The Greensboro Record* on street corners and worked as a copy runner and stringer for the nighttime sports editor. At seventeen, while still in high school, he went to work at a department store in Greensboro, writing ad copy for the newspaper and dressing window displays at night. During his senior year at Greensboro High (my alma mater), he played second team halfback on the football team that went to the state finals in Durham, where his team lost (Dad knocked himself out cold by running into the goalpost), but a businessman who saw him play and admired his hustle offered him a job at a Durham department store and a chance to attend the university in his spare time.

He stayed at Chapel Hill for one year, attending mostly night classes in journalism. He thought he might want to be a political columnist or the next Ring Lardner. Instead, he met an airplane mechanic who agreed to teach him how to fly, and soon after that someone recommended him for a job at a department store in Washington. He dropped out of college and caught the train north, arriving on the streets of the nation's capital with fifteen bucks in his pocket. The job didn't pan out and he was down to his last dime when he won a blueberry pie in a raffle. "I was walking out of the store eating the pie," he once told me, "trying to figure out where I would go next when I physically ran into your great-aunt Edna." Edna was Walter Dodson's other older sister (the noncrazy one, I liked to think of her), a government secretary.

Aunt Edna took my father home to Bethesda, Maryland, and installed him in her guest room, and a week later he found a job selling advertising for *The Washington Post.* That job led to a bigger job at *The Cumberland News,* where he doubled as ad salesman and aviation writer. One day in 1940 he strolled into McCrory's Five and Ten to purchase a pocket comb and spotted Janet Virginia Kessell, who was twenty years old, the youngest of eleven kids, and who had recently won the Miss Western Maryland Beauty Pageant. She had been offered either a thousand-dollar prize or an all-expense paid trip to the 1939 World's Fair, the theme of which was the World of To-morrow; she took the trip. Now she was back home selling big-band records and wondering if she should marry a local boy named Earl. Though he didn't own a record player, my father bought a Benny Goodman disk. He went back a few days later and bought an Artie Shaw record and asked the beautiful sales clerk out. She told him she was engaged to marry a guy named Earl.

My father proved his gumption by going back to McCrory's until she agreed to go out with him. They went to a place called the Crystal Palace to hear Kay Kyser and his orchestra. After their second date, my mother broke off her engagement to Earl. Earl moved to Baltimore. My parents got married less than a year later.

After hurriedly putting out on Birkdale's eighteenth green, Dad and I legged it into the clubhouse, where a kindly steward permitted us to use the men's locker room to dry off a bit and then showed us into an empty dining room, where he brought us some warm toast and hot tea. Under the agreed terms, Dad had won the match once again but he insisted we call it a draw.

I was sorry Norman Crewe wasn't around to fill us in more on Birkdale's evolution as an Open site, and then I realized something a little embarrassing. We'd come a day earlier than I'd informed our missing host we would be there.

This wasn't my only gaffe. I asked the steward why there was no

longer a plaque commemorating Palmer's masterful recovery shot on
fifteen, and the steward smiled. "That's because it's on sixteen. Sixteen was fifteen in Mr. Palmer's day."

After tea, we snooped around the empty clubhouse a bit, looking at framed photographs of Trevino, Watson, and Miller battling
Birkdale's winds and dunes. I left a five-pound note on the table for
the steward, and we drove back to Southport to check into the
Prince of Wales Hotel, maybe England's most famous golf hotel.

There were lots of elderly people scattered about in the Prince's
lobby, most taking naps in chairs. A Welsh businessman was checking out. "Look at this," he insisted to the clerk, tapping his finger on
his bill. "You charged me for a bottle of champagne."

"Right." The young lady didn't seem surprised. "Is there a problem?"

"Yes. I didn't order a bottle of champagne."

"Very well then." The clerk gave a little sigh. "I'll remove the
charge."

"Thank you."

The Welshman looked at us and shook his head. He seemed to
be holding out for a more formal apology from management, but
obviously none was coming. When the clerk presented him with his
revised bill, he slashed his name on the credit card slip and said, "In
case you're interested, the only reason I would have ordered a bottle
of champagne is if I'd learned this hotel was going to be torn to the
ground. Have a nice day."

He turned to us and said, "Good luck, you two. You'll need it."

My father and I looked at each other. Dad shook his head ever
so slightly, a silent advisory to keep my smart mouth shut. I politely
gave the clerk our name and asked specifically for Arnold and Winnie Palmer's regular room. The clerk smiled at me as if she had a gas
pain, disappeared briefly into a back room, and reappeared with a
large key that looked as if it could open a Spanish galleon chest.

Ours was a dim tower room on the Prince of Wales's second floor. The ceiling was high enough to permit pole vaulting, and the air was warm enough to bake bread. I tried to open a window, but it wouldn't budge. The huge windows were painted shut, and the radiator clanked like Marley's ghost.

How could this dump be the most famous golf hotel in England? I wondered as I sat down on one of the twin beds and sank to the floor. The answer, of course, was that the Prince had *once* been a superb hotel—maybe even a great one, as its dim elegance suggested—but was clearly now feeding off its own fame as a place the world's best golfers stayed when they came to Lytham and Birkdale Opens.

My father entered the room carrying his suit bag and medical case.

"How's it look?" he asked cheerfully.

"A little tired. Maybe I should go ask for Jack and Barbara's room."

"Forget it. At least it's dry and warm."

"Very warm."

While Dad unpacked his medical stuff in the tiny, weird tropical-pink bathroom, I turned on the small black-and-white television and found two guys playing snooker on one station, the early evening news on another. An Arab terrorist group had exploded a bomb on a West Bank bus, killing twenty, and a postal worker in Yorkshire had beaten his wife to death with a rubber mallet. A medical study estimated that five percent of the British population could be suffering from something called mad cow disease, while back home in the land of the free, a poll showed a third of Americans believed they'd personally encountered space aliens; Barbra Streisand had been given a foreign policy briefing. As a poet William Wordsworth said when he passed this way en route to the Lake District, the world was still far too much with us.

"Do you think Arnold and Winnie really ever stayed here?" I wondered aloud. Outside and two floors down, I noticed, a young man was trying to pry open the door of a green Sierra in the car park with some kind of thin metal contraption.

"If they did," Dad replied, "it was probably before Arnie won the Open."

After our showers, he suggested we amble across the street for a predinner drink at the Scarisbrick Hotel, which looked to be in an even more advanced state of decay than the Prince of Wales.

"That used to be a swell place to go on a Friday night," he remembered fondly as we walked down the Prince's wide staircase to the main lobby, where even more old people were snoozing in chairs and a baby grand piano was pounding out Sinatra's "My Way" all by itself. "That was a real Air Force hangout in those days," he said, "with lots of good-looking local girls and great swing music."

We walked across the street to the Scarisbrick and found a dark wood bar, illuminated principally by beer signs and a blinking fruit machine. A number of elderly men sat alone in booths staring mood-ily at their beers. Dad slipped into a booth, and I went to the bar and ordered us beers. "How about this," I said, handing him a pint of Old Speckled Hen, "a funeral home with a bar."

I sat down, and he sipped his beer and said, "Now, now. Your turn is coming, dear boy. Someone said that to an old man, anyplace that's warm is a homeland. Especially after playing Birkdale on a day like today."

"In that case, you should be very happy with our room. It comes with its own sauna. Or maybe I forgot to tell you. It *is* the sauna."

He told me how he'd first come to the Scarisbrick with the daughter of a local man named A. H. Tarbuck, whom he'd met by chance on the train. "A charming Jewish gentleman. He'd owned jewelry stores all over Europe before Hitler took over. I offered him a Lucky Strike, and we fell into a conversation about FDR, and he invited me here for a drink. He was an older gentleman, with a wife and a married daughter whose husband was in North Africa. He invited me home for dinner. Tarbuck belonged to the Conservative Club and knew Churchill. He once showed me a bag filled with South African diamonds."

"What was the married daughter like?"

"She was attractive. Very attractive. Her name was Miriam. She and I used to go out for a drink sometimes at night. We'd come in here—this place, as I say, really got swinging. I think Glenn Miller did a show in here one night." Opti reminded me of what an absolutely awful singing voice he had by breaking softly into an old war song, something to the effect that a fella who was going to fight had a right to a little romance.

"You seemed to spend a lot of time during the war going to the movies or dancing with attractive English women. Did Mom know?"

"I suppose, though I never mentioned it. She went to USO shows all the time back in the States. There was an admiral at Annapolis who was nuts about her. Good thing I wasn't in the navy."

"Did you ever have a wartime romance? If you were going to fight, you had the right, as they say."

My father looked at me. It was the kind of brazen question he probably never expected me to ask. Until recently, I probably never would have had the nerve to ask it. Part of me would be shocked to hear he had a fling. Part of me wouldn't be the least bit surprised, because I might have, too.

He didn't seem either surprised or bothered, in any case.

"Are you asking me if I ever fell for a woman I met over here? The answer is no. Absolutely not. I was married to your mother, and I loved her."

That, of course, was not what I'd asked him. I'd asked him if he'd ever had an *affair*, a wartime dalliance, some horizontal refreshment in the cause of liberty, a good old English leg-over. Women were always attracted to my father, I knew, and even at eighty they found his breezy charm almost irresistible.

"I'm not going to pretend to you that I was a saint over here," he said quietly, fingering the rim of his pint. "The war was on, and we were a long way from home. That's no moral justification for anything except, perhaps, to say I believe I honored my vows to your mother. I knew she was the woman for me."

"Was there anybody in Paris?"

He gave a vague half smile. "As a matter of fact, yes. I used to hang out with a Canadian nurse named Helen. We went to some plays, saw the sights. She helped me buy a couple hundred dollars' worth of perfume for your mother the week before I shipped home. Believe me, it was all pretty innocent. I'm sure you can't even imagine it."

Having said this, he drank his beer silently. He was right, I couldn't. Or maybe I could. At any rate, I believed what he said. He and my mom had been married almost fifty-four years and still liked to put on big-band records—well, CDs now—and dance in the kitchen, like in the old days at the Crystal Palace. That's when it suddenly came to me how we could have a little more fun.

I dropped a Titleist on the thick hall carpet of the Prince of Wales. I unwrapped a water glass from its sanitary paper ("Says here that Winnie Palmer used this very glass to gargle with, maybe that's why they never washed it") and walked to the other end of the corridor, placing the glass upside down on the carpet. Then I strolled back.

"The object," I said, "is to see how many chips and putts it takes you to hit the glass. We'll play nine holes. Best of nine wins the match and buys dinner."

My father looked wary. "I don't think this is such a good idea. People could be trying to rest."

"Dad, this place makes the city morgue seem busy. Why do you think the real Prince of Wales is always in Scotland massacring birds? It's so he never has to come *here*. To quote Camilla Parker Bowles, 'Quit dawdling, Charlie. Be a man and *shoot* the blimey little critter.' "

"You shoot."

"Oh, for Pete's sake . . . coward."

I took aim with my pitching wedge, drew the club back, and made (if I say so myself) an excellent chipping swing. The ball ricocheted off the hallway's ornate wallpaper just below a Constable reproduction and struck the leg of a small table halfway down the corridor, coming to a stop twenty yards from the glass. If it's true that it's better to be luckier than good in golf, I'd just gotten a really lousy break.

"Good grief," muttered my father. "You're destroying the place."

"You're right. I probably should have used a longer iron."

He dropped his Top-Flite and took a quick jabbing chip as if he expected an enraged floor manager to come wheeling through the staircase door at any moment. None came. His ball rolled neatly down the corridor and stopped four feet from the water glass. The man could have chipped on the hood of a Buick.

I made him putt it out anyway. We walked back to the end of the corridor. He was one up with eight to play. He duplicated the chip and left his next shot only about three feet from the glass. My turn, I decided to putt rather than chip and smacked my ball hard enough to send it bouncing off the baseboard at the far end of the corridor, a resounding crack that made my father wince.

"Finesse doesn't seem to be your long suit today," he said. "Something chewing at you?"

I shook my head, then admitted I was annoyed that our room

was so disappointing. The angry Welshman had a point after all.

"Forget it," Dad said. "We've both stayed in worse. Why waste time worrying about it? We'll be out of here before you know it. Let's play."

Opti was right, of course. We played another "hole," this time halving, and walked back to the end of the corridor again. I said I'd enjoyed our strange abbreviated round at Birkdale. My father nodded.

"You held up really well," I said. "Mom will be pleased."

"I doubt that. She wasn't thrilled about this trip. Let's keep the details of our adventures a little vague, shall we?"

I agreed, then I told him what was really bothering me. I said I'd spent a lot of the round thinking about my grandfather and his grandfather and how much he now seemed to be like them. I wasn't really bothered, I said, so much as thoughtful.

"I'm flattered you think so. They were good men. Pop could barely write his name, but he was the most civil man I ever knew. He never turned anybody away from our door during the Depression, black or white. Uncle Jimmy was quite a charming old gent. I never heard him raise his voice."

We chipped again. Dad's runner ended up five or six feet from the glass. Mine also got close to the target for a change. As we approached our putts, I said, "I remember when Pop died. You said you had to go to Florida to take care of him for a few days. The next thing I knew, Mom said he had died. I couldn't believe it."

"Well, you were only eleven or twelve. Death doesn't seem possible at that age."

"You're right. It's funny what goes through a kid's head. I recall being fascinated by the idea of death. I always wanted to ask you what it was like being with him when he passed away."

"He died with a lot of dignity, just sort of ebbed away. His kidneys were failing, but he was pretty clear-headed right up to the end. We sat and talked a lot. I remember he said he was going to get out of that bed and take you and your brother fishing. The last thing he asked me to do for him was give him a shave. I tried to find a barber who could do it, but no one would come to the house, so I did it myself. I lathered up his face and used his old straight razor."

The hallway doors opened, and a young man in a dark suit approached us with a strained smile on his face. *Uh-oh,* I thought. *The management cometh.*

"Good evening, gentlemen," the man said, clearing his throat. "I'm Weeks, the hotel floor manager. Seems we've had a bit of a noise complaint about your . . . *golfing.*"

"Really?" I said, the picture of innocence abroad.

"I'm very sorry," said my father, blushing. "We'll stop right away." He padded off dutifully to retrieve the water glass and our balls, and Weeks smiled after him like the pleased headmaster who's caught the boy scribbling dirty words in the hymnals.

"Are you a golfer, Weeks?" I asked him.

"Actually, I am not. Sorry to say." He sounded as if I'd asked him if he enjoyed beheading small animals.

"So you don't know who that is?" I indicated the elderly figure scurrying to please him. Weeks looked at my father with slightly less disdain, and I looked at Weeks wondering if he possibly suffered from mad cow disease.

"Actually, no. As a matter of fact, I haven't a clue."

"Ever heard of Sam Snead? They called him the Slammer. Winningest golfer who ever lived. Won more than a hundred tournaments worldwide, including your Open at St. Andrews in 1946. Called the place a cow pasture and never came back again." I waited for this critical information to penetrate his bony Anglo brow. "You see, Weeks, we got rained out over at Birkdale this morning. Dad just felt like chipping a bit, for old times' sake. You've got champions' names written all over that mirrored wall downstairs. This guy was the best of the bunch."

"*Really?*" he murmured. "I had no idea."

"That's okay. Please don't make a fuss over him." Dad was headed back our way now. "He hates for people to make a fuss over him."

"I understand." Weeks switched on a five-star smile for my father.

"Sir, if it would be of interest to you, we could perhaps make one of our larger reception rooms available to you for your practicing."

"That won't be necessary," Dad said contritely. "Our little game is done. I'm sorry for any trouble we may have made."

"No bother whatsoever," Weeks assured him. "And if there's anything further you require, Mr. Snead, please don't hesitate to call me personally." He bowed and left us.

My father handed me the balls and the Winnie Palmer gargling glass and frowned.

"Mr. *Snead?*" he said.

I gave him the same defiant grin my son sometimes gives me when he's been caught clobbering the dog or bashing a lamp with his "indoor" golf club. Why bother trying to deny you did the crime, seems to be Jack's strategy—when you can simply rejoice in it!

"I guess something I might have said made him think you were Sam Snead," I said, patting him gently on the back. "Isn't that funny?"

"Not really. Next thing you know, they'll be asking me to sign that ridiculous mirror downstairs." An entire wall in the hotel's pub was covered with signatures of the world's most famous players; everybody from Ray Floyd to Nick Faldo. The previous evening, we'd wasted half an hour debating over the authenticity of the signatures. Dad was of the opinion that they might be genuine, but (call me a cynical cuss) I was pretty sure a kid named Bruno from the kitchen really painted them.

"Don't worry."

As we strolled back to our sauna, I told my father what Sam Snead had once told me—us country boys always stick together. I said dinner was on me because he'd whipped my tail at Birkdale, which made me one-for-three in our matches, not counting the interrupted Prince of Wales carpet contest. That didn't count, I said, due to an unauthorized spectator on the course.

"When we reach Scotland tomorrow," I promised him, "I'll take me revenge."

"Dream on," he said.

All the Lovely Wee Places

A winding road from Dumfries, Galloway, took us to Southerness, a marvelous short links course unknown to most Americans overlooking the Solway Firth, where we met up with a retired vet named Dr. Jupp and his wife Freddie for a late Saturday afternoon round. The Jupps were on a "weekend break," as Freddie Jupp called it, staying at an inn nearby. Our first day in Scotland was rain-free, the sun gloriously warm on our shoulders.

"We've been to America quite a number of times," Dr. Jupp pronounced loudly as we marched off the first tee together. He was a tall, thin man with a wisp of duck fluff waving from the crown of his bald head. "Got some foreign friends in St. Louis named Kellogg. She's all right, husband's a bit of a lush. Know 'em?"

He was frowning at me, though I quickly realized frowning was Dr. Jupp's natural expression. His scowl fell somewhere between that of a disapproving owl and a constipated eagle. I admitted I didn't know the Kelloggs of St. Louis; I said that the only Kelloggs I knew came from Battle Creek. I paid homage to them every time I ate my cornflakes, I said. *Ta-dump.* No one but my father seemed to catch my little funny.

"Where's that?" wondered Freddie primly.

"Michigan," I said, "land of wolverines, big two-hearted rivers, and Henry Ford. A budding northern golf mecca, too. You might want to check it out on your next trip."

"Right," snapped Dr. Jupp. "I've eaten lobsters from there."

I decided not to tell him lobsters came from Maine, not Michigan. He didn't seem like the sort who could handle being corrected by a *foreigner,* and I didn't fancy having my appendix taken out with a mashie niblick. We watched Freddie tee up and crack her ball a hundred yards down the fairway with a big loping swing.

"Get your arse lower to the ground, Freddie!" Dr. Jupp shouted helpfully at his wife through a pair of bony cupped hands. "Arse to the ground, that's the ticket!"

"Fizz off," Freddie said.

I smiled at my father, wondering what it was about Brits and their arses. He seemed to be thinking the same thing. Was getting your *arse to the ground* anything like getting your *bum into the shot?*

Southerness is considered a "plain" course by some devotees of Scottish linkslands. For one thing, it's one of the most contemporary seaside creations in Britain, having been built by MacKenzie Ross during the same postwar years he was restoring Turnberry's links, seventy miles up the coast. There Ross used earth-moving machinery to marvelous effect, sculpting the dunes and hummocks that give the Turnberry player a powerful sense of the land's whimsical elevations.

For one reason or another—but probably economic in nature—Ross left the lovely green earth at Southerness alone, routing his course over relatively flat pastures and hayfields. The whole enterprise cost less than two thousand pounds to create and was turfed, not seeded, the soil being almost identical, the story goes, to that found in the fens of England. There is, at any rate, an unhurried grace about this little-known linksland—evidenced by the fact that, upon a golfing barman's strong recommendation, we'd simply dialed up from a local pub where we were having lunch and been politely invited to drop in.

Southerness was a bonus. It was supposed to be an "off day" for Dad to rest his wheels, but the hot lunch and cold beer seemed to give him renewed enthusiasm for the game, and what ensued from this unscheduled side trip was a lively round with the Jupps. Dad chatted amiably with Dr. Jupp, who hailed from the Cheviot Hills, about the war, and Freddie pointed to the rumpled green-gray line of the Solway's distant shore and said to me, "That's Silloth, dear. Do you know Silloth?" I admitted I didn't. "That's England over there, the place where the great Cecil Leith came from. Do you know her? She was quite a champion lady golfer back in the teens, though someone said she was, you know, a strong-willed and rather peculiar girl."

I said I knew a bit about Cecil Leith. Some said she was the first lady golfer who struck the ball as well as a man, and had been the first undisputed queen of women's golf until a tall, pallid twenty-year-old from Surrey named Joyce Wethered challenged her in the finals of the British Ladies' championship at Turnberry in 1921. They met a year later at Prince's, Sandwich, and the roles neatly reversed. The shy Wethered became the dominant lady of the golf world until a new crop of American female golfers rose up in the 1920s, led by a powerful-swinging Rhode Island girl named Glenna Collett, who became Glenna Vare.

"Fancy you know all that," Freddie said with surprise.

I admitted I'd been lucky enough to know Glenna Vare before she passed away.

A stiff breeze was whipping off the Solway, but snuggled under my checked wool cap, and swinging a club much better than I had all week, I'd run off a string of pars almost before I even realized what was going on. The unhurried pace and flat terrain seemed to suit my father, too. He pulled his trolley along Southerness's gentle undulations with a minimum of trouble, firing off some excellent approach shots, making his usual share of ten-foot putts.

I went out in 38, my best score of the trip, and Freddie Jupp demanded to know if I was a "professional American player." I smiled, thanked her profusely for thinking such an absurd thing, and admitted that I was just a humble golf scribe playing above his head for the moment.

"A what?" She fingered her pearls.

"I write about golf."

"Ted," she said sharply to her husband, "this young man says he is a *golf* writer. What do you think of that?"

"A *what?*" Dr. Jupp was halfway through his backswing on the tee of the handsome tenth, a short par-three backdropped by a lovely view of the Hills of Galloway. He topped his ball and glared at his wife.

"He writes about *golf!*" she said, a good deal louder, to her husband, causing her pearl necklace to hop at her throat. "I'll bet he knows that big boy you like to watch. You know the one I mean. The one they call Wild Thing. Bad temper. Strange hair."

"Oh. Right," Dr. Jupp growled.

A few moments later, I was teeing my ball when Dr. Jupp came and stood a few feet away. He was easily within my peripheral field of vision.

Crossing his arms on his chest, Dr. Jupp clearly didn't think there was any problem except perhaps that I was dawdling. I could hear air roaring in and out of his nostrils. I glanced up at him and smiled—hoping he'd get the message to back off a bit—but he refused to move, so I swung, pulling the shot and missing the green badly twenty yards to the left.

"That certainly wasn't your best," he pronounced. I saw my father, just behind him, quietly laughing.

"So what's the story on the lad she means? You know the one."

I admitted I didn't. *Bad temper, strange hair?*

"Do you mean John Daly?" Dad suggested.

"*Delly!* That's it," exclaimed Freddie Jupp. "What's he really like?"

I said I didn't really know, explaining I'd only "interviewed" John Daly once, if you could call it that—a twenty-second conversation before he stormed out of the locker room at a prestigious tournament in Texas after shooting a 75 and missing the cut. Mostly I knew what everybody knew, that Daly had his problems—a history of alcohol abuse, emotional instability, a barber who seemed to work with pruning shears—but in my view, I said, Daly was the most exciting player to come along since Arnold Palmer. I'd seen him electrify crowds. I liked the way he played fast and never took prisoners in competition. It was his life off the course that was such a mess. Not yet thirty, he'd been married three times, accused of wife abuse (a charge he strongly denied), been banished by the PGA Tour for various offenses ranging from picking up his ball during play to fighting with spectators, nearly lost his sponsors, faced up to his alcoholism, and once considered driving his Mercedes off a cliff. For all that, I had a soft spot for Daly because as a kid growing up in Arkansas, he knew the name of only one famous golf course—the Old Course at St. Andrews. I asked Dr. Jupp what he thought of John *Delly.*

"I think he's a big fat *git,*" Jupp declared, and for a moment I thought he might spit at my feet to emphasize the point. "It's an absolute dis-*grace* how that lad behaves." Freddie rolled her eyes at me.

"If he ever cleans up his act, though," observed my father, "he could be a real appealing fella. Golf needs characters like him. The public can relate."

"Wouldn't wager on that if I were you." Dr. Jupp shook his head, resuming his aggressive bowlegged walk as we headed toward the tenth green. "I don't think someone of his doubtful character even belongs in the game."

"He really loves Wild Thing," Freddie assured me quietly as we walked side by side. "I do wish he could do something about that funny bit of hair, though."

I asked if she meant John Delly or her husband the vet. Freddie Jupp burst out laughing and slugged me on the arm with a balled-up fist. She told me I was a "big cheeky lad." The lady had a good right.

It was nice to be in Scotland finally with my father. My son was already talking of the day I would take him there. At the moment Jack was more interested in bagpipes than golf bags, but I could happily picture the day we would hack around the land of half his ancestors on a similar adventure together. The great linkslands by day, the great bagpipe bars by night.

Dad and I drove to the village of Kirkoswald the next morning, a cool cloudy sabbath, and attended services at the little stone kirk where Eisenhower had supposedly worshiped. The minister was a potato-shaped man with wild gray eyebrows. He gave a cracking sermon about the evils of permissive living that had something vaguely to do with telecommunication satellites running amok overhead and polluting impressionable Scottish minds with German porn. Twice he halted the proceedings dead in their tracks and ordered us to sing hymns louder.

After church, as the clouds peeled back and the sun came out, we drove a few miles up the coast road to Turnberry.

To our left, eighteen miles offshore, the Ailsa Craig, where the world's greatest curling stones used to come from, rose up on a tranquil sea. It was a bonny afternoon with abundant warmth and virtually no breeze. The Turnberry Hotel, when it finally appeared, resembled a wedding cake sitting on a green hill. We checked in and ran into an old friend of sorts in the hotel's handsomely refurbished lobby.

"Well, I'll be doggone," said Dr. Bob Tanner, the Birmingham dentist, pumping my hand like a long-lost cousin from Dogpatch. He wrung my father's hand, too, and introduced us to one of his traveling pals, another dentist named Bob. The Bobs were dressed in the kind of elaborate multihued golf outfits that made me think that cricket, with its simple white shirts and trousers, might not be such a dumb sport after all.

The Bobs were going down for an afternoon round on the Ailsa course and invited us to join them. "We could have a little best ball match," Bob Tanner proposed.

I looked at Dad and was pleased when he said, "Sounds fine to me."

An hour later, we teed off on the Ailsa course. We even had caddies. Dad's was named John, a scrawny older man with a filterless cigarette dangling from his lips. John mumbled "hallo" and scarcely said another word for the next two hours. Mine was named Mike. Mike was almost mahogany from a fortnight's vacation on Cyprus. "Why would you want to go to Cyprus in October when the weather here is so lovely and the gorse in bloom?" I asked Mike.

"Because it's not Scotland, mate," he replied.

The start of our match was highly inauspicious. I hooked my opening drive fifty yards into the hayfieldlike rough on the left. Dad topped his drive and trickled his ball maybe fifty yards off the tee. The Bobs smashed power fades past the bunkers on the left, finding the heart of the fairway. I required three attempts to return my ball to the short grass. Dad topped his second shot and sent his ball scampering another hundred yards. Turnberry's opening hole is only 350 yards long, one of the easiest on the course. The Bobs were waiting for us to hit our *fifth* and *third* shots respectively and my caddy Mike, perhaps daydreaming of Cyprus, was looking at me with genuine sympathy—though for me or him, it was difficult to tell. I was reminded of the old joke where the American golfer, mentally unglued after a round in which everything has gone wrong, finally lashes out at his Scottish caddy, "Angus, by golly, you're the worst damn caddy this game has ever seen!" Angus thinks for a moment, shakes his head, and calmly replies, "Oh no, sir. That would be *too* much of a coincidence."

By the third hole, we were already three down. The Bobs had made consecutive pars and a birdie and apparently decided we were irrelevant. They were busy talking about a promising timeshare condo project on Marco Island, and I whispered to Dad that my game was about to get on track. Turnberry was the site of the greatest shot-making exhibition in the history of the game, a brilliant duel between Jack Nicklaus and Tom Watson at the '77 Open championship, which Watson won at the seventy-second hole, shattering the old British Open record of 276 in the process. I reminded my father that in the final round Nicklaus birdied the fourth hole to jump out to a commanding three-hole lead, only to see young Tom come roaring back and overtake him at the wire. If Tom could do it, so could we.

The Ailsa's fourth hole is an aptly named par-three called Woebetide, a fairly short swat of 160 yards to a slightly elevated "pulpit" green.

I'd been to kirk that morning. I'd said my prayers. If God is a just God, I thought, *here's* where I'll finally make a hole-in-one. What an ideal spot! At the Pebble Beach of Scottish golf courses! An ace would turn the whole match on its ear, vanquish the obnoxious Bobs, and woe betide them.

One Bob's shot was already in the front right bunker; the other had flown the green. Dad's shot lay on the apron just in front of the green. I made a smooth pass with my six. The ball drifted up into the air currents, rising from the cliffs to the left, and then dropped on the green. One of the Bobs murmured, "Christ. That's close."

"You bet it is, Mate," said my faithful caddy, Mike.

It wasn't in the hole—*inches* short again. My life story. Charter member of the HIN Society. I tapped in. At least we'd won the hole. Mike handed me my ball, and we slapped hands like Greg Norman and his caddy, Tony Navarro.

The Bobs weren't talking condos anymore, but Dad's legs, I could see, were already giving out. That was too bad. I was sure I was finding my game and we could beat the Bobs.

But it simply wasn't in the cards. After the fifth hole, which we halved with pars, I suggested they proceed without us and we'd settle up later. Dad protested, but it wasn't much of a protest. I could see he felt bad trying to compete with the Bobs. I told them we really wanted to slow down and enjoy our stroll around Turnberry because we were headed to Glasgow in the morning and this was our only chance to see the course. The Bobs said they understood. We shook hands and watched them tee off and head down the fairway after a group of Japanese with bags as big as cruise missiles.

When they were gone, Dad admitted he didn't feel like playing anymore. The remark set bells off in my head.

"Are you okay? Shall we just head in?"

"Relax, Bo," he said. "I just want to walk and watch you play."

Mike reminded me that the halfway house was just up ahead at the ninth, a good spot to sit and have a rest and some refreshment. I thanked him and said I would prefer to carry my own bag from that point on and would settle up with both him and John later, too. "No problem, Mate," Mike said, waving a hand. Breaking his silence, John said he would make sure Dad's clubs got cleaned and taken back to the hotel.

On the way to the halfway house, I played the next four holes pretty well—par par bogey par. The ninth is Turnberry's most majestic hole, with a championship tee that lets you drive from a narrow headland two hundred feet above the rocks and churning surf. I smacked a nice drive over the cairn marker that shows you the proper line and just missed making par. We walked to the halfway house and ordered beers and sat on a bench overlooking the remains of Robert Bruce's castle. Families were picking whelks off the rock below, and people were out walking their dogs in the balmy evening light.

Dad said, "Doesn't feel like the end of September, does it?"

"Not September in Maine, Mate."

"How's your house?"

"Almost finished."

He smiled drowsily. "I've heard that one before."

My house in Maine was an ongoing saga and something of a complicated subject between us. It had all started nine years before, when my wife and I got it into our heads that our children should be raised in Maine. The fact that we didn't even *have* children at the time didn't prevent us from packing up, fleeing Boston, and moving a hundred miles up the Atlantic coast.

We purchased five acres on a forested hill, and I cleared land with a chainsaw, learning firsthand why guys who do this kind of work for a living usually have missing body parts and low career expectations. When I informed my father that I planned to build our period-correct post-and-beam house with my own hands, he reminded me that the rough theory behind attending college and finding a good job was that you could earn enough money to *pay* someone who knew what he was doing to build your dream house. He urged me to seek serious professional help—either a real carpenter or a shrink.

I laughed at him and told him to think of the project merely as a phase I had to go through—my Bob Vila period. I said it was what happened when a yuppie watched too much *This Old House*. An insatiable hunger to own, to build, to *create* something in the wilderness took possession! Besides, I'd heard him say many times that he would dearly love to build his own house with his own hands.

"That's true," he agreed. "I meant a log cabin somewhere in the Smokies, though. I used to say I wanted a little farm, too. That doesn't mean I'm going to start raising cows and pigs in the backyard."

For reasons that now slightly eluded me—but undoubtedly had more to do with my father than Bob Vila—I Sheetrocked the walls, laid the pine plank floors, finished the windows, hung the doors, made the cabinets, laid the tile, varnished essentially everything in sight, and hammered and sawed and power-glued myself into a period-correct state of exhaustion.

Now the house was finished—well, okay, we were about to add two dormers, ever tweaking—and I was in the process of cultivating the estate. I'd basically squandered my children's college money on evergreen shrubs and perennials, cultivated two acres of Kentucky blue fescue grass, and planted sixty or seventy rosebushes around our New Age homestead. There was no truth whatsoever to the silly rumor circulating in town that I had plans to create my own little nine-hole executive golf course up in the forest. *One* hole was all I really needed.

Before I could steer the subject safely away from my house and back to the golf in Ayrshire, though, Dad changed it for me.

"You know who would love this place?" he said, as we loitered on the sunny Turnberry bench.

"Jack and Tom?" I said, thinking of Nicklaus and Watson, who were probably too busy that week in '77 to notice the place anyway.

"No. Bill and Bob." He meant his old golf pals. "We could really go at each other in a place like this."

The remark made me think of the match we'd just bailed out of. "We could have whipped the doctor Bobs, you know," I said.

"Maybe so," he said, closing his eyes, lifting his face to the breeze. "It doesn't matter, does it?"

No, I thought, *it doesn't*. In a year, Dad would be gone. In five years, someone else might own my dream house. This moment, though, however imperfect, would never come again. That larger point was even finally beginning to sink into my head. Opti had a gift for always returning me to the importance of the moment. I made a note to tell Bill and Bob how my father had mentioned them one glorious evening on a bench at Turnberry.

From where we sat, I could see that the fifteenth tee was open. I suggested we skip holes ten through fourteen and play in from the fifteenth. Dad seemed a bit reluctant, but being a seasoned hole-skipper, I prevailed on him to risk such a cardinal breach of ethics. I birdied the hole, a tough par-three called Ca Canny, and told him the gods themselves approved of a little creative hole-skipping every so often.

Ailsa's sixteenth is one of the nicest par-fours in creation, a medium-length straightaway hole that challenges you with a steeply shouldered ravine in front of the green. Watson nearly gave the Open to Nicklaus here in '77 by bravely shooting for a pin cut in front. His ball landed on the hill and for a heartstopping moment seemed about to tumble back into the little burn. Somehow it didn't, Watson got up and down for par, and both men went to the seventeenth dead even. I played the hole nicely, with a gorgeous drive, a well-struck six-iron approach, and a twenty-foot lag putt that permitted me a safe tap-in for par.

"You did that like a pro," Dad commented, zipping up his jacket as we exited the green. I saw his leg bag was leaking again and realized he must be getting cold.

"Which pro?"

"Which pro do you like?"

"Let me think about it," I said. "I'll tell you after the next hole."

Turnberry's seventeenth, a handsome par-five, was kind to Tom Watson in 1977. A birdie there moved him one shot ahead of Nicklaus—a lead he held to the title. My own lengthy putt for birdie came up three feet short of the cup, and I missed an easy putt for par. I'd neglected to putt like a kid.

"I'm putting like the old Tom Watson," I said. "Not the young and fearless one."

"It happens to us all," Dad commiserated, replacing the flag-stick.

"Hasn't happened to you," I accused him, causing him to smile.

We stood on the green, and he reminded me of Nick Price's recent magnificent fifty-five-footer that had crossed the green as if it had eyes and rattled the cup during the final round of the Open in 1994. That brilliant eagle snatched the claret jug from Jesper Parnevik and fulfilled Price's childhood dream of winning the British Open. No champion I could think of except perhaps Watson was more deserving.

I told my father something interesting that Price had recently told me. His father had died when he was ten. They'd been able to play only two rounds of golf together. Price, a father of two small children, still thought about his father a great deal and obviously wished they could have had more time to play the game. If you asked Nick Price to name his ideal four-ball group, he would tell you Bobby Jones, Byron Nelson, and his father.

"That's lovely," my father said. "What would yours be?"

"That's tough. Probably Snead, Nelson, and you, or Palmer, Watson, and Price. You'd unfortunately have to watch. I wouldn't say no to Crenshaw, Love, and Curtis Strange, either. You?"

"Jones, Julius Boros, and Sam Snead."

"Some nice swings there."

"Save one of your own for eighteen."

As we walked off toward Turnberry's home hole, I thanked Dad for playing when I was sure he'd rather be resting. He said the pleasure was all his. We went back to our room, and he showered and quickly fell asleep on the bed. I called downstairs to the dining room to confirm our dinner reservation for eight, then hopped into a steamy shower myself. When I got out, I heard the magical skirl of a bagpipe being played . A piper strolls the grounds at the Turnberry Hotel each evening at dusk. It was dusk. I picked up the telephone and quickly dialed home. When my son finally got on, in the midst of having his Sunday lunch, I held the receiver out the window so he could hear it.

The next day we drove up the Ayrshire coast to Prestwick, where I convinced a hesitant pro-shop attendant to permit us onto the ancient links for a few holes—the day being gray, cold, and windy and the old course where the first twelve British Opens were contested being virtually empty of souls. Prestwick is a good illustration of how the game has outgrown many great golf courses. It's short (6,740 yards), sweet, and eccentric. The first hole goes off hard by a busy commuter rail track. There are blind holes the likes of which no modern club membership would tolerate. Parking space is nil. The early Opens were played here over twelve rather than eighteen holes. But the place is a monument to the game's glorious history.

My favorite Prestwick hole is the famous *blind* par-three fifth, called the Himalayas. A bogey there, I've found, is a good score. We played to the fifth hole, achieved bogeys, then stopped and walked back to warm up in the Omega.

We drove up the road to Royal Troon and each had a pint of wallop in the empty members' bar. I would have loved to take a crack at Royal Troon, a ruggedly difficult layout that has been unusually kind to Americans in the six Open championships the club has hosted. Four were captured by Americans, including Palmer's brilliant Open title defense in 1962, Tom Weiskopf in '73, Watson in '82, and Mark Calcavecchia in '89. Unfortunately, I hadn't written ahead to make any arrangements with the club secretary and the afternoon was too cold and blustery for golf anyway.

Next day, we pushed on to Bridge of Wier, where we hooked up with Kate Bennie, my mother-in-law, and her longtime friends Tom and Elizabeth, for lunch at a place called the Fox and Hounds. Kate was making her annual pilgrimage home to Glasgow, and she asked my father if I was behaving properly. "Depends on what your definition of proper is," he replied. "He's made the staff at every hotel deliriously happy at the sight of our departure."

"The boy can be a devil boy," she said, giving me a look she usually reserves for her fourteen-year-old scholars caught excavating their noses. I wondered if she was still holding a grudge about the window I'd recently knocked out of her house. It was a brilliant sand-wedge shot, fired through the window of her two-hundred-year-old farmhouse from 180 yards across the pond in front. Mum had been reading a book in her favorite chair by the window when the ball crashed through the glass and came miraculously to rest on the table next to her tea. As I'd told her, I'd never come close to hitting a sand wedge *that* well.

Mum ordered haggis, neeps, and tatties, so I ordered them, too. Despite what you hear in Scotland, nobody on earth really likes haggis—a dish made from sheep guts, dishrags, and old Glasgow daily papers—and I reminded everyone at the table about Chateaubriand's famous quote about Scottish haggis—*I thought it merely smelled like shit until I tasted it.*

Tom and Elizabeth laughed, and Mum, heroically suppressing a smile, would have laughed, too, but this would have granted me the haggis high ground, and no self-respecting Scot ever yields the high ground on haggis or any other subject pertaining to civilization as we know it.

The neeps and tatties (turnips and potatoes) were excellent, but the haggis was dry and tasteless, which may have been a culinary break. "The only way to fix a bad haggis," my mother-in-law rose brilliantly to the moment, "is to order a nice extra sauce made of Drambuie. You drink the sauce and throw out the haggis." Mum was suddenly in lively spirits, and I asked Tom and Elizabeth if she was behaving properly.

"Well," said Elizabeth, "she seems to have grown a wee bit more *American* with each passing year."

I assured them Mum's full assimilation was utterly impossible. For one thing, she'd been on American shores for thirty-five years and stubbornly refused to eat peanut butter or charcoal-grilled steak, or to drink Pepsi. She had never watched a Super Bowl, given the finger to an umpire, or voted for a Republican. She was to true American citizenship, I pointed out, what a tropical heat wave is to Olympic bobsledding.

Somehow, the subject got around to golf. Tom suggested that my father and I play a club he was thinking of joining called Ranfurley Castle, with a man named Big Jim Patterson, a "crack player" whom he graciously offered to phone up on our behalf.

My father begged off, saying he needed to rest for Carnoustie, but I was eager to play a match against anybody named Big Jim. Foolish me. The next day, while Dad poked around Glasgow, I played Ranfurley Castle with Big Jim Patterson through a driving mist storm, which Patterson insisted on calling "a nice Scotch mist."

Patterson was a true Scottish patriot, and a heck of a golfer. As we played up and down the picturesque hilly track, he beat my brains out and talked endlessly about all the swell things Scots had given the world—the steam engine, scotch whiskey, asphalt roads, the Macintosh raincoat (one of those, I kept thinking, sure would be handy), and something about the world's first self-service restaurant. Even Neil Armstrong, the first man to visit the moon, Big Jim said, was part Scottish—which explained why he'd played golf there.

Struggling to find either my game or my dignity, I decided not to break the news to my host that it was Alan Shepard who played golf on the moon. But I did let slip that I'd heard that Texas has more people claiming to be real Scots than Scotland does, and I idly wondered if there were any truth to the rumor that Scotland used the guillotine two hundred years before the French. I *could* have pointed out that Scotland also has the highest rates of lung cancer and alcoholism in Europe—not to mention the most statistically unsafe roads. But, hey, who wants to be an ugly American when you're playing as somebody's guest?

In the end I found neither my game nor much of my dignity at Ranfurley, though I did scare up a hare big enough to have given Jimmy Carter a lethal coronary. After the proper thrashing, Jim and I shook hands and had a beer to balm the pain and wet down any body parts that had somehow avoided getting soaked in the Scottish mist. Big Jim and Little Jim parted friends, more or less.

"How'd it go?" Dad asked pleasantly as I slogged into the hotel room, dumping my drenched golf bag on the floor. He'd had his feet up for much of the afternoon, browsing an anthology of British poetry he'd picked up somewhere, sipping ginger ale and watching Ricki Lake. A guy who looked as if he couldn't wait to get offstage to stick a heroin needle in his arm was saying he lived to have sex with overweight women. He was surrounded by overweight women. The audience shouted gleefully at him, and Ricki Lake, leering, announced a commercial break. A perky spot for dish detergent came on. The British send us *The Mayor of Casterbridge*, I thought, and we send them Ricki Lake. My attention came back to Dad's question.

"Remember what happened to the English troops at Bannockburn?"

"Think so. The Scots wiped 'em out entirely."

"Correct. Let's just say they had an easier afternoon than me."

The next day, I took a measure of revenge on Scotland by beating up the new Jack Nicklaus-designed Monarch's Course at The Gleneagles Hotel, in the Perthshire hills, by putting like a kid, chipping like my old man, and shooting my way to a 77. My old man chipped and putted like himself to a highly respectable 91. The rest had clearly done Dad some good and our companion for the round didn't hurt, either. His name was Jimmy Kidd, a lively conversationalist, passionate golfer, son of a Glasgow greenskeeper, and the Director of Development for the famous sporting hotel. Kidd and I had met a couple years before when I visited the hotel shortly after the Monarch's Course opened to great fanfare. He told us funny stories about the creation of the course, and even funnier ones about how European guests—particularly well-heeled Germans and Brits—were so enamoured of the novelty of riding carts they couldn't keep them off tee boxes and greens.

"You seem to have a knack for coping with it all," Dad complimented him. "Whether it's Jack Nicklaus or Germans in the bunkers."

"Glad you think so. I try not to get too excited, Brax," Jimmy said, looking at him. "That's a gift I got from my father. I never knew a man I admired more than him. His name was James. They called him Jimmy. I was called Jim in my younger days. I was the oldest of his seven children. Dad was six feet tall and eighteen stone, a powerful figure. He was a genuine character, a big-hearted man who always had time for people, and I idolized him but I could never somehow find the way to tell him that until the end of his life. I suppose I was determined to somehow prove to him how good I was at business. I worked so bloody hard at my career and being successful we somehow lost valuable time to be together. When my mother died I think it broke his heart.

"I brought him here to the hotel for the Scottish Open in 1990. That meant a lot to me, and to him, too, I think. I spent the last two days of his life with him. I took him to the hospital on the Sunday night before he died. We had been talking a fair bit by then, making up, I guess, for some of the lost time. He told me stories about his father and even his grandfather. Things I'd never heard. It deeply enriched my life, I must say. Being a father didn't come all that easily to me but learning these things from my own father was like a final gift. Our lives have got better, as a result. My son now works in the business with me."

"Bravo," Dad said, clearly moved. He toasted Jimmy with his raised wine glass.

We went on to Cameron House, by the southern shore of Loch Lomond, to have dinner with Douglas Dagleish and his son Colin. Douglas was president of the Scottish Golf Union and Colin a former Scottish amateur champ and Walker Cupper who now operated a successful golf tour company called Perry Golf, with his Atlanta-based brother Gordon. They brought thousands of Americans like my father and me to Scotland and Ireland every year, pumped us full of good real ale and links golf, and sent us home soggy but contented customers.

The Dagleishes had an interesting family golf story. "None of us played golf till we moved into a house across the street from the course at Helensburgh," Douglas explained, as we settled into over-stuffed chairs near a crackling fire in the drawing room, after supper. I couldn't recall what we'd just eaten, but it was highly tasty. A waiter brought us all single malt whiskeys.

"The boys were small when they wandered across the street and started to play the game. Next their mother went across the street and took it up. I was forced to go join them finally—just to keep the family together, you realize. My wife became the club champion, the boys went on to become very fine players and attend school in the States, and I became captain of the golf club, then president of the county golf association, then the Scottish Golf Union . . . all because the boys wandered across the street. Most sons follow their fathers into the professions. I followed my sons across the street to an entire new kind of life."

"That's a charming story," Dad said, and began rattling off one of his own about his hopeless efforts to give my mother golf lessons. She'd been playing now forty years and wasn't any better at it than the first day she swung a club. "But at least she's very consistent."

There was much laughter.

My eye kept drifting to the window, my attention drifting, too. A cold autumn night was pressing against the darkened windows, and the shore of Loch Lomond was less than a full wedge shot down the hill.

All this family talk got me thinking about Sam Bennie, my late father-in-law. As a boy, Sam had grown up fishing this end of Loch Lomond with his favorite uncle. On an entrance wall of my home there was a rather mystical-looking framed photograph of Sam, who was called Campbell by his family, taken at about age eighteen, just after the war, standing beside his uncle's boat, looking at once innocent and canny, on the south shore of the famous loch.

Sam grew up to roam the world. After completing his military service and leaving the Royal Engineers in the late 1950s, he and Kate emigrated to Canada and then to New York, where Sam, a brilliant electrical engineer, went to work for ITT. A romantic posting to Alaska followed. He worked on the Distant Early Warning System, sometimes called the DEWline, in the late 1960s and early 1970s, by now the father of three small kids—Fiona, Alison, and Ian. The family lived in Anchorage and flew a pontoon plane out to a cabin on a wilderness lake on weekends.

Sam and Kate hungered for a bit of Scotland and found it, after an intense search of rural New England, in the highlands of Maine, a village called Harmony, population 800. They purchased a three-hundred-acre farm overlooking sprawling Moosehead Pond and moved into the ramshackle farmhouse one snowy day in March. In summer, the view from the house's porch eerily recalled Loch Lomond's southern shore.

I was thinking about the last time Sam came home to the farm, just a few years before. He'd been traveling the world for more than a decade, keeping apartments in places like Dallas, Istanbul, Sri Lanka, and Papua, New Guinea, but always coming home for a few months each year to Kate and the farm. And *always* for Hogmanay, the Scottish new year.

The family ritual called for tuning the shortwave radio to the BBC live broadcast of Big Ben striking the new year, followed by lots of eating and hopping about to traditional highland reels. When Sam came home for good, Maggie, his first grandchild, was approaching her first birthday. Whilst Maggie was still in her mother's womb, Sam had nick-named her Stardust and brought her a collection of stuffed animals plucked from junk stores and jumble sales all over the world. He dubbed this ragtag collection the Stardust Fan Club.

It turned out to be Sam's last gift. He was gravely ill with throat cancer that final Hogmanay. We'd known this for only a matter of months. In weeks he was gone. One snowy March morning, with the sun coming up over the highlands of Maine, Sam passed away. We were all with him.

Finding myself now by the shores of Loch Lomond made me think of Sam, and that made me think of my own father, and that made me veer off dangerously into the bogs of my own impending sadness. Fortunately, Opti was there to bring me back.

"You all right?" he asked, picking up vibes from my uncharacter-istic quietness. The Dagleishes were looking at me, too.

"Yes," I said. "Just thinking."

"About golf courses, I should imagine," said Douglas affectionately. The words rolled off his tongue as if he were an ancient clan chieftain.

"That's right."

The Dagleishes gave us a list of their favorite hidden gems of Scottish golf, places off the beaten path where Americans seldom ventured—Boat o' Garten, Bridge of Allan, Golspie, Tain, Brora, Oban. It was good information to have. I'd actually visited a couple of the courses they mentioned. Douglas described them aptly as "lovely wee places you truly ought to see."

"By the way, have you ever been to Islay?" asked Colin.

As a matter of fact, I explained, we were thinking of going out to Islay because Kate Bennie's people, the Sinclairs, hailed from Islay, and she'd sprinkled her father's ashes on a hill overlooking some golf course out there. He'd worked for the Linen Bank and belonged to an old club in Glasgow called Williamwood. I hoped to check out Williamwood, too.

"The course on Islay is called the Machrie. It's excellent—very rough and original. lots of blind holes and complicated terrain. You won't find much in Britain to compare it to. You must look up my good friend Murdo Macpherson. A complete character. Runs a small hotel and manages the links. He's kind of a one-man show on Islay. But I saw in yesterday's *Herald* that Nick Faldo was just out there. The rumor is he's out to buy the place."

"A lovely wee place indeed, that," rumbled Douglas. "Better go before Nicky gets his hands on it."

I promised we would try and visit the Machrie, perhaps after St. Andrews. I glanced at Dad and smiled. Would we make it that far? He smiled and nodded. Maybe so.

"I'll give old Murdo a ring tomorrow," said Colin.

"So where's your next stop?" Douglas wanted to know.

"Carnoustie."

"Ah, *Carnoustie.*" The name rolled solemnly off his tongue as if it were an oath. His smile broadened again.

"We're all sons of Carnoustie, you know."

The Game Within Us

There were smiles all over Links Parade Road. A woman passed me, led by a prancing boxer dog. She smiled engagingly. The dog glanced up but didn't smile, although it's always difficult to tell with a boxer.

"Isn't it simply the *greatest* news?" she trilled to me, a stranger with a golf bag slung on his back, which could accurately describe about every third person you met on the street on a mild autumn morning in Carnoustie.

"Yes, ma'am. Long overdue. Congratulations."

"Thank you very much indeed."

We passed without even breaking stride. The great news, heralded in the morning edition of *The Scotsman,* was summarized by the headline "Open Returns to Carnoustie."

Five British Opens have been decided at Carnoustie, a fairly gray and nondescript village by the Firth of Tay that has probably done more to foster the growth of golf outside of Scotland's borders than even St. Andrews, its principal rival an hour to the south. One of the great mysteries of recent times, however, was the fact that there had been no Open championship held at Carnoustie (the sternest test in all of Britain, some feel) for two decades.

Such decisions, made by the longbeards of the Royal and Ancient based at St. Andrews, flew in the face of Carnoustie's evangelical pedigree. Around the turn of the century, a couple hundred of Carnoustie's sons left their native land to teach golf to the world, effectively becoming the Johnny Appleseeds of the game. A proportionately high number of them settled in America, including Stuart Maiden, who taught the game to Bobby Jones, and the brothers Smith, Willie, Alex, and Macdonald, two of whom (Willie and Alex) became early champions of America's national open championship. Macdonald Smith, whom Herbert Warren Wind called one of the great ball-strikers of all time, also came within a hair of winning the American championship. Not surprisingly, several of the men who helped found the fledgling United States Golf Association were Carnoustie sons.

Carnoustie's most famous native son, Tommy Armour, who supposedly once threw his clubs in disgust out the window of a train crossing the Forth Rail Bridge, won the first British Open held in his hometown in 1931, followed by Henry Cotton in '37, Ben Hogan in '53, Gary Player in '68, and Tom Watson in '75. Each win possessed significance larger than almost anyone could properly fathom at the time.

Armour, blind in one eye from mustard gas in World War I, captured his last major title here before shoving off to America to become the preeminent teacher of his day, and Cotton, the well-born suave scrambler who elevated the status of lowly club pros everywhere and first advocated pupils hone their swings by hitting against an old car tire, collected his second Open title at a moment when

Americans Snead, Nelson, and Sarazen dominated the game and British hopes for a home victory were at an all-time low. His final-round 71, on a day when torrential rains and swirling winds blew most of the other scores over 80, stands as one of the most heroic finishes in Open history. Cotton needed only twenty-six putts to salvage Britain's pride and earn the adoration of his countrymen.

Ben Hogan's feat in '53 came on the heels of his miraculous U.S. Open comeback victory in 1951 but stands mighty in the game's folklore because of the shot-making clinic the Wee Ice Mon put on before the gallery at Carnoustie. Gene Sarazen persuaded Hogan to enter his first and only British Open that year, and Hogan arrived two weeks early to perform his customary thorough preparation for battle. He practiced with the smaller British ball, studied Carnoustie's windswept undulations, and concentrated his work on fairway woods and low irons, feeling they would be the key to victory. On the first day, watched by a throng of eight thousand that included singer Frank Sinatra, Hogan fired a 73 in a stiff westerly breeze. He followed up with a 71 on Thursday, ending two shots out of the lead. On Friday morning, he missed the course record 69 by one shot and broke the record that afternoon with a five-under-par 68. It was peerless golf—rounds that got better as the tournament progressed. Carnoustie was the climax of Hogan's career and possibly the greatest tournament he ever played. He promised the locals he would come back, but he never did, one explanation goes, because he had nothing further to prove.

When Gary Player, who once slept as an unknown on the beach at St. Andrews, came here in '68, he was a full-blown star in search of his second Open title—and Carnoustie boosted him to the marquee level of a Palmer and Nicklaus. In weather he called "absolute rubbish," Player held off Billy Casper, Bob Charles, and a charging Nicklaus to capture the Open on a links he called "the toughest course in the world." No one rushed to dispute the opinion.

Tom Watson, on the other hand, had never won much of anything when he came to Carnoustie in 1975. Jack Nicklaus was the heavy favorite. On fairways baked rock hard by weeks of drought, South African Bobby Cole went out on day one and eclipsed Hogan's record by firing a 66 but was topped by an Australian named Jack Newton, who putted his way to a blistering 65—yet another record. Almost no one noticed a polite red-haired lad from Kansas lurking in the large pack just behind Cole and Newton. The media, in fact, focused almost exclusively on Nicklaus and Johnny Miller, expecting them to be the Yanks who broke from the pack.

Instead, on a gray Saturday when none of the contenders broke 70, Watson quietly birdied eighteen for a finish of 72, which placed him in a tie for the lead with Jack Newton. Carnoustie had its first-ever playoff, and local odds already had Newton the winner nearly three to one. Coming to eighteen, the contenders remained level. Newton fired his two-iron to the greenside bunker, while Watson coolly uncorked a high-flying shot to the heart of the green—capturing par and earning the first of his five British Opens.

With this kind of pedigree, it was reasonable to ask, why had the all-wise Royal and Ancient bumped sweet Carnoustie off the Open rotation, like a rough but favorite uncle being kicked out of the wedding?

Theories abounded, but there was a man I hoped would give me the real lowdown, and maybe a proper lesson on how to execute the famous "Carnoustie run-up shot" to boot. His name was Tony Gilbert, and he was supposed to be waiting for Dad and me at Carnoustie's starter house.

You can't miss Carnoustie's clubhouse, which is really just an administrative building with pullcarts stashed beneath the stairwells, a small, drab concrete structure that possesses all the monochrome charm of a municipal incinerator. It's the town's leading eyesore. I walked up to the window and asked for Tony Gilbert, one of Carnoustie's best-known teaching pros, paid my seven-quid guest green fee (the clerk was expecting me, I was playing as Tony's guest), and was informed that my host was waiting for me in the putting green area.

There I found a trim, lean-faced man with youthful blue eyes and the kind of complexion that comes only from strolling for years in the sea wind. He was dressed in a red windbreaker and wearing a striped necktie, industriously rapping ten-foot putts into a hole with depressing repetition. I introduced myself, we shook hands, and I asked Tony straightaway about the Open controversy, wondering if perhaps having the ugliest clubhouse in creation could explain the R&A's distorted logic. The only other plausible explanation was that blue-collar Carnoustie lacked the posh hotels and other luxury amenities many foreign golf travelers seem to require.

"Could be, could be," Tony murmured as we set off down the fairway from the first tee, leaning into a gathering east wind, "but I think it's a wee bit more political than that. For one thing," he explained, "there has always been a heady competitive spirit between the golfers of Carnoustie and St. Andrews, Scotland's two leading municipal layouts. These things are fairly cloaked in mystery, but I have a sneaking suspicion that the decision came down purely to personalities. Golf is a character-builder, they say, and the burghers of St. Andrews perhaps simply think they've got the superior character."

The way he chuckled, I could tell he found this notion simply laughable. "For one thing, " he added, "our Carnoustie golfers regularly beat their St. Andrews counterparts in regular competitions."

Tony stopped in his tracks and gave me a quizzical look, as if we'd forgotten something.

"Say, aren't you supposed to have your father with you, laddie?"

I explained, somewhat uncomfortably, that my father had run into some "unexpected difficulties" and would possibly join us later. Tony nodded and left it at that, and we played on, striking long irons dead into a rising wind at a flag flapping wildly just over the hummock, guarding the first hole at Carnoustie's championship course. My three-iron shot flew about a hundred yards through the air. At Carnoustie, as at most seaside links, wind is the eternal enemy.

I realized I was trying not to let my concern show. My anxiety wasn't over my pitiful golf shot. My nerves were frayed from an incident that had just taken place back at the hotel. Our rooms at the Glencoe Hotel faced the links, and when I'd barged excitedly into my father's room without knocking, babbling on about my eagerness to play Carnoustie finally, I'd been horrified to discover him stripped naked, red-faced, with a stomach that appeared to be, well, *exploding*.

That's what it looked like to me, at any rate. He'd shouted at me to either "invite the whole world inside or please shut the door!" and I'd swiftly obeyed, unable to take my eyes off the huge fleshy bulge on his abdomen and the angry red welt. "Good God, what's going on? Should I call a doctor?" I stammered. "For chrissake, calm down," he snapped at me. "I've just blown the gasket that holds the flange to the stoma-bag in place. No big deal, except I seem to have left my spare at home."

"But what's that—that big thing on your stomach? And that red *thing*?" "This?" He patted the bulge and smiled ruefully. "This, dear son, is what's called a colostomy. And this red thing is my intestines. Please forgive me for being a little *indelicate*, but when you conduct your bowel movements into a little bag, it's important to have a bag that properly works. That, in a nutshell, is my big problem at the moment."

I was momentarily dumbstruck, watching his frustrated ministrations in a kind of detached horror. It was just the kind of unexpected development my mother had forecast and that I, somewhere in the back of my mind, feared might scuttle our trip. As he cleaned his stomach with a damp bath towel, I told him I would go phone Tony Gilbert and cancel our round.

"Don't be *ridiculous*," Dad said sharply. "You go on and play. I'll take care of things here." He glanced at me and explained that he'd already spoken with the hotel manager, who was phoning up a chemist in Dundee. There was a large medical facility there.

"Go, go, *go!*" he snapped at me, and I involuntarily began to back up. I bumped into the door, paused, turned to look at him once again, and then left him with a sinking feeling in my own gut.

Tony and I finished the first hole with a par and a double bogey respectively, then walked to the second tee, nestling in crumpled dunes and hummocks of sea grass. The hole, a long par-four aptly called Gulley, was a narrow doglegged corridor that cut left to right. "Position A would be just to the right of that large bunker in the middle left. That's called Braid's bunker," said Tony, and proceeded to slug his ball there as if he simply did it every morning before eating his porridge. I teed up my ball and buried it under the lip of Braid's bunker, or position F, which stands for a word rhyming with *ducked*, which matched my darkening mood. Tony watched me slam the sand and advance the ball a meter or two into the fairway.

"You're workin' mooch too hard on that shot, laddie," he said calmly.

With that, he climbed down into the trap and dropped a ball

and showed me how to strike it smoothly out of the sand, using mostly my arms. His ball soared, leaving only the smallest indentation in the firm sand.

"You have a loovely swing, Jimmy," he said soothingly. "Stay back on your heels now, relax, and let the shot coome oot." I dropped a ball and stroked a decent shot out of the bunker, though nowhere near as fine as his. "You're a good teacher," I said.

He smiled, extended me a hand up from the trap, and said, "You're a good pupil. Tell me now, where did you learn that big nice strong swing of yours? Your father, I expect?"

I shook my head and explained that my father had introduced me to the game but refused to give me lessons, insisting that I learn from a real teaching professional. My first teacher had been a man named Aubrey Apple at a club called Green Valley, in Greensboro, where I grew up. "Eight kids lined up with hand-me-down clubs. I didn't remember much about the lesson except that Apple yelled a lot. That meant he really liked us."

Tony smiled. "Aye, I've known a few teachers like that in my time. Your dad's approach was a wise one. He let you come to the game—and the game come oot of you. There's a good game within us all, laddie. I try and do the same thing with my wee ones, encourage the game to come oot of its own accord."

"You teach kids?"

For some reason I'd assumed he worked with older and more skilled players. Somebody had told me Tony Gilbert was the best teacher in Carnoustie.

"Aye. That's who I teach, in the main. The little ones, the wee ones. I march 'em down to the beach to learn the sand game, and we have a nice day of it. They're usually fearless in the sand after a day at the beach with old Tony."

"How many young pupils do you teach at once?"

"I have ten or twelve pupils at the present. Some of my older lads are doing quite well up in the ranks, I'm proud to say."

The wind slackened, and we both played the next three holes in even par. At six, called Long, a murderous par-five with out-of-bounds all the way down the left side and bunkers in the middle of the fairway, Tony, pointing at the turf, showed me the exact spot where Hogan eschewed the safe driving line during his "mystical" four rounds in '53, landing his tee ball daringly on the narrow sliver of grass *left* of the treacherous bunkers, a target no more than fifteen or twenty yards wide, an area now popularly called "Hogan's Alley." "Pinpoint precision it was, absolutely incredible. Each time he improved his drive a little bit, and each round his score got better. I'll never see anything like that again, I feel safe to say."

"You were there?"

"Indeed so. I saw almost every shot the man made coming home. He appeared to be in his own world. It was bonny golf."

I liked that—*bonny golf.* I heard echoes of Sam Bennie's voice in Tony's words. I liked the way the wind abruptly died, too, and the way the day was becoming sunny and mild . . . and my father's situation slipped momentarily from my mind.

Tony and I chatted amicably and played. Par bogey par par. I was just getting the hang of the game when we stopped at a rustic snack shed after nine and had a cup of tea and an egg sandwich. Thinking once again of my father, I asked Tony about his family particulars.

I learned Tony had once been a championship archer, a greenskeeper at Burntisland in Fife, and had just missed qualifying for the British Open by two strokes in 1967. His interest in the game had come from his father, Ted Gilbert, a Glasgow thread-buyer who won the Calcutta championship while doing his military service in India in 1927. "I have his medals at home," Tony explained. "Dad didn't think highly of my decision to turn golf professional. He was strictly an amateur guy, if you know what I mean. But golf is a working-class game in Scotland, and I thought I was king of the working-class guys." Tony chuckled, sipping his tea in thoughtful silence.

"The irony is," he continued, "I thought my son Timothy might well be the best of the lot. Big strong lad, an excellent player, a long striker like you. Broke m'heart when he decided to go another way . . . aye. But what a pro young Tim could ha' been."

I asked what Tim Gilbert did now.

"Manages a casino aboard a cruise ship based in Miami." Tony smiled cordially at a trio of golfers strolling up; they looked defeated, either by the wind or their games, it was difficult to tell which. "Can you imagine that? But he loves it, which makes his mum and me happy. Lovely lad, Tim."

We started on Carnoustie's infamous back nine, probably the roughest home walk in golf, especially if the wind is up. Tony asked where Dad and I were headed next, reminding me once again of the disaster at the Glencoe that was awaiting me. I decided not to say "Probably Edinburgh Airport." So I replied, "Muirfield. A man named Archie Baird is getting us a game there."

Tony nodded. "Aye. I know of old Archie. Good man. So you'll have a day with the mad colonels at Muirfield. Good for you."

I asked him why the colonels at Muirfield were mad. He responded with a joke:

The old colonel invites the young lieutenant down to his snooty golf club for a drink on Wednesday night. "I'm sorry, sir," says the young lieutenant, "but I don't indulge in strong drink." "To hell, man, you don't take a decent dram?" says the astonished old colonel. "Well, perhaps in that case you should come doon on Thursday evening. That's when the ladies come in, and we get up to a fair bit of frolic." The young lieutenant shakes his head. "I'm sorry, sir," he says, "but I'm afraid that kind of thing just wouldn't do for me." "God *help* you, lad," cries the bewildered colonel, "you're not a bloody *poof*, are ye?" "No, colonel, I am *not* a poof," replies the indignant young lieutenant. The colonel shakes his head. "In that case," he says ruefully, "you may as well skip Friday night *altogether!*"

I played horribly on Carnoustie's difficult back nine, but picking Tony's brain about when and how to teach my own wee ones was a pleasure. He showed me the Carnoustie run-up shot—a shot in which, by adjusting your stance and keeping your hands firm, the club face of a lower-lofted club is kept low, and the ball scampers forth with a low trajectory and a beautiful overspin—and he told me tales of Carnoustie's former commercial life as a center of the jute trade. He talked about the internecine politics of the local clubs, about proposed grand hotels along the sea front, rumors of big deals being made in anticipation of the '99 Open. I was bending over a twenty-foot birdie putt at eighteen, concentrating hard, when Tony commented mildly, "There's a man who seems to be waving at us. Could that be your dad?"

I turned around and saw my father standing on Carnoustie's acre-sized practice putting green, where George Lowe, Jr., the famous putting wizard, had supposedly learned his technique. He was wearing a fresh change of clothes, his old Ping putter was in hand, and his soiled green St. Andrews cap was jauntily cocked.

"That's him."

I made the putt, and we shook hands and walked over. I introduced Tony. "It's too bad you could not join us, Brax," Tony said, "but I would love for you to come by the house to meet my wife Julie. We'll have a drink and a proper visit, if you like."

We agreed to come at seven.

After Tony left us, Dad and I conducted another putting examination on Carnoustie's empty putting green, two spins around the eighteen holes. We finished in darkness, and he beat me yet again, winning by three holes. "I trust you're feeling better," I said as we started across the street to the Glencoe. "Much better," he said. "Thanks."

"I gather our next stop isn't the departures lounge in Edinburgh, then?"

"Be kind of a shame to miss Muirfield and the Old Course, wouldn't it?"

I knew no further questions were required or desired, so I told him Tony's joke about the colonels.

Dad was laughing as we entered the lobby of the hotel, where owner Joe McClorey was still walking around like a man in a daze. Joe explained that he'd just taken a phone call from Karsten Manufacturing, the Arizona firm that manufactures Ping golf clubs, booking every room in the hotel for Open week of 1999. He invited us into the bar for a celebration drink, which we didn't refuse.

Tony Gilbert's house was on Kinloch Street in Carnoustie. He met us at the door wearing gray slacks, another striped necktie, and a green Carnoustie sweater. We'd planned to stay twenty minutes but lingered three hours. Tony showed my father his father's golf medals and the beautiful crystal glasses upon which he carved club crests. Crystal carving was a modestly profitable sideline of Carnoustie's most agreeable golf teacher.

Julie and I made small talk about son Tim, cruise ships, vacations in Greece, and public accountancy, her professional trade. She was a handsome energetic blonde, a chartered accountant who didn't really care, as she put it, "a jot for golf" because she had "another love besides Tony."

I asked what that was. "I'm a lawn bowler and toxophilist!"

This turned out to be a championship archer. Julie had also bowled in the Scottish Nationals.

The Gilberts both walked us to the door, Julie standing close to Tony. We shook hands, and Tony urged us to come back for the Open championship in a few years. I looked at my father and smiled.

"We'd love to," Dad said, without hesitation.

"Excellent," said Tony. "It's settled, then."

"Maybe I'll even bring my wee ones," I said, "for the Carnoustie run-up and a lesson on the beach."

"Even better."

Julie kissed us both, an accountant's no-nonsense buss on the cheek. She promised to teach my wife lawn bowling if she agreed to come, too, so Alison wouldn't have to "spend the rest of her natural life listening to you silly men rattling on forever about golf."

Mystery of the Hole

"Right. Here we go."

Archie Baird took a deep breath.

"We'll begin at the beginning. The first stick and ball game we know about was a Roman game called *paganica*, which came up through Europe, through France and Germany and into Holland, where the Dutch made the most of it, playing a game they called *kolf*. We have evidence the Dutch played something they called *kolf* going back to 1300. There is no evidence of golf in Scotland before 1450. *Kolf*, a game played on ice in winter and fields in summer, died out completely around 1700. It was probably Scottish wool merchants who brought the game back here. Scotland was a poor country, Holland was a rich country. The merchants took their wool across and sold it and sometimes encountered unfavorable winds, and so it was perhaps inevitable they would fill their time playing *kolf*. They brought the game home with them, and it was here the game changed forever and took root. Here, on the east coast of Scotland, with an abundance of land, we transformed the game from playing to a stake on ice to playing on natural land to a rabbit scrape . . . a *hole*. I truly believe the game as we know it today would never have evolved without rabbits. The rabbits, you see, would gather in the hollows and nibble the grass down smooth and prevented scrub vegetation like buckthorn and hawthorn bushes from overrunning the linksland. In the middle of the scrape, the buck rabbit would create a hole and urinate in it to mark his territory, and the early golfers played from one hollow to the next. The hole was usually marked with a gull feather. It was very simple golf."

Baird paused, took another breath, and peered at us somewhat skeptically. "I can go on for hours and hours about this stuff. Are you sure you're up for it?"

I nodded. "Fascinating," said my father.

Archie Baird, former R.A.F. fighter pilot, retired fourth-generation small-animal vet, golf collector par excellence, and Muirfield's redoubtable archivist, gave us a small proprietary grin. I'd heard about Archie and his dog Niblick for years from friends and always intended to look them up. Among other things, Baird's wife Sheila's great-grandfather was Willie Park, the famous club-maker who won the first British Open at Prestwick the year before the outbreak of the American Civil War. But more interesting to me was the fact that Baird operated the best private golf museum in the world.

Archie was a ruggedly fit seventy-year-old with rawly barbered hair and a brisk no-nonsense manner. Niblick was a small wiry-haired Border terrier whose face uncannily resembled Clement At-lee's, the former prime minister. We were standing in Archie's little museum, a small, damp, chilly room of artifacts housed in a former cart shed near the pro shop of Gullane Golf Club, on the west end of Main Street in the sleepy East Lothian village of the same name.

We'd been in town two days, and thanks to Archie, I'd already had a match I'd never forget. In fact, I was having difficulty devoting my proper attention to Archie's history lesson because I was still thinking about it. The day before, while Dad rested and wrote some cards at Greywalls, the fine coaching inn located just off Muirfield's tenth tee, I'd played Gullane Number I, at the opposite end of the town, with a charming rogue named Sandy Williamson.

Archie had arranged the match as a prelude to a trip around Muirfield with Dad, but he warned me to watch out for Sandy Williamson. "Sandy's a sly one. His age is a bit advanced, but so's his game. Best play with one hand firmly attached to your billfold." I quickly learned why. A large, stoop-shouldered, white-haired man in his seventies, dressed in a frayed navy parka and baby-blue socks, there was nothing the least bit elderly about Sandy's game. He'd been Gullane's perennial club champion in the 1950s and 1960s and had me four holes down before we'd even reached, huffing and puffing, the brow of Gullane Hill at hole seven, a famous spot writer Jim Finegan says is one of the half-dozen "most enthralling spots in all the world of golf," a spectacular rise from where you can see fourteen counties on a clear day, distant Edinburgh, the Forth Bridge, the Kingdom of Fife across the gray waters of the Forth, and the green fairways of Muirfield nestling against the village less than a mile away.

Gullane Golf Club, founded in 1882, offers its four hundred members three eighteens, not to mention a fine little six-hole children's course in the center of the village that pretty well summarizes the place's raison d'être. British golf architect Donald Steel is on record as saying that of all the world's golfing centers, Gullane may be the most influential and natural. Among other things, the village environs are a leading bird sanctuary, though most of the birds you'll see on the narrow main drag are golfers. On a high summer day, it's said with great affection, there are more golfers than inhabitants in Gullane. The place is golf mad.

Sandy Williamson was clearly afflicted. He told me he managed only seven or eight rounds a week nowadays, which was nowhere near the pace he had maintained as a younger man. Playing as if he owned the place, Sandy had the peculiar casual habit of dropping his bag on the green, no matter where he happened to be putting from. Sandy's putting routine was even brisker than my father's, and I watched him spank several balls almost nonchalantly into the depths of the cup, including one *forty*-footer. Congratulating him on his birdie at the eleventh, aptly called Maggie's Loup (so named after the legend of a brokenhearted local lass who tossed herself onto the rocks far below, perhaps during a mixed singles match with Sandy Williamson), I admitted I was a bit in awe of my elderly opponent's game. He touched his flatcap and nodded. "It's a fine combination—to be lucky and good, but I used to be quite a sensational putter back when I was the only bald Boys Open champion."

Bald Boys Open champion? I swallowed the bait.

Sandy explained that he first won the Boys title in 1939, just before the war. No photos were taken of the winner that year, and the Boys champions were not rounded up again for a group photograph until 1946. "By then it was too late for me," Sandy remembered solemnly, removing his wool flatcap with immaculate timing, revealing a bald dome surrounded by shaggy gray locks. "I was the only bald Boys champion Scotland ever produced."

He gave me his first smile of the day, and I managed to give Gullane's former Boys champ a decent game on the back side, somehow managing to draw the match even by sixteen, at which point Sandy fired off two consecutive birdies to dash my foolish hopes. My father joined us by the eighteenth green, and I introduced him to

Britain's only bald Boys Open champion. They shook hands, and Sandy invited us to come back for a rematch before he lost the rest of his hair.

"Very well," Archie resumed his museum spiel. "Here we go again. A word or two, then, on historical golf equipment. We must mention the featherie ball. It took one man an entire day, and two top hats full of feathers, to make just two featherie golf balls. The ball would fly about 150 yards. It cost more to produce than a club. The first club heads, by the way, were made of apple, beech, and blackthorn, with a bit of lead in the back. The first iron clubs were made by blacksmiths. This was how the game was played for more than three hundred years. Obviously it was not a poor man's game. In 1850 there were still only fifteen golf courses in the world—all but one of them in Scotland. That year the gutta-percha ball was introduced, and everything changed. Gutta-percha is a tropical gum-like material that acts like a thermoplastic. When it's hot, you can mold it; when it's cold, it goes hard. Dentists still use it to make temporary fillings. Gutta balls were cheap and durable as opposed to the fragile and expensive featherie balls. For that reason alone, golf suddenly exploded in popularity. By 1900 there were more than two thousand golf courses in the world. Next came the Haskell rubber-core ball, invented by a clever American in the early part of the century, but frankly a bit bouncy and erratic—so they started marking the face of clubs to put a bit of helpful spin on the ball. Control became a central part of the game. Club-makers replaced blacksmiths. The so-called modern game was born."

Archie showed us a practice ball with a parachute, a metal-headed driver dating from 1900, a pitching iron with a hole cut into the face ("Meant for playing out of the water. Didn't work, I'm sorry to say, which explains why they're so rare."), and a "flicker book"—a flip-action instruction manual that animated the swing of Bobby Jones, a sort of crude portable home golf video. "The Americans are a very simple people," Archie said, handing me an odd-looking iron with a novel wooden face. "They knew their woods went farther than their irons, so they cleverly put wood *on* their irons. That didn't work either, to no one's great surprise."

"What a place," said my father, pausing to examine a print of a pale gentleman decked out in a lacy eighteenth-century waistcoat. He was swinging a crude golf club. "You must get lots of tourists in here."

Archie shook his head. "Funny thing about that, Brax. When I opened this place, I thought that's exactly what would happen—they'd come in droves. I thought they would be lined up to learn a wee bit of history. But you know? That's not the case. The Golf Museum over in St. Andrews can't seem to draw respectable crowds either. Difference is, theirs is a business enterprise while mine is purely a labor of love. I'm not so brokenhearted if only a few people come by asking for a tour each year. That means they're really interested. You'd be surprised who's been in here, lots of ordinary Americans and even some of your top American professionals. Ben Crenshaw always makes an effort to come by. Now there's a man who loves his history."

"This print looks very old," my father said.

"That print is very interesting. The clothes are wrong. The club is wrong. And it's a modern swing the man is using. The print's a total fake, but there's so much blessed mystery surrounding this game, you can make a handsome living peddling fake art and replicas of old clubs. On the other hand, I think the mystery is why we love it so much. Take, for instance, the mystery of the hole."

"The hole?" we both said in unison.

"Right. What you Americans sometimes unfortunately call a *cup*. We know the hole was invented by a Scot when the Dutch or Roman game came to these shores and became golf. The rabbits were critical to the process, but somewhere along the line someone had to come up with an actual *hole*. We just don't know who that clever individual was." Archie gave us a slow solemn look and then shook his head. Niblick sighed and leaned against my leg.

"It remains one of golf's greatest mysteries—lost forever, I'm afraid, to the mists of time."

Fourteen British Opens have been contested at Muirfield, home of the Honourable Company of Edinburgh Golfers. Descended from the "Gentlemen Golfers" who had played at Leith Links in Edinburgh since the fifteenth century, the Honourable Company's "Rules of Golf" were adopted almost word for word in 1754 by the society destined to become the Royal and Ancient Golf Club of St. Andrews—rule-makers of the modern game.

Nicklaus made his Walker Cup debut at Muirfield at age nineteen in 1959 and captured his British Open here seven years later. Player, Trevino, Watson, and Faldo also took home the claret jug from history-steeped Muirfield, a linksland that sits well above the sea and features beautiful turf and a visual honesty better players find irresistible. There are no forced carries, no water hazards, no ruinous outcroppings of prickly gorse to speak of. "The good shot is consistently rewarded," Jim Finegan writes, "the indifferent shot is just as consistently chastised." Before Nicklaus and Watson won at Muirfield, Harry Vardon, James Braid, Walter Hagen, and Henry Cotton anointed its greatness.

For the good player, the primary challenge at Muirfield lies in the ever-daunting sea winds, a bearded rough that can resemble the wheatfields of Kansas before harvest, and far too many exquisitely constructed sod bunkers to make a passage round pain-free. My first drive hooked badly out of bounds left, prompting Archie Baird to recall fondly that the great James Braid of Elie, first born of the Great Triumvirate that included Vardon and J. H. Taylor, also miserably hooked his opening drive over the wall on the left the year he won the first of his two Open championships at Muirfield, in 1901. He seemed to be telling me there was always hope at Muirfield. My next swat from the tee found the fairway, but a subsequent poor long iron shot from the fairway left me facing a difficult fifth shot from the bottom of a bunker in front of the green. I staggered off the hole with a triple bogey.

Archie made par, Dad a surprisingly easy bogey.

"You seem to be off to a poor start," said Archie, as they headed for the riding cart Archie had thoughtfully arranged for Dad. "I hope old Sandy didn't exhaust all your good shots at Gullane yesterday. How much did he take you for?"

"Three pounds."

"Aye. Could have been much worse."

"Jim always starts late," my father chipped in, smiling at me. The rest at Greywalls had done him good. I heard a lilt in his voice and saw renewed vigor in his swing. "Takes him a while to figure it out, but once he gets his head on straight, he can post fine numbers."

This was nice of my father to say. Unfortunately, it didn't turn out to be the case. I played somewhat indifferent golf on the outward leg, which had nothing to do with the quality of the course. Muirfield was outstanding, a pleasure to play and an inspiration to behold. Something else was bothering me. Walking off the second tee alone while the two older men sped ahead to their balls in the cart, I realized what it was. I was keyed up and worrying again about the outcome. Not just the outcome of our round here at Muirfield—but of the trip. We'd been away thirteen days. Something told me Dad wasn't planning to go much farther.

Muirfield's second hole is considered a "breather," a 351-yard par-four some players have a go at if the wind is favorable. I drove my ball into the right rough, shouldered my bag, and started after it. As the East Lothian sun shone down, my mind slipped back a few weeks to a useful "lesson" I had learned on another dramatic faraway coast in the company of a friend named Laird Small. Laird is the head professional at Spyglass Hill Golf Club, Pebble Beach's famous sister course among the tall coastal pines of the Monterey Peninsula. He is also one of America's finest young teachers, responsible for fine-tuning the games of several promising young tour players.

I also started miserably at Spyglass that day, double bogeying a fairly easy par-five opening hole. Another double followed at number two, a short par-four that was exactly the same length as Muirfield's second. As we climbed the hill to the third tee, I was almost ready to give up and head back to the clubhouse. Laird suggested we sit on the grass of the third tee for a few moments and talk. The spot, he said, meant a lot to him, so we sat down. The tee sits high among the dunes where Scotsman Robert Louis Stevenson supposedly used to walk, trying to get inspiration for his work, while living briefly in Monterey in the late 1800s. The green sits below, framed by a glorious panorama of the Pacific Ocean. Spyglass Hill takes its name from *Treasure Island,* and its majestic beauty and rugged difficulty make it one of the most admired—and feared—golf courses in America. I'd hoped to play so well there that day instead of so miserably. I apologized to Laird and admitted I was kind of rattled. This was mere days after my father had called to tell me he was dying of cancer and our trip to Britain would have to be postponed indefinitely.

I rationalized my poor start by admitting I'd hoped a memorable round at Spyglass would take my mind off my problems. Laird smiled and said he understood. That's why many folks played golf. Unfortunately, their mind usually *was* the problem.

As we sat looking at the view, he proposed a little experiment. He asked me for the scorecard, and I handed it over. He tore it up and said, "Let's see if we can get you into NATO."

"NATO?"

"That stands for *Not Attached To Outcome.*"

He said the idea wasn't original with him—a blind golfer pal had thought of it—but that every good teacher knew that the more you pushed against the game of golf, the more the game tended to elude you.

I told him he sounded like my own father, with his talk of "everything contains its opposite" and how trying to "create the magic makes it vanish."

"There're really no new ideas, are there?" Laird agreed. "It's all how we choose to look at things." He suggested that we look at the rest of the round differently, proposing that we play merely for the simple pleasure of each other's company and the opportunity to be out on such a fine morning, unburdened by thinking about our scores and trying to determine the outcome.

A memorable round did indeed follow, though I can't remember exactly how I did on most of Spyglass Hill's romantically named holes. We walked along striking shots and talking about our wives and my children and the baby he and his wife Honor hoped to soon be adopting. I recall us stopping to watch seabirds and listen to the way the wind soughed through the famous Monterey pines. A fog rolled in on the back nine. Deer crossed our paths, pausing to wiggle their noses at us. I vaguely recall, in the midst of all this, a string of pars and even a couple birdies happening. It may have been the finest round of my life, but I'll never know for sure.

It was an exercise worthy of Opti the Mystic. I'd come to Spyglass tense and worried, hoping to bury my sadness by beating a great golf course into submission. Instead, I'd submitted and left relaxed and reminded once again of things I'd known since I was a boy, lying on the soft green fairway of my father's golf club.

At Muirfield's tenth hole, one of Nicklaus's all-time favorite holes, a mammoth 475-yard par-four, I unleashed my best drive of the day, a three-hundred-yarder that Archie Baird said compared favorably to anything the Golden Bear had done on the hole.

He and Dad rolled down the fairway in their sputtering cart, with Niblick trotting importantly just ahead and slightly to starboard. Golf didn't seem to be the particular aim of either man. The weather was mild and sunny, the tall rough leaning beautifully in the slight breeze off Aberlady Bay. It was a day, in some respects, that eerily recalled my lovely day with Laird Small at Spyglass Hill.

I took out my scorecard and tore it up, immediately feeling better. I looked at Dad. He was laughing and obviously having a good time. In the honorable company of Archie Baird, a voluble host and a fellow veteran of the air war, sharing stories and reminiscences that had little or nothing to do with golf or the greats who had trampled this turf, my father seemed thoroughly in his element at last. In Archie, he'd met a Scottish version of himself.

I lagged back a bit, noting the solemn beauty of the turf (the best in the world, according to Nicklaus, for making iron shots with the kind of spin you want) and the geometrically perfect bunkers, which my worry had made me too blind to appreciate on the front side.

We came at last to seventeen, the difficult par-five where Roberto de Vicenzo once holed a two-iron for an albatross, and a hole that possibly altered the playing career of Tony Jacklin. In the final round of the '72 Open, Lee Trevino and Jacklin approached the hole tied for the lead, just one stroke ahead of the ever-present Nicklaus. Jacklin played two solid shots within a few yards of the green, but Trevino sprayed his shots all over the place. First he drove into a bunker, was forced to play a second "safe" shot out, then trap-hooked his third to the deep rough in front of the green. Discouraged, certain he'd handed Jacklin the tournament, Trevino slapped an indifferent shot over the green. Jacklin chipped his third shot to within fifteen feet of the cup. Trevino went to his ball and hastily struck another poor shot—which raced across the green and jumped into the hole for par. It was the Merry Mex's third "miracle" shot that week.

Recently, while visiting with Jacklin at the home he was selling in the Scottish border country to prepare for life on the Senior Tour in America, he told me that Trevino's "lucky" shot at Muirfield had effectively ended his career. Shaken by what he'd witnessed, Jacklin, never the best of putters to begin with, missed his birdie at seventeen that day—and then missed his par. The wild reversal of fortune handed Trevino his second consecutive British Open title. "I'm convinced my own confidence died on the spot," Jacklin reflected quietly. "I mean, I'd played the best I could, I'd done everything required of a champion . . . only to lose it all on a man's careless lucky shot. My God, that broke my spirit."

My father finished with a 93, which made him visibly happy. I finished with . . . who can say? I was happy, too.

Buoyed by our bonny trip around Muirfield, Archie drove us through the village and explained a bit more about the history of East Lothian, then whizzed us up a residential lane in his little Ford Fiesta very nearly to the crown of Gullane Hill. He wanted to show Dad the grand view and even gave us a snippet of verse for the occasion.

"It's up the hill," he recited, *"and doon the hill,*
And roond the hill and a'man;
And ye should come to Gullane Hill
If you can golf at a'man.
We'll cure you of a summer's cold
Or of a winter's cough,
We'll make you young even though you're old,
So come and play at golf."

We applauded, Archie bowed slightly. We climbed back into his cramped car and sped down the hill with Archie telling us how he met and courted his wife Sheila, about the years he spent studying in America prior to the war, and how he'd given up his veterinary practice due to the changing nature of that trade. We parted with a drink at the Old Club House Pub, which overlooked the children's links, where several future Sandy Williamsons were out shooting at red flags. Archie wanted to know where we were putting up that night.

I mentioned we had a couple rooms at Greywalls, right next door to the hole where I drove a ball like the Golden Bear.

"Oh, splendid," Archie said. "If there's a good moon tonight, be sure and look out at the golf course. It can be quite an extraordinary sight."

My father thanked him for his hospitality. I added my hear-hear.

We touched our glasses, drinking to Trevino's luck and Jacklin's misfortune and the eternal mystery of the hole, whoever invented it.

"That's why we love this game, you know," said Archie. "The bittersweet mystery of it all. The uncertainty of what we shall discover. . . ."

"It's new every time you go out," agreed my father. "Wasn't it de Vicenzo who said golf is like love—one day you feel too old, the next you want to do it again?"

"Right you are, Brax." Baird felt his own familiar quotation coming on. " 'A tolerable day, a tolerable green, and a tolerable opponent supply, or ought to supply, all that any reasonably constituted human being can expect in the way of entertainment,' " Archie recited. "That's Lord Balfour. The rest of the quote goes thus: 'With a clear course and fine sea view the golfer may be excused if he imagines that golf, even though it be indifferent golf, is the ultimate end of man's existence.' " He looked at me and said, "He was thinking of Gullane Hill when he said that."

I started to raise my glass to Spyglass Hill and Gullane Hill, both of which had *cured* something in me, and to Laird Small and the laird of Gullane Archie Baird, genuine custodians of the game, but I wasn't sure anyone in the Old Club House Pub but me would get the connection. I simply hoisted my glass and said thank you to Archie.

Several hours later, I had a clear view of the course and the sea beyond from my room at Greywalls, a cozy cell overlooking Muirfield's tenth. The moon, shining on the water, made me think of a Zen belief that enlightenment is like the moon reflected on water: The moon does not get wet nor the water broken; the light is wide, but a whole sky can be reflected in a single drop.

True to Archie's word, I could see a great deal of the linksland, washed blue by the moon and stars. My room had green wallpaper and floral drapes, a small reading lamp, five prints of soldiers on the walls, a single bed, a Finlandia TV, and a slipcovered chair. I sat in the chair and flipped on the TV, just to see if there was still a world beyond Muirfield. The late news was on. A woman who hadn't spoken in seventeen years had finally broken her silence, asking for a ham sandwich. Britain's oldest chicken had died after a ripe old age. The fratricidal factions in Bosnia were at least talking about talking again. Mu'ammar Gadhafi had graciously repeated his offer to have his son marry Chelsea Clinton to improve diplomatic relations with the United States. On the local front, former president George Bush was visiting St. Andrews to attend the annual autumn meetings of the Royal and Ancient and play a little golf.

Thinking what an ironic twist *that* was, I turned off the set and walked down the narrow hallway to my father's room to see if he wanted to go down for a nightcap in the bar, but he wasn't in his room.

I strolled downstairs, past the empty front desk and the photo wall where Greg Norman was giving a Greywalls chef a midnight golf lesson. I found my father in the library, playing old war records on an old wind-up record player sitting on the piano.

"Look at this," he said, as I entered. "Great stuff here."

He showed me several 78-RPM records from the war years and reminded me for the umpteenth time how he'd met my mother in the record department of McCrory's, how he'd gone back for weeks to buy classical and big-band records and hadn't even owned a record player. Then he told me another story I'd never heard: that my mother made a recording of "I'll Walk Alone" and had it sent to him overseas. During the war he used to take the record to village libraries and play it on their record players.

He handed me one of the records. "Look. Tony Martin singing 'To Each His Own.' "

"Who's Tony Martin?"

"Big Hollywood star in the thirties and forties. Not much of a soldier, though." I asked how he knew this.

Dad smiled. "Because he was in my outfit at Chanute Field. Funny guy. Used to flirt with your mother a lot. Told her she looked like Alice Faye, the movie star. I think Alice Faye might have just divorced him. Your mother sold cigarettes at the Buckingham Palace PX—that was the name of the place, believe it or not—and I was teaching at the parachute training school. We lived off base. Martin was the kind of guy who wasn't above having other buck privates shine his boots and make his bunk. Guess they thought they'd get into the movies or something. I can't say I ever really knew the man, though I might have yelled at him a few times."

We played the Tony Martin record. Tony Martin had a superb voice. I pictured slinky women with cigarette holders and eyelashes that could wound.

"So how was Mom?" I knew he had vanished to his room after dinner to call my mother. I'd stayed downstairs chatting with a young newlywed couple from Phoenix whose parents had mysteriously given them a trip to Scotland for a honeymoon. Neither played golf. "I guess I'll have to learn to play golf now," the bride complained with a note of doomed resignation. "Kevin wouldn't know which end of the club to hold." She indicated the groom, who had his nose safely buried in a copy of *Country Life.*

"Your mom is fine," Dad said. "She's having a man come and waterproof the wooden fence in back. I told her she ought to go buy Thompson's because that's the best water sealer, but she said the man at the hardware store suggested Olympic because it has sunblock in it. So she bought the Olympic." He held another record up to the light and squinted at the title. "I guess she's learning she doesn't need me around quite as much as she first thought."

I started to say something but didn't, either because my tongue wouldn't get out of the way or because I simply couldn't think what to say. So I said I was going to walk out and stand on Muirfield's tenth tee in the moonlight and admire the hole where I'd made my Nicklausian blast earlier that day. He said he might join me in a minute or two. As I left him, Tony Martin was crooning that he'd found his one and only love.

I walked out back and stood on the little stone wall above the tee, looking out at the Muirfield links, thinking about the Mystery of the Hole. The hole was critical to golf, yet a hole was really nothing more than ten ounces of air, a divine nothingness. The object of the game was to reach this place of nothingness as economically as possible, to pass through nature with as much grace and dignity as we could muster. Less really was more, and even if golf wasn't the ultimate end of man's existence, it struck me that a small, ever-shifting, mysterious nothingness was precisely what gave the game its essential glimmer, balance, and allure, impregnated it with a power that was simultaneously as visible and elusive as moonlight on the water.

I decided to step down onto the grass and, stepping forward off the wall, kept going, falling about four feet. I landed directly on my back and lay there, the wind knocked out of me, on a pillowy pad of fragrant grass, feeling really dumb but far more startled than injured, staring up at the moon.

So much, I thought, *for Buddhist woolgathering*. After a few minutes I got up, rubbed my backside, climbed back over the wall, and went inside. My father was just heading up the stairs and paused to wait for me.

"How was the golf course?" he asked mildly.

"Very comfortable."

He smiled and slipped his hand through my arm, mostly to give his knees a bit of support as we slowly climbed the steep stairs together. I started to say something about my mother being brave under the circumstances, but he seemed to read my mind and spared me the effort.

"Your mother will be all right," he said as we neared the top. "Change is difficult for her, but she's a surprisingly tough lady."

The corners of his mouth turned up slyly.

"You know, it's only been the past five years I've gotten her to sleep in the nude. You sleep much better in the nude. I've told her that for years. I think she's finally beginning to believe me."

Haunted Ground

On our first full day in St. Andrews, my father and I strolled down to the first tee of the Old Course to watch 20-handicapper George Bush tee off.

It was a cool, overcast morning, and a large crowd had gathered in anticipation of seeing the former president. Standing in the crowd near the front steps of the Royal and Ancient's famous sandstone clubhouse, I heard snatches of several languages—French, Japanese, and someone who was clearly from Brooklyn. Bush and his entourage of fellow Royal and Ancient members finally appeared, accompanied by Secret Service men and a small drove of reporters. The former president turned and waved to the crowd, prompting modest cheers and a volley of clicking cameras. Reporters and photographers jock-eyed with the spectators to get a better angle on the proceedings, or else they ignored the protests and sprinted ahead out onto the course to get a better view.

Bush, whose father was a USGA president and whose maternal grandfather, George Herbert Walker, gave the prize cup to the international amateur matches that bear his name, teed up quickly and slapped a respectable little drive to the right side of possibly the most generous opening fairway in the world. The crowd cheered as if Greg Norman had just unleashed one of his patented monster drives.

"This must be a little strange for you," my father reflected. "To cross paths with your old friend Mr. Bush like this."

I admitted it was a little like looking at the ghost of Christmas past. But then, I thought, this whole trip had been a journey into the past.

I said, "I doubt if he would even remember me. I was just one of several hundred faces shouting questions at him in those days."

"Oh, I bet he would. Seems like a pretty thoughtful guy. You liked him, as I recall."

I didn't deny it. In some respects, that was part of my problem. Privately, Bush was one of the most engaging figures I'd spent time with as a reporter. He talked straight and laughed a lot, loved to tell stories, and always looked you in the eye. His politics were centrist, sensibly middle-of-the-road. He seemed genuine and hopeful. He reminded me eerily of my own father and even resembled him a bit.

In this respect, political reporters and golf journalists have the same kind of dilemma—how to get close enough to a subject in order to understand what he's about without falling under his spell or finding an ax to grind. Maybe I'd fallen a bit too much under Bush's spell. At any rate, as the tone of politics turned decidedly uncivil in the mid-1980s, when *unnamed sources close to the campaign* began to replace the traditionally valued identified sources, which so much of responsible journalism used to rely upon, I'd learned there really is no such thing as an "objective" reporter. The challenge is to simply make yourself be a *fair* one.

Now, these years later, watching the reporters jostle around Bush made me recall the hectic weeks I'd spent with him on the campaign trail in 1980. One morning in Puerto Rico, relieved to be away from the slush, opinion polls, and high-wire tension of the New Hampshire primary, Bush and I jogged a couple miles alone together on a tourist beach, talking about the campaign and his grandchildren and other things, when we came upon a man who was practicing his sand-wedge game on the beach in front of his hotel. I was impressed that Bush didn't feel obliged to stop and introduce himself and press the flesh. As we passed, he merely wished the man good morning and quipped over his shoulder, "Now there's a truly committed golfer. I wish I had a sand game like that." A few paces along, he murmured to me, "I wish I had *time* to do that."

Well, thanks to America's voters, George Bush finally had the time to work on his sand game and be with his grandchildren. And watching the former president smile and shake hands with Scottish dignitaries who'd turned out in full force to greet him, I didn't get the impression he really missed the grind of the presidency, any more than I missed being in the press pack. Both of us had moved on to kinder and gentler jobs that allowed us to play the game we loved most.

After Bush and Company were gone, Dad and I walked over to the little white starter's house to see if our names had made it through the Old Course daily ballot. The man inside informed us that the results of the drawing wouldn't be known until later that afternoon. It was only noon. We had several hours to fill up.

About forty-two thousand rounds a year are played on the Old Course, almost half of them reserved for the citizens of St. Andrews, an inalienable right they've enjoyed since Archbishop John Hamilton of St. Andrews, one of Scotland's leading churchmen during medieval times, signed a decree in 1552 granting them unhindered access to the town's linksland—in effect, creating the world's first municipal golf course.

The balance of Old Course teetimes are made available to visitors, but demand for the precious slots grew so fierce several years back that Links Trust Management, which operates the town's six golf courses on behalf of the town, was forced to institute a daily ballot drawing that determines who will get a teetime on the most famous golf course in the world. There are 450 golf courses in Scotland, and five other splendid tracks in the town of St. Andrews itself, but pilgrims who find they've made it through the daily ballot feel as if they've been granted a special dispensation from the gods.

In the five or six times I'd played the Old Course, I'd never encountered the slightest difficulty getting a teetime. That's because I usually appeared alone and was penciled in to fill out some other group's foursome. As a result, and proof of St. Andrews' international stature, I'd gotten to play the Old Course with golfers from several nations, including several Brits and Americans, a Japanese newlywed couple, and a charming Italian man who hummed arias the whole way round and insisted that Arnold Palmer's family originated in Sicily, where their family name was Palmeri. My best score on the course was 80. My goal was to shoot 75—what Sam Snead shot in the final round to win the British Open here in 1946.

Snead's St. Andrews story is a typically colorful one. The Slammer hadn't wanted to play in the British Open that year, but under the terms of his contract with Wilson Sporting Goods, he was forced to enter. While leaving New York, his airplane caught fire and had to be evacuated. Arriving in bomb-ravaged London, he found that hotel rooms were scarce and he had to sleep on a public bench before catching a train for Scotland. When he arrived, he was angry to learn he couldn't use his favorite center-shafted putter because the R&A had banned that style after Walter Travis won the 1904 British

Amateur using his famous Schenectady putter. Upon seeing the stark, spare Old Course for the first time, Snead turned to someone and asked, "What the devil is that? It looks like an abandoned golf course." His problems mounted when his caddy, said to be one of the canniest at the Old Course, showed up for work drunk; Snead had to fire him on the spot. His replacement proved no better—whistling through his teeth every time Sam prepared to shoot. Despite all this, the Slammer ran away with the title, firing 290 for seventy-two holes, beating his pal Johnny Bulla and Bobby Locke by four strokes.

Officially, you're supposed to have a 28 handicap or better to get on the Old Course, evidenced by some kind of official documentation—a USGA certificate, say, or a letter from one's home club pro—but visitors work diligently to subvert this essentially fair-minded system, producing letters from nonexistent pros back home or, in the case of some overzealous guests, submitting Scottish-sounding names in the doomed hope it will somehow improve their chances of acquiring a desired teetime.

My own method of subverting the system, if it came to that, was a caddy I knew named Bruce who said he could make sure I got on the Old Course anytime I wanted. Bruce was one of St. Andrews' most respected loopers and had carried the bags of lots of tour pros and famous folk. His office was a barstool at the Jigger Pub, beside the Old Course Hotel, and when Dad and I arrived there after watching George Bush tee off, I was sorry to learn that Bruce was still out on the course with a client. We ordered sandwiches, and I left a message for him to call me later at the Scores Hotel.

We took our pints out to the Jigger's little courtyard and stood beside the gray stone wall overlooking the knoll where I'd first come and stood and stared out at the Road Hole in the rain, twenty years ago. Dad sipped his beer and seemed pleased to be looking once again at this venerable, embattled turf. Then he turned to me and said, "Why is it so important for you to hook up with your friend Bruce?"

I shrugged and explained to him that regardless of how we fared in the daily ballot, Bruce could probably make sure we got on the Old Course. He knew the right people and had proved helpful in the past.

"Why would you want to do that?" my father said puzzledly, watching a group of golfers now approaching their balls around the green. One golfer's ball was in the Road Hole bunker, and two more were well short of the putting surface. A fourth was apparently somewhere over the back near the pebble road that borders the green and makes the approach so lethal. No one, I noted, had found the putting surface in regulation.

"That should be rather obvious. We didn't come all this way *not* to play the Old Course, did we?"

He thought for a moment. "Do you think it's fair if we ignore the rules and get to play the Old Course while someone who follows them doesn't?"

"That's not the issue, Dad. The issue is, half those people don't really care about *playing* the Old Course. To them it's just a trophy, something to boast about back home. They'll remember more about the shop where they bought five cashmere sweaters with the Old Course logo than they'll remember about the Old Course itself."

I felt like I was twelve years old, trying to explain that I'd only *glanced* at that week's spelling list, which Donnie Alberson, a guy with a great future bagging groceries at Winn Dixie, had "somehow" gotten his hands on and passed around on the school bus.

"So why do you want to play it? You've played it plenty of times."

We looked at each other. It was me who finally blinked; I looked away, shrugged again, and shook my head. I didn't agree with him, but he had a point. I had played it many times. Why was it so all-important now? Of course, I *knew* why. We both did. But I didn't want to have to say it, and I'm sure he didn't want to have to hear it. At Muirfield, I'd feared my father was going to say he had to go home after St. Andrews.

Now at St. Andrews, I was certain of it. It was possible, even likely, that any round on the Old Course would be our final round of golf together. It would be a fitting way to finish, but a finish is a finish, and that's what I feared most.

"If that's how you want it," I said. "We'll put all our hopes on the ballot."

"That's the only way I want it, and you would, too, if you'd just think about it."

We emptied our pint glasses and walked into the adjoining pro shop at the Old Course Hotel, where a friend of mine, Neil Paton, works as the head professional. Neil and I had once played a delight-ful round on the New Course (laid out by Old Tom Morris in 1895 and a track, some feel, that's an even sterner test of character than the Old), during which he'd helped cure a wicked shanking problem of mine, and I wanted my father to meet him. Neil and I were about the same age and we both had young children.

I liked to think of Neil as a genuine son of St. Andrews in the tradition of Young Tom Morris, who in 1868 succeeded his father, Old Tom (the Old Course's most famous caretaker, a four-time Open champion) in capturing the British Open championship. Young Tom won the Open three more times and brought champion-ship scoring to new levels of brilliance before learning, during a big money match against the Park brothers (Willie and Mungo, them-selves both Open champions) at North Berwick in 1875, that his wife Margaret had given birth to their baby but lay gravely ill. Before Tommy could reach home, both Margaret and the baby were dead. Three months later, on Christmas Day, Young Tom Morris died, too. The popular legend holds that Young Tom died of a broken heart, though strong drink may have played a part. Young Tom was a teetotaler until his wife and child died.

I told my father this tale as we waited in line to see if Neil Paton was anywhere about. Growing up in St. Andrews, Neil had been a good amateur player in his own right but preferred, as he once told me, to "have a wee bit more civilized kind of life" than chasing the game all over Europe, as the modern golf prodigy bent on a professional playing career must do. His shop was full of American and Japanese customers who seemed to be clearing the shelves of any item bearing the St. Andrews logo, keeping the cash register awhirl. When it was finally our turn, my father bought my mother a pin with the St. Andrews cross (a symbol later adopted by the Confederate States of America for use on their battle flag), and I purchased an Old Course ballcap for my son. I was disappointed to learn from the harried sales clerk that Neil was "off to Edinburgh" and probably wouldn't be back for a few days.

To kill more time, I suggested we take a stroll down to the Himalayas, the eccentric public putting course situated between the Old Course and the wide sand beach where filmmakers had shot the opening scenes of *Chariots of Fire*.

"That's such a sad story about Young Tom," Dad said as we crossed the Old Course's wide finishing hole via the little public walkway that bisects it. "I suppose the moral is, Don't let golf take over your life." He walked a few paces and added, "Speaking of which, how's your own beautiful wife doing these days?"

It was a gently loaded question. I knew he worried about my "modern marriage," as he called it—the long hours and frequent travels and busy professional schedules Alison and I both kept, attempting to strike the proper balance between careers we loved and the full demands of parenthood. This was not an area of my life I was in any rush to open up for general floor discussion with my father, perhaps because his marriage was so unlike mine and I knew he had opinions about the dangers of the modern two-career marriage. I knew he didn't think unions where the partners poured as much of themselves into their work as their family life—or each other—stood much hope of making it over the long haul.

In some respects, my ten-year marriage to Alison seemed almost too perfect. She was beautiful, smart, funny, a great wife and mother. The ten years of our marriage had whizzed past, and I could count the number of serious arguments we'd had in a decade on just one hand. Friends often commented how strong our relationship seemed. They admired the way we talked everything through. They admired our individual and joint work ethics, our house, our children. Lately, though, something had grown a bit fuzzy between us. We were both to blame. Alison was working more hours than ever, and I was feeling neglected and resentful. It had been many years since our last family vacation. My resentment, on the other hand, made her feel unloved and stretched even thinner. Fissures had appeared in the rock. Wiser heads assured us this sort of thing was inevitable and that all good marriages endured difficult stretches. Give it time, they counseled, be patient, *keep* talking to each other. Rough weather makes good timber, as they say in Maine. Our marriage was simply too strong to fall apart, they said, and would eventually get back on course. All we knew was that we loved each other and adored our kids. We were still talking, and that gave me hope.

But I didn't want to dump this complicated stuff on my father. Not before I understood what it meant myself. Especially not now that his time was so limited.

So I kept to safe generalities. "She's fine. Working far too hard. But it seems to be what she wants right now." I explained that she'd just been made associate vice president of the college where she worked and that executive recruiters seemed to phone the house almost as frequently as telemarketing operators.

"I wish I could somehow slow you both down," he said, slipping into Opti mode. "Ambition is a kind of siren song. Especially in a job like yours. The danger of great ambition is that you'll work so hard, you may someday wake up and find that the things you really wanted were the things you had all along."

We walked along. As usual, he'd just put his finger on one of my biggest fears—the nagging worry that our thriving careers were gently wedging us apart. I said nothing.

"Well, in any case," he said, "give her a big kiss for me. As Young Tom Morris found out, you can never kiss your wife enough."

"I will," I assured him.

At the Himalayas, we ran into Fred Lockhart. Fred was putting with his small grandson Ewan. Fred was retired from the Royal Post and belonged to one of the lesser known golf clubs in town that decidedly *wasn't* the Royal and Ancient. His opinions of the R&A, the ruling body of golf everywhere in the world except North America, were neither shy nor high. I introduced Fred to my father, and my father asked what he thought of the swank new clubhouse being built less than a thousand feet from where we stood. Workmen were busy attaching a green metal roof to the sprawling new structure, which was supposed to be ready for the next Open championship in July.

"A blight in the Almighty's eye," Fred grumbled without hesitation. "Uglier than a carbuncle on a pig's arse."

Dad smiled. I knew Fred was dead serious, though. A lot of locals felt that travel agents, members of the R&A, and others who had something to gain from commercial development were compromising the integrity of the Old Course and the character of St. Andrews itself by allowing golf's birthplace to be transformed into a commercial shrine. The opposite view, not unreasonable in my opinion, was that as golf's popularity continued to grow, the wisest approach was to try and accommodate as many visitors as possible while trying to maintain the qualities that make St. Andrews so special. To that end, a new golf course designed by Peter Thomson had been recently opened, in hopes it would help relieve the burden on the Old Course. The opening of the highly controversial clubhouse was long overdue in the minds of some visiting golfers who were forced to change into their spikes in the car park.

Fred would have none of it.

"It's all a bloody whitewash, a power play by the Royal Ancients," he said, intentionally twisting the name of the governing body whose famously photogenic clubhouse sits beside the Old Course. Many people think they own it—including some R&A members, as Fred will tell you.

Fred saw conspiracies afoot all over the Old Grey Toon. According to him, the R&A had basically "infiltrated" the Links Trust and was now bent on nothing less than controlling the teetimes on all of the town's golf courses but most particularly the Old Course—a profane and even parliamentary violation, in his view, of the ruling democratic spirit of St. Andrews. Protest committees had been formed, petitions sent around. Legal remedies were being considered. Meanwhile, construction of the clubhouse merely symbolized the gathering conflict.

"It's going to get nasty," Fred predicted, dourly tapping the ground with his putter. "There's rumors Links Trust is planning to cut a secret deal with a big London travel outfit that would take control of the visitors' teetimes," he explained. "Mark my word, it'll be a dark day in St. Andrews if tha' comes to pass. First thing those buggers'll do is double or even triple the fees and cut the time of the locals." He shook his large head in disgust. " 'Tis nothing less, I tell you, than a cultural abomination."

"I remember playing the course for two shillings and six," Dad volunteered hopefully.

"Aye," Fred rumbled somberly. "Those were the days. Now we're *aboot* greed and power, pure and simple."

I asked Fred who was winning their putting match.

"Ewan," Fred said, patting his grandson firmly on the back. "He'll be playing for Scotland before we know it." Ewan was about my son's age. He gave a small grin at this news bulletin.

We followed them onto the Himalayas, using a pair of old hickory-shafted putters rented at the admission shed for one pound fifty each, and played another thirty-six-hole match that I once again lost. Losing putting matches to my father next to the great golf courses of England and Scotland appeared to be my real *dharma*.

On the way back to the Scores, we paused once again at the little white starter's shed to see if the results of the ballot had been posted. A group of Japanese men whose shoes and bags looked as if they had just been purchased at Neil Paton's shop were busy posing for photographs on the tee. The results were in. Our names weren't on the list.

That evening, I took my dad to a place I knew in the hills just east of town for dinner. The restaurant had a lovely view of the town and the sea. Its beams were low, the fire blazing. The barman brought two expensive French brandies (Churchill's favorite breakfast tipple) to the table and surprised us by suggesting we bring our golf clubs into the restaurant. When we asked why, he explained that a week before, thieves had sledge-hammered the window out of a van in the car park and looted six sets of clubs from the back of a Saab in less than thirty seconds. The latest strategy of the bandits, he said, was to follow golf pilgrims from one place to another, waiting for the opportune moment to strike. St. Andrews was a favorite spot because the streets were often crowded with tourists, creating headaches for police. The problem, he said, was epidemic, but the travel industry refused even to acknowledge it.

"It's a sorry world out there these days," he said with a shake of his head.

"It's pretty certain you won't get out alive," Dad tried to cheer him.

The barman looked to see if he was joking. Dad was joking, but the barman couldn't tell. I wondered vaguely if he served on one of Fred Lockhart's citizens committees. I pictured members of the R&A being led to the guillotine the way French peasants had led lace-shirted aristocrats to their makers.

"That may be, sir," the barman said with slight indignation, "but it's not like it used to be round St. Andrews. Next thing, they'll be knocking off the hotels, too. Then you laugh."

On this note he left us, disgustedly wringing a terry towel with his hands.

"Poor fellow," Dad said. "He looks as if he's never laughed."

"Face like a well-made grave," I agreed. "He should shoot his TV."

The barman's prophecy prompted us to consider, not entirely seriously, how the world had changed since Dad's last visit to St. Andrews.

"The world has doubled twice in population, but polio and smallpox have been eliminated. That's real progress," Dad said.

"South Carolina built three hundred golf courses, posted legal speed limits, and outlawed marrying your sister," I volunteered. "That may be even greater progress."

"A glass of really good French brandy now goes for twenty bucks."

"How much was it in your day?"

"I don't know. Only Churchill could afford to drink the stuff."

"I've got one," I said. "Anxiety now kills more people than wars."

"Is that true?" asked my father.

"I don't know," I admitted. "But it's doing the barman or his towel no good whatsoever tonight."

My father laughed and grew quiet, scanning the menu. We both settled on Angus steaks. He preferred his slightly rare, I preferred mine slightly burned. I pictured me receiving my steak about the time he was finishing dessert.

"I'll tell you another way things have changed since I was over here," Dad said.

"How's that?"

"Back when I was a soldier over here, I used to wonder what it would be like to be a father." He was looking out the window at the roofs of the town. He turned his head to me and smiled. "Now I spend my days trying to remember."

Our dinners arrived, and the conversation shifted back to the war, to the months he spent running a small prisoner of war camp in the forest of Compiègne after the liberation of Paris. The camp was on the outskirts of the town where Joan of Arc's military career came to an end in 1430, and German prisoners were used to sort and pack up weapons, uniforms, and other materials the German army had abandoned as it fled France in 1944.

The camp, my father explained, had no barbed wire or even fences to speak of because the German soldiers were weary of war and receiving two hot meals a day. Out of the sixty or so prisoners in the camp, there was only one card-carrying Nazi, an unapologetic sergeant named Krauss.

"Krauss was a problem. He was Bavarian, a bully, and a real belligerent son of a bitch. We had to watch him pretty closely. The captain who was really in charge of the camp was never around—he

had a girlfriend over in Soissons, the next village—so I made most of
the decisions. Krauss didn't like me very much, and I didn't like him.
You probably know that Compiègne was where the Germans surren-
dered to end World War I. The first thing Hitler did when he
occupied France was order the railcar where Germany had signed the
Armistice in the forest of Compiègne to be dismantled.

"You may not know, though, that the little rail station in Com-
piègne was used by the Nazis as the embarkation point for sending
French Jews to concentration camps in Belgium and Germany.
That's why there were so many reprisal killings after the Liberation.
The Free French wanted revenge on some of their own for collabo-
rating with the Germans."

"How many people are we talking about?" I asked.

"I don't know exactly. I heard it was well over fifty thousand
people. Men, women, and children. Many of them came through
Compiègne. A lot of them were gassed. People in the town told me
the story. They were sickened by it—they'd been helpless to do
anything, I guess. It was still fairly unknown what had happened. But
once locals started coming around to the camp, the story got out
pretty quick."

"Why'd locals come to the camp? To mock their German cap-
tives?"

"Goodness, no. They were starving and freezing to death. It was
almost winter. A lot of them were farmers who'd lost everything. I
remember one man who showed up with his little girl one morning
in late November. He was barefoot, if you can imagine. I gave him
some German army boots and some sweaters and jackets. I may have
even given him a rifle and ammunition to hunt rabbits with in the
forest. He was so grateful. A few days later, he showed up with
another child, a boy slightly older. I gave him more boots and
clothes. I wish I could remember his name. . . ."

Dad thought for a moment. "He came back several times. He

had six children. One day he brought me a giant mushroom he'd grown beneath his house. I remember how proud he was of it—how much he wanted me to have it. He said it would make an excellent omelet. We didn't have any eggs, so I had a cook named Walter slice it up and fry it. It was delicious. Our cooks had been German army cooks. Walter was just eighteen. He used to look after my apartment. Nice kid. Said he wanted to be a chef at the Paris Ritz someday. Had a wallet full of family pictures. His favorite thing was to read palms. He used to read my palm and tell me the same thing. He told me I would someday be very wealthy."

Dad smiled at the memory. "Fortunately he cooked better than he read palms."

"Wasn't that against military regulations, giving boots and stuff away to civilians?" I asked.

"Sure it was. They could court-martial you for that offense. Nobody really cared, though. The captain was with his girlfriend. Paris was liberated. I used to drive there in a jeep on weekends, parking behind the Opéra, and walk around the city. What a place it was. Everybody wanted the war to be over—everybody except maybe Krauss."

"What happened to him?"

Dad sighed. "I gave him to the Belgians."

"*Really?* Why?"

"As I said, Krauss and I had this thing going. He tried to get my goat by saying that Americans were weak people—too sentimental for our own good. That would be America's downfall. He never put a cork in it and always gave the Nazi salute. I finally told him if he gave me another Nazi salute, he would have to do it with his feet because his arms would be in plaster casts. His real gripe, though, was with Walter—the kid who kept my apartment. One day Krauss used a forklift to crush Walter to death against a wall. He thought nobody saw him do it. But his own soldiers turned him in. I personally marched the bastard to the town jail with a machine gun at his back. If he'd said anything, I might well have shot him right there. The captain, as usual, wanted nothing to do with the matter. He was having a good time elsewhere. It just so happened that we had some Belgian underground fighters passing through on the way back to their country. I gave Krauss to them."

"A death sentence?"

"Probably."

"Did you regret it?"

"I've spent years wondering."

A large, cheerful waitress brought our steaks. She had a mountain of red hair piled on her head and gaps between her teeth, a Scottish Wife of Bath. "You two must be Americans," she insisted. "Americans always order the steak. Who's pink and who's black?"

When she was gone, I said: "Something's just occurred to me. I'll bet you got your palm-reading thing from Walter."

One of Opti's oldest party tricks was to read palms.

Dad set his fork aside and sipped his cognac. He nodded. "You may be right. I never really thought about it until now."

"I'll tell you something else you never thought about. You never read my fortune," I said. "Wrong gender, I guess."

"I guess." He ate some more of his steak and then said, "Give me your hand."

I stuck out my hand, palm up.

He was always adept at reading the palms of attractive women. He told them outrageously positive things—*You are deeply admired for your great beauty and loving intuition; I see an extraordinary career in public service blossoming in the very near future, perhaps an ambassadorship or a successful run for the United States Senate; I don't believe I've ever seen a more intriguing life-line—have you ever been to Khartoum during the rainy season?*

He studied my palm, continuing to nip at his cognac.

"Am I going to be rich?" I asked. "Please don't tell me I should run for the Senate."

He shook his head. "This is very interesting."

"Interesting good or interesting bad?"

"Good and bad. You're already rich but may not realize it. I see other things."

"A hole-in-one? A new Chevy Blazer?"

He shook his head. "Those aren't important. I see some interesting changes coming in your life, some important connections of the heart you will finally make . . . things you will pass along to your children . . . your children are your real job, you know."

"Right, right," I said impatiently. "How 'bout at least a little ambassadorship to Ireland or a riding lawn mower?" Out of the corner of my eye, I saw the Wife of Bath closing fast from three o'clock.

"He's telling my fortune," I explained to her.

"Get *on,*" she said smartly. "I thought he was proposing. Is he any good at it, the fortune-telling bit?"

"He predicted the end of the eighties and the demise of the leisure suit," I assured her. "Even before they happened."

"Brilliant. Would you care to do mine, love?"

"Delighted," Opti said, releasing my hand like a stone.

Her name was Beth. He told Beth of Bath she was going to have a long life, several gorgeous children, and a nice house by the sea and possibly would win some kind of big contest involving Border collies. "Good heavens, I *have* two Border collies!" Beth shrieked deliriously and went away to fetch our dessert puddings as if she'd just won the Scottish National Dog Trials.

"You sure know how to warm a big bonny lassie's heart," I said to him.

"That's my job," Opti said, with a wink.

. . . .

The next morning, we drove over to the nearby village of Elie and played the short but cunning links there, a gently elevated seaside course, laid out by Old Tom Morris in 1895, that featured sixteen par-fours and measured just 6,233 yards against a par of 70. In my view, the course is distinguished for two other reasons, though. First, the links at Elie has never been closed in its entire history.

Second, because the first hole is a blind tee shot over a steep hill, play cannot proceed from the first tee until a little man pops out of a shed that features a submarine periscope on top and announces, "Please play away, gentlemen." The periscope is used to make sure the forward grouping is safely out of cannon range. Except for the first and finishing holes, the sea is always in view at beautiful Elie.

The village was also the birthplace of James Braid, he of Muirfield hooking fame, the local-boy-done-good who won five Open championships and later built some of the finest golf courses in Britain. Almost as important to the social development of Scotland, Elie was where my mother-in-law used to spend summer fortnights as a child while her papa played golf.

The day was kind to us at Elie. The sea air heated up nicely, and Dad limped around to a highly respectable 91 while I, attempting to stay put in NATO, managed 78 and seemed to be finding a respectable game. We played with a local baker named Malcolm who claimed he was visiting only to warm up "in private" for his evening men's league match, up the road at his regular club in Anstruther. Malcolm had the most violent hook swing I'd ever seen, but he got results. He routinely aimed a hundred yards *right* of every target off the tee, took a windup as big as West Texas, and found the heart of the fairway. It was quite impressive. He also drove two of the shorter par-fours and finished with a smart 75 on his scorecard, then bid us adieu with a muscular handshake, urged us to wander up the road to

Anstruther sometime, then hurried off to his elderly Cortina as if he feared his fierce adrenaline rush would leak out like motor oil before he reached Anstruther's first tee.

We drove back to the Scores, and I phoned up the Links Trust and learned that our names had once again failed to make the Old Course teetime list for the next day. There was a message from Bruce the caddy, though, and a phone number.

"This is ridiculous," I murmured, looking at Bruce's number, wondering if I shouldn't just call him and ask him to do something for us and hope my father didn't find out. I wadded up the paper and tossed it into the wastebasket.

Dad came out of the bathroom, where he was running a tub of water for a bath. He was holding a Bible and the little leather notebook where he jotted down thoughts for his weekly men's Bible class. He'd been moderator of the class for fifteen years. I broke the news to him that we hadn't made the ballot once again.

"Well," he said, not particularly dismayed, "let's give it another day and see what happens."

He picked up his fountain pen and headed back to the bath.

"And then what?" I said after him, perhaps a bit sharper than necessary.

He paused and looked at me. "Well, I think after that, if we don't have any luck, Bo, it may be time for us to move along."

I said evenly: "You mean go home."

"Correct. I really think it's time. I've got some things to do."

"So Islay and Williamwood and France were never part of your plans?" I regret to say that this came out more like an accusation than a question.

"They would have been nice. We've had a great time. Let's give it one more day and keep our fingers crossed."

He disappeared into the bath, and I went out for a walk, and after a hike up to the remains of the town's old cathedral, where both Tom Morrises are buried, I found myself standing above the stone steps leading down to the first tee at the Old Course, enviously watching the final players of the day tee off. I wondered if the players were legal because the starter's shed was empty and locked tight. Other players were visible out on the course, but darkness was perhaps only an hour or so away. The wind had been blowing all afternoon, pushing ragged gray clouds across the streaky autumn sky. The sleeves of my windbreaker flapped sharply in the wind. The two players were wearing knitted ski caps. I watched them tee up and hit their drives and hoist their bags and march off to battle as long as the light permitted. I stood there feeling more than a little sorry for myself. Sulking the way I used to do when I was thirteen. We'd come all this way, I told myself, for nought.

Just then a voice behind me remarked: "I'm told golf has been played out there for almost five hundred years and that by law anyone is basically entitled to walk these public grounds."

My father was standing behind me dressed in fresh clothes. His windbreaker was zipped to the chin, and his St. Andrews cap tilted jauntily.

"That's the story they feed the public," I said. "The truth is, they keep a goon squad handy to remove any violators who haven't paid a proper green fee. They make the goon squads of Brazil look like rank beginners."

He gazed out at the old linksland. "Want to risk it? I thought I would at least take a stroll around the Old Course, just to see if the place has held up without me."

"I guess so. Sure."

By the time we reached the first hole, where the two players had just finished, the winds had slackened off a bit and the clouds had peeled back toward the neighbouring village of Leuchars to permit a few rays of the sun to spill across bay and linksland. Ahead of us, I saw holes where nobody was even playing—the wind or the cold had driven them off.

It's said you can really only see the glories of the Old Course at sunset, when shadows reveal the character of a piece of ground that has influenced the thinking of more golf course architects than any other place on earth. The first time Pete Dye played it during the 1965 British Amateur, he labeled the Old Course a "cow pasture"— only to play it twice more and come away convinced it was the greatest golf course in creation.

The Old Course was built by no man, shaped only a bit by Old Tom Morris and others, and it therefore abounds in eccentricity: massive double greens, crisscrossing fairways, target lines that seem to shift with the ever-shifting sea winds or don't exist at all. You aim for distant church steeples, nubs of fairway, eruptions of gorse. The dangers are mostly hidden from view. Caddies will tell you that the smart play on the outward leg is to the right—that approach gives you the best angle to the greens—but conversely all the decent bailout room is to the *left*, wryly favoring the man who hooks the ball. The Old Course has 112 bunkers, many of which are so well disguised and lethal that they have ominous monikers—Principal's Nose, Coffin, Grave, Hell. As a result of these factors and the ever-present blowing wind, you proceed cautiously and *learn* to play the Old Course perhaps more than any course on earth, your respect deepening with each circuit. "You have to study it," Bobby Jones advised. "And the more you study, the more you learn. The more you learn, the more you study."

We walked slowly all the way out to the Eden estuary, careful to keep well shy of greens and fairways where players were engaged, and eventually came to the eleventh green, the 172-yard par-three called High Hole, one of the most dangerous holes in all of golf, where Jones began to learn this lesson the hard way as a young man during his first Open championship in 1921. He took 43 on the outward nine and bunkered his tee ball in fearsome Strath bunker by the eleventh green. He finished with a triple bogey, ripped up his card, and stalked off the course. The incident, though, had a transformative effect on Jones. He was so thoroughly ashamed of himself for quitting, he vowed to set the highest standard of sportsmanship for the rest of his career.

Since nobody was near the hole, my father and I stepped up to the tee. I explained to my father that the hole always caused me all sorts of grief. Strath bunker had caught my ball several times, and the green looked indecently puny with the Eden estuary spreading out behind it. Moreover, the wind usually came straight off the water, knocking anywhere from two to three lengths off your club. I'd tried everything from a six-iron to a two-iron at High Hole and almost always came away feeling low.

"Try it now," Dad said. "The wind is down."

I smiled at him. "I don't have a club."

"By all means," he replied, "use one of mine." He handed me an imaginary golf club.

It was another of Opti's little exercises.

"What is it?" I asked.

"What do you think you'll need?"

I looked at the hole. "Four-iron flush."

"It's a four then. Hit it flush."

I took my stance and made a swing, finishing with my hands held high, as Jones used to do in his prime.

"That's the way," Dad said soothingly. "Think that little darling has a chance to go in the hole?"

"Not a chance," I said, and explained about my Hole-in-None Society plans.

"Oh, well," he replied mildly, "that makes two of us. Maybe I can join."

He motioned me to vacate the tee. A trio of fast-moving players who looked like local teenagers were closing from the tenth green. We walked off the tee and started to cut across the empty twelfth.

"I never knew you never scored an ace," I said. "Considering how well you play your irons, I guess I naturally assumed you had an ace—probably several."

He said, "Oh, I came close a few times. It just never seemed to be my moment. After a while I just quit worrying about it and accepted what the game gave me. That's the key to a good round of golf, you know—let it happen. Besides, if you don't have an ace, you always have something to look forward to."

On the way down the side of the twelfth fairway, I told him about Laird Small and Spyglass Hill and the importance of learning to stay in NATO.

"That's a wonderful story," he said. "Someday you can pass it along to your kids."

"Was that what you meant last night when you cut short my palm reading to shamelessly curry favor with the Wife of Bath? You said I would pass something important along."

"I wasn't talking about passing along your old Blazer, Sport."

Dad paused again and touched my arm and nodded at a group on the thirteenth green. Thirty yards to the left, a tall guy was anguishing over a five-foot putt on one of the Old Course's famous double greens. He stroked the putt, and it went in the hole, causing a portly man behind him to let out a modest little war whoop. They slapped hands like NBA warriors, retiring from the green. We followed them at a discreet distance to the par-five fourteenth and watched them tee off toward the church steeple in the town, hoping to avoid the out-of-bounds on the right and the infamous cluster of pot bunkers called the Beardies on the left. All four players found the safe landing area called Elysian Fields and hurried off at a brisk pace toward their balls, racing the darkness home.

As we stood there watching them, a plane flew low overhead. It was an old-fashioned biplane, the kind often used for aerial photography. I wondered if someone was taking pictures for the upcoming Open. Pictures you see of the Old Course are almost always taken at sunrise or sunset. It reminded me of the day all those years ago when a plane had flown over us at Green Valley, prompting Dad to mention Saint-Exupéry and opening a brand-new world to me.

"Tell me something," I said. "Why did you give up flying?"

This was something else I'd never thought to ask my father. Why was that? Flying had been his first love, but something had made him give it up, and I was embarrassed to say I didn't know what it was.

He smiled and shoved his hands into his windbreaker.

"Cold?"

"A bit," he admitted. We started to walk down the fourteenth fairway. The foursome were now well ahead of us.

"It's a funny story. Or maybe it's not so funny. I almost killed myself and your brother."

"You're joking." It seemed to be an evening for revelations.

"Unfortunately not."

He told me the tale. One day in the early spring, when my brother was about a year old, my father decided to introduce his firstborn son to the joys of flying. He strapped him into the seat of a Cessna plane and took off to visit an old friend at an airfield near Chapel Hill. The friend was the airplane mechanic who had once given Dad flying lessons while he was briefly a student at Chapel Hill.

"I wanted to show him my brand-new son," Dad said, "and I thought Dickie would get a thrill out of the ride. The thrill was a bit more than I anticipated."

After taking off for the forty-mile return trip to Greensboro, the plane suffered a sudden power loss and began to lose altitude—the engine was having difficulty getting fuel. Dad sensed a fuel line blockage and began desperately trying to fix the problem but couldn't.

"We were barely flying over the tops of the trees," he remembered. "I was looking everywhere for a place to put her down, but there wasn't a field or road that looked right. I couldn't figure out what the hell was wrong."

"Did you think you were going to die?"

"Sure. That goes through your head. Mostly I was thinking about your brother. How damned unfair it was if we crashed and he died."

"What'd you do?"

"Flew along trying to avoid treetops and plowed-up fields. A freshly plowed field in the spring, you see, gives off cold air. Old-time aviators were terrified of freshly plowed fields. They can knock you right out of the air. I followed roads and fallow fields. We zigzagged all over the place."

"Like that time you flew Mom down the New River Valley."

"Right. I terrified her. This time I terrified me."

"But you made it back. . . ."

"Yep. That's when I found the problem. I'd forgotten to switch on the heater that keeps the carburetor from freezing up. It was a beginner's mistake. But if I was making mistakes like that—risking my own son's life—I told myself it was time to quit. I thanked the good Lord for getting us back in one piece, took your brother home to his mother, and never flew again."

"That's quite a story," I said. "Did you ever miss flying?"

"Not really." We walked a few paces, and he added, "Well, yes. I did. But life goes forward, doesn't it? You trade this for that." He smiled. "I did fantasize, though, about taking your mother up in a hot-air balloon sometime. I pictured us floating around up there with a good bottle of French champagne. Smooching a bit. Singing old love songs from the war."

"On behalf of songbirds everywhere, I beg you to leave the singing to Miss Western Maryland. That's her job."

"I promise." He fell silent, then said, "Well, well. Look here, Bo."

We were standing on the seventeenth tee of the Old Course. The Road Hole.

The sun was gone, the air was cold, and the course lay almost fully in the embrace of a blue twilight now. A few faint stars were visible above the clouds, and there were lights on in the Old Grey Toon. The group we'd been following had hit their drives and disappeared rapidly down the fairway.

"This is where I wish we had our *real* clubs," I said.

"Aw, who needs 'em? " Dad said. "Let's play anyway."

"You're right," I agreed. "We could play air golf with the ghosts of St. Andrews the way I played air guitar with the Beatles. Please play away, Mr. Dodson."

Dad teed up his air Top-Flite, took his stance, and swung. "There," he said. "Right over the sheds. Just like fifty years ago."

I teed up my air Titleist and asked, "How fast did that fifty years go by?"

"Stick around. You won't believe it."

I struck my shot and outdrove him, as usual, by at least a hundred yards.

We walked down the darkened fairway side by side. For a change, I wasn't really thinking about all the greats who had walked this way to immortality: Old Tom and Young. Taylor and Braid. Jones and Snead. Nicklaus and Lema. Ballesteros and Faldo. Watson, who had crossed this spot with a record-tying sixth Open within his grasp—to just miss.

I was thinking, instead, how simply fine and proper it was that my old man and I were finally playing the Road Hole together. Now came Opti and son.

From the heart of the fairway, Dad used an air three-wood to lay up short of the infamous Road Hole bunker. From the left rough, I swatted a beautiful air four-iron to the lower half of the green. We were playing our own games, if I may say so, magnificently.

He walked up to his air ball, just shy of the bunker, and announced he was using his air sand wedge, then lofted his ball sweetly to the green, stopping it within a few feet of the cup.

"Very nice," I said. "Before we putt out, though, tell me about your birdie."

He looked at me, then nodded solemnly at the bunker.

It took a few seconds for me to realize what he was telling me. He'd somehow made birdie from the Road Hole bunker!

"That's unbelievable," I said, shaking my head. "I've never heard of anybody doing that."

"It came as a major shock to me, too."

I demanded that he describe in detail this miraculous little feat, on a par in my mind with anything Jones had done at Lytham or Palmer at Birkdale.

He said the details were kind of foggy, but he seemed to think the hole was considerably different back then. "For one thing, the bunker was a lot shallower than it is now. The sod wall was nowhere near as high as it is here. You could escape pretty easily with a decent shot." He took a step closer, sizing up the wall, which was higher than a man's head. "I don't see how anybody could come out of this thing."

He added that the pin he'd shot at that day fifty years ago was on the lower half of the green. The greens were thicker grass in those days, before modern lawn mowers came along. That made a big difference, too.

"You still made a hell of a shot," I said to him. "And it wasn't an air ball."

"No," he said a little wistfully, "it wasn't. Sometimes, though, it takes on the quality of a dream. Perhaps, I simply imagined it."

"No," I said. "Not a chance."

We putted out rather quickly. I made an uncharacteristically fine air lag from the lower part of the green and tapped in for four—a brilliant air par! Dad sank a clutch five-footer to halve the hole.

"Two air pars on the hardest hole in golf," I said as we shook hands.

We walked to the eighteenth tee, struck fine drives into the darkness, then moseyed down the fairway of the most famous finishing hole in golf, crossing the little arched stone bridge. For weeks I'd been so fearful of this moment, anticipating how awful I would feel when it finally arrived. But strangely, I wasn't the least bit sad now. I was *cold* as blazes but almost unnaturally happy to be finishing a round of golf that only I would ever remember. No card would ever show the score. Our match would vanish into the air.

"Call me sentimental if you like," my father said, taking my arm as we approached the Valley of Sin, the dangerous swale that guards the front of the eighteenth green. "I think it's been a hell of a journey."

"You're just being sentimental," I replied. "The showers were much worse than expected."

"You're talking about the trip," he said. "I'm talking about the journey."

·   ·   ·

The next morning, I drove my father to the airport in Edinburgh for a dawn commuter flight to London. We decided to leave St. Andrews before finding out if we'd made it through the Old Course ballot that third day. Three times might have been a charm, but nothing could have topped the round of air golf we'd played the evening before.

On the way to the airport, my father proposed to me that I finish our golf trip alone, push on to Islay and France to see what I could find. I told him that was pointless without him, but by the time we'd crossed the Forth Road Bridge, he'd persuaded me to change my mind. I agreed to go on for another week or so.

At the airport, a boisterous group of Scottish teenagers were headed for Texas. The scene was one of tearful mayhem. The kids were whooping it up excitedly, and the moist-eyed parents were desperately attempting to check bags, collect hugs, and issue brilliant nuggets of travel wisdom.

It vaguely reminded me of the day my father drove me to the airport to fly to Europe for the first time. Then something else really brought that moment rushing back. I glanced at my watch.

"Son of a gun," I said. "It's stopped again." My watches always stopped when I needed them to run. Perhaps because I always wore fifty-dollar watches—watches you could toss into a golf bag or briefcase and never think twice about losing them.

"Here," Dad said, unbuckling his, "take mine. I don't need it anymore. Besides, I've been meaning to give it back to you for a while."

It was the ugly blue Seiko watch he'd given me twenty years before for college graduation. He'd been caretaking it all these years, and I'd never even really noticed. I looked at it now and shook my head. It really wasn't ugly at all. In fact, it was classy blue and almost elegant. "Holy cow. I was just thinking about that watch," I told him.

"Well, put it on, dummy," he insisted. I took mine off and strapped his on.

I kissed my father on the cheek, and he kissed me. We hugged, and then he was walking away, leaving a whiff of his Aramis after-shave, falling in step with a gawky fifteen-year-old girl carrying a Pearl Jam backpack and a small black boom box. I saw him speak to her and saw her turn her head to a friend, a shorter girl on her right. Both girls giggled, and then the shorter girl skipped around to my father's unaccompanied side and took his arm. I half expected to see her stick out her palm.

Opti was up to his old tricks.

La Forêt de l'Amour

Six weeks later, my father suffered a stroke.

I was seated beside him at the Thanksgiving table in Greensboro, when food suddenly started tumbling out of his mouth. At
first I thought it was a messy gag designed to amuse his grandchildren, and obviously they did, too. Maggie and Jack immediately
burst out giggling as the adult conversation ebbed away. I remember
looking at Alison; she looked so sad.

By the time we got him to the emergency room at the hospital,
his blood pressure was two hundred over sixty, a runaway train. They
placed us in a curtained alcove next to a man whose girlfriend had
stabbed him in the abdomen with a kitchen knife.

"What are we doing here?" Dad quietly asked me. Memory loss
often accompanies a stroke.

I took his hand. It was unusually cold. His breathing was shallow and labored, his skin splotchy pink and pale.

"Waiting for a guy to come check out your heart," I said.

"Oh." He added, calmly: "Where's your mother?"

I explained she was out in the emergency room lobby harassing the hospital staff, trying to separate the heart specialist from his Thanksgiving dinner.

"Is it Thanksgiving?" he asked.

"Yep." I explained I knew it was Thanksgiving because we'd played golf that morning at Sedgefield. Some American males traditionally watch football in a turkey-induced stupor; we play golf on the nation's turkey day. I was pleased our actual final round hadn't been at St. Andrews but at Sedgefield, where he'd first walked onto a golf course as a caddy seventy years ago. We'd finished where he'd begun the game.

"How'd we do?"

I said we did okay. The course had been deserted. I shot 79. He'd played every other hole, made some nice putts as usual. We passed some men playing with their daughters and sons. We talked about his work and mine. We saw the Tracy house. It looked much smaller than I remembered.

He asked me where I'd been traveling. Speaking seemed to be a strain for him. I explained that I'd just come from Fort Worth, where I'd spent a nice afternoon talking with Byron Nelson. It was the anniversary of Nelson's eleven straight PGA wins in 1945, one of which occurred at Greensboro, and I was writing a piece for *Golf* about that.

"You have a job men would die for," he whispered.

"Are you trying to get my job?"

He managed a dim smile. "Funny boy. Keep that sense of humor. You'll need it." He closed his eyes and then opened them again.

"Tell me about the rest of the trip," he said, pausing to take a breath. "I mean Islay and France."

I hadn't brought up the trip to him while we were playing that day. I pulled up a chair and sat down, still holding his hand.

After dropping him at the airport, I said, I'd driven into Edinburgh and looked up Torquil MacNaughton. Torquil was the son of Kate Bennie's best childhood chum, Margaret Ann, who now went by Lady MacNaughton because her husband, Calum, a Glasgow University professor and physician, had been knighted by the Queen. Torquil, who worked for the Bank of Scotland and had once played all five of Scotland's British Open courses on the same day ("It was for a charity fund raiser, we had to use a helicopter, sunrise to sunset. I wish I could remember most of it. . . ."), graciously declared a golfer's holiday upon my arrival and drove me to the Dalmahoy Golf Club, where the European Solheim Cup squad had recently mashed their American female counterparts into the mud. We played a close but friendly match, our own version of the Solheim-Ryder Cup feud, that fittingly came down to our final shots at eighteen. I laid a pitching wedge shot two feet from the cup on my approach, and Torquil impudently placed his shot a foot inside that. I congratulated him, called him a cheeky bastard, and conceded the putt. He thanked me, said it took one to know one, and conceded mine—nicely reversing the roles of Nicklaus and Jacklin at their famous Ryder Cup finish in 1969. We shook hands and had a beer and agreed to settle the issue on my next trip through town, perhaps even slipping over to the Old Course where Torquil, during his distant university days at St. Andrews, obviously got to play far too much golf.

Next I went to Williamwood Golf Club in Glasgow, Kate Bennie's father's club, a middle-class club you entered through the car park of a Shell station. There I hooked up with three older members who squabbled with each other about the big upcoming soccer

match between the city's archrival professional teams, Rangers and
Celtic. At one point, the one named Billy insisted I turn and
wave to a small figure standing at the upper window of a Victorian
row house at least a quarter of a mile away. I dutifully waved. The
figure waved vigorously back. "That's ma' loovely wife Helen," Billy
said proudly. "She always likes to see who I'm playin' with." "What
Billy means," chipped in the one named John, "is Helen always likes
to see that Billy's not playin' with any *lay-dee* members." We all had a
good laugh.

The next day I'd taken a flight through heavy fog over to Islay
and met Murdo Macpherson, a bald, charming hotelier who could
have passed for Sean Connery's younger brother and shuttled his
own guests around town in a mud-splattered van. Bouncing through
potholes at alarming speed on the way to the hotel, a stark white
structure set down among several rustic self-catering cottages on the
vast peat barrens of the island's beautifully stark west side, Murdo
explained that Nick Faldo had decided not to purchase the Machrie
Hotel and Golf Club, apparently in part because the island's current
air service could accommodate only seventy paying customers a day.
According to Murdo, Japanese businessmen—the Japanese owned
two of the eight major distilleries on the island—accounted for a
large number of the occupied seats in the daily flights, and Faldo
obviously had a grander retreat in mind. "Considering all of the
rather unfavorable press the man has received, I found him quite
pleasant to converse with," Murdo explained. "We struck no deal,
but I think it's safe to say he found the links out back quite beguil-
ing."

If he didn't, I soon found myself thinking, Brother Nick ought
to find another line of work. The Machrie course was a rough-cut
gem, everything I could have hoped for in an unspoiled seaside links,
as remote and challenging as anything I'd ever played, featuring tumbling fairways, punchbowl greens, and at least half a dozen blind

approach shots over heaving eruptions of earth to hidden greens. A place of freedom and solitude but, in a word, the average American country clubber's living *nightmare*.

Laid out by Willie Campbell of Musselburgh in 1891 and revised by Donald Steel in the 1980s, the Machrie was once seriously considered as an Open championship venue until it was decided that the *two-day* journey from the mainland would exhaust players and spectators alike. Overjoyed by my discovery, I played the Machrie three times in two days, through gales of wind and rain and periods of such tranquil sunshine, you could actually see the coast of Northern Ireland rising up like a fairy kingdom thirty miles away.

Being a devoted fan of "blind" holes—no less than Tommy Armour, who once growled that anyone who doesn't care for them is no true fan of golf—my favorite Machrie test was hole number seven, a 395-yard par-four that almost defies proper description. You tee off in a little dell, aiming for . . . well, *where* exactly? An immense dune rises fifty feet above you, and no fairway is visible in any direction. Your target on this masterpiece of mental torture turns out to be a zigzag of overgrown footpaths winding whimsically up the dune. Beyond the shaggy peak lies an uneven fairway that tumbles pell-mell down to a sunken green concealed by a low ridge. A broad dune behind the green provides the only perspective for the scary approach shot. Jim Finegan aptly calls Machrie's seventh "grand opera, though some may call it opéra bouffe." The Paps of Jura rise in one direction, the Mull of Oa in another. Most players I know would call it the toughest hole they *never* want to see again. I call it heaven.

In golf heaven, of course, there are no crowded links, and fittingly, I spotted only two other players on the course during my visit. One of them was a local boy and his dog. The other was Murdo, getting in a quick few holes during an afternoon lull before the hotel dining room opened for dinner. He spotted me and waved.

I informed him I was madly in love with his seventh hole. "Glad to hear it," he said, "but it's only mine on paper. The links belongs to the game, not to me."

We strolled to the mighty seventh and played a one-hole match that I somehow won, and Murdo bought me a delicious mutton dinner in his restaurant, telling me about the golfing exploits of his son Andrew, who was presently working as an assistant to the legendary professional John Stark at Creiff Golf Club, in Perthshire. I asked Murdo if he nurtured hopes of Andrew returning to Islay to take over the Machrie. "To tell the truth, it's not a hope I hold out too terribly much," Murdo admitted, reaching down to pet one of the two Jack Russell terriers that were never far from my host's feet. "Andrew's a clever and ambitious lad. Kids like him leave Islay and never come back." He smiled somewhat wistfully, and poured me another finger of a peaty local malt. "Cheers, here's to your further travels," he said, lifting his glass.

I took my soggy clothes on to France, rented a car, and drove to Compiègne, checked into a small dark hotel next to the medieval city's main bridge and the train station where the Germans, I soon learned, in fact deported close to 80,000 French Jews to concentration camps during the war. On my second day in town, I visited Napoleon's sprawling summer palace and went searching in the vast adjoining royal forest for the beech tree where Dad had once carved my mother's initials.

"Did you find the tree?" Dad suddenly asked, as he lay on the emergency room bed waiting for the heart specialist to arrive. His eyelids fluttered. For a moment I thought he'd dozed off.

"I think so."

I explained that I'd found a broad lane vanishing into the yellow forest, but I'd unfortunately discovered *thousands* of lovers' initials carved into the skins of the ancient beeches there, decades of declared *amour*. It had seemed fairly hopeless. After an hour or so of searching, though, I'd come upon what appeared to be *JKD* and another set of illegible initials encased by a crude heart and the date 1945, halfway up a large leaning beech. I decided this must be it— even if it wasn't. I opened my Swiss Army knife and carved my own and my wife's initials and the date below them.

As I worked, an elderly man in a wool topcoat came shuffling down the gravel path. He stopped, leaned on his cane, and watched me finish the carving. He was shabbily elegant: brown felt bowler, cashmere wool scarf, a figure from a Delacroix. He studied my hand-iwork and made a comment in French that I didn't understand. I explained to him that my French was very poor. He nodded and smiled with brown broken teeth. "C'est la forêt de l'amour," he declared, waving his arm expansively. *The Forest of Love.*

After that, pleased by my discovery, I'd strolled farther into the beautiful forest via the bridle path and walked for well over an hour, enjoying the sights and smells of the blazing autumn woods. After a while, I realized I might be lost and turned up another well-trampled path and walked along till I came to a small creek, a pretty wooden bridge, and a row of bushy poplar trees. I saw a patch of green beyond the trees, and white rail fences. It looked like an old race-course. I pushed through the limbs and stepped out onto the grass just as I heard a solid metallic *thwack* and someone shouting angrily in French. I turned and saw two men standing thirty yards away, gesturing furiously at me. They were holding golf clubs. One of them had just fired his tee shot a few yards over my head. I'd stumbled out of the Forest of Love onto the Golf Club of Com-piègne.

I apologized as best I could and hurried across the golf course toward a white stucco beamed structure that I assumed was the clubhouse. I walked into the clubhouse and found an attractive middle-aged lady who hadn't a clue what I was trying to ask her— namely, How long had the golf course been there? Had it been around in my father's day in Compiègne? Did anyone around perhaps *parlez-vous anglais*? Could I play it?

"You see Dick," she said.

"Dick?"

"Yes, Dick." She bustled away, and a nice-looking chap in a brown sweater came back. His name was Stephane. We shook hands. Stephane was Golf de Compiègne's Directeur and spoke *anglais*. I could have kissed him on both cheeks. "You must meet Dick Di Salle," Stephane said cheerfully. "He is our *président sportif*. He is American." He motioned me toward the clubhouse bar with a large smile. "I call. You wait."

I went into the bar and ordered a Coke and watched the dining room fill up with attractive-looking people from Compiègne. They kept turning their heads to smile at me, so I smiled back. I felt like the stranger in town in a spaghetti western.

Soon a robust-looking gray-haired man rambled in with an attractive woman by his side. "I hear we've been invaded by the Americans again," he said, offering a brisk handshake. Dick Di Salle introduced me to his wife Rolande. We found a table and ordered venison sausage for lunch. I learned Dick and Rolande had met just after the Liberation when Dick, a first lieutenant from Colorado who arrived in France three months after D-Day, helped set up a hospital in nearby Soissons.

I explained that he'd arrived about the same time as my father, and I told the Di Salles about the months my father ran the "prison" camp on the outskirts of town. "I remember the camp," Dick said, "but I don't remember your dad. That's not so surprising, though. There were so many Americans coming and going around here at that time." For the next hour or so, we talked about the war. Rolande talked about the horrors of the German occupation, and Dick, now a retired hospital administrator, explained how he'd met the love of his life on a tennis court in Soissons and decided to stay put and build a life in France. Rolande had been a champion tennis player, but now the couple also golfed. I asked them about the handsome golf course outside. "Oh, it was here during the war," Dick said. "You just couldn't see it. The Germans parked their trucks on it, and the Allies later bombed it." He said a bunker on the eleventh hole (near the spot where I'd barged onto the course) was in fact the remains of an old American bomb crater.

It was an unexpectedly bountiful day. As I left, the Di Salles urged me to come back again someday with my father or my wife or my children, and Stephane reappeared, smiling and handing me a packet that contained the club history, a visor, and an attractive blazer patch with the official Club de Compiègne emblem. I thanked him and said I would wear it with pride.

The next morning, a dreary rainy Thursday, I played Compiègne's golf course with the only people who were about, Jean and Michel, ironically the same two blokes whose match I'd interrupted the day before. They turned out to be Gallic versions of American golf nuts and seemed to have entirely forgotten or forgiven my transgression. Only Michel spoke English. He kept complimenting my shirt: *"Nice shirt, Jeem."* This was odd because my shirt, per usual, was plain white. Finally, near the end of our round in the rain, I figured out he had been graciously complimenting my *shots.* I thanked Michel and invited him and Jean to come to my home club in Maine someday. Michel translated this to Jean, who seemed very pleased and said something to Michel, who asked me if *Men* was anywhere near *Pee-ball Beech.* I replied that both were at least on the coast. I just forgot to tell them *which* coasts.

That afternoon I drove to Chantilly, where there was a great château and a famous racetrack and an even better golf course, where the European Open had been played. I played one of the two courses there alone through a fog. Somewhere near the end of the round—I wasn't playing well or having much fun—I looked at the Seiko and realized it had stopped. Fearing I'd killed yet another watch, I drove into the town proper and found a jeweler named Pagette, who held up the watch and gently shook it, producing a disturbing rattle. Chevy ball bearings seemed to be rolling around inside it.

Gently prying apart the watch at his little table, Monsieur Pagette stared at the innards like a worried surgeon. He finally shook his head and said something I was pretty sure wasn't "Heck, it was only a dumb ole battery." He closed up the watch and presented it back to me with a delicate shrug. He murmured something consoling, which his wife Hélène helpfully translated. "He says, um, he cannot, um, *comprehend,* how this, um, timepiece could, you see, have, um—how you say?— have worked for so many years." We all stared solemnly at the watch for a moment. Then I thanked them and left.

I drove on to Paris and checked in to a small hotel behind the Opéra and walked around the City of Light for a day, thinking about my father and his great affection for the French and their famous river city. After that I met Bertrand Dubeigny, a golf pal of Murdo Macpherson's, a doctor of tropical diseases who graciously took me to his golf club in the western suburbs of the city and later accompanied me to the Musée de la Grande Armée and showed me Napoleon's tomb and told me about the hardships his family, some of whom served in the *Résistance,* had endured during the war. We parted on Le Pont Neuf with a firm handshake and a promise to meet and play again sometime. Touchingly, Bertrand gave me some antique postcards from the war era and asked me to give them to my father as a little token of gratitude from the liberated French people. It was a moving gesture, and we actually embraced.

D-Day summer was finally over—but I'd finally finished a pilgrimage the way I'd hoped to. The autumn rains had come. Reunions were breaking up. On my last night in Paris, clear and cold and starry, I sat on a set of wooden bleachers by the Arc de Triomphe and watched a parade of World War II veterans from Britain,

France, and America pass in review beneath the arch, elderly men with too-tight uniforms and forgotten medals pinned to their chests, shuffling down the Champs Elysées.

The next morning I flew home.

My father was sleeping now, taking very shallow breaths, still holding my hand.

I wasn't sure how much of this he'd even heard. A nurse appeared, followed by a young doctor with a clipboard, nervously rocking on the balls of his spotless Nikes; a tennis player, I thought. He offered me a listless hand and simultaneously consulted his chart. He scarcely glanced at me and invited me to wait outside while he examined my father.

I was reluctant to go but finally went and sat in the emergency room lobby, where a young woman in running gear was sobbing quietly in the arms of an older woman and a three-hundred-pound man in a NASCAR tank top sat reading *Scuba Diver* magazine. A television set was playing, sound down, Packers versus Cowboys. I picked up a women's magazine and opened it to a sneaker ad that assured me: *Your childhood isn't lost, you just misplaced it somewhere.*

My father did not die, though I had honestly expected him to.

Instead, he pulled off another small resurrection feat. Two weeks later, after a brief restless rest, he went back to work with only a faint slur in his speech, cracking jokes about tippling on the job.

For Christmas, he took my mother to the Grove Park Inn, F. Scott Fitzgerald's old Smoky Mountain haunt. He asked us not to come to Greensboro for the holidays because he wanted a "quieter" holiday with his wife. Our evening phone call once caught them breathless. They'd been hoofing to Benny Goodman in the den while Molly the dog chaperoned from Dad's favorite armchair. They spoke of taking drives up to the Blue Ridge, of rising early to visit the farmer's market. They behaved like two people caught up in the first blush of courtship.

My father went to Florida for his annual winter sales meeting. The meeting was a success. His territory, as usual, was one of the top earners in the country. We spoke on the phone—I was in California doing interviews at a tournament site—and he was ebullient, predicting the new year would be his best ever. He was already a sales legend in his company, but like Macbeth he had plans to expire in harness.

Two days later, my brother reached me on the West Coast to say Dad had come home from the Florida meeting and gone straight into the hospital. I flew east to pick up my daughter at her ballet lesson, then packed a larger bag and flew south to be with him.

Steve Blieveneick, my father's longtime friend and surgeon, asked me to step out of the hospital room. Steve was a big burly Catholic, a brilliant cancer specialist, a poor golfer but an avid outdoorsman. He placed the X-ray on the illuminated panel and asked me to take a look. As I stared at it, he said, "I've almost never seen anyone with cancer so pervasive. It's everywhere. His pelvis. Intestines. Liver. His back. I don't have a clue how he's gone on this long. The man should have been dead months ago. Your father astounds me."

He turned off the panel light and looked at me straight in the eyes.

"These things are mysterious. We're in God's realm now. The medical establishment is basically helpless at this point. Your dad's a racehorse. When he decides it's time to go, I have a hunch he'll go the way he lived—no complaints, no questions. I'd like you to be there."

I assured him a stable of racehorses couldn't drag me away.

"Good."

An ambulance brought Dad home from the hospital. We set him up in a special bed in my old room. A large black woman from the local hospice came to help us learn to take care of him. With the assistance of another hospice technician named Colin, I became my father's live-in nurse, chief medicator, changer of bed linens, bather, feeder, and head porter—maneuvering his wheelchair slowly through the narrow hallway and kitchen and den, the traffic cop of his vastly diminished universe. My mother stood back, a hand to her throat, a face holding back tears, helpless to do anything more than watch and wait for his requests for meals—requests that were rapidly diminishing.

Together, my brother and I became Dad's late-night companions. Little by little his days and nights turned inside out, and ours went with them, a phenomenon the people at the hospice call sundowning.

Montaigne had wanted death to find him planting cabbages. With Dad, we became couch potatoes and watched the NCAA basketball season drawing to a close, players executing brilliant baseline pivots and jump-shots as we moved from prime time into the long, eerie late-nights of cable TV. The UNC Tarheels were playing tough. Dad, turning grayer by the day, was pleased.

My mother, who moved quietly around the periphery of this vigil, suggested that I get out of the house—go play golf with my childhood buddy Pat or attend a movie. I went out and drove aimlessly around Greensboro in Old Blue. There were so many new streets that I didn't know now, gourmet coffee bars, a rush hour that was staggering. Where, I wondered, had all these *people* come from?

I drove out to Bryan Park, the city's fine public golf facility, but I didn't want to play golf. I walked over and found a large man sitting in the starter's cart. He was wrapped in a blue windbreaker, sucking on a smoldering stogie. Once again, I introduced myself to Aubrey Apple and asked if he remembered me.

"Oh shit, yeah," he said, squinting at me. "You write about golf. How the hell's your daddy?" *Yo deddy.*

I told him my father was dying. Aubrey shook his head and said he was sorry to hear that. He told me they didn't make gentlemen like my father anymore. I thanked him. I also asked him how he liked being the club's starter, prompting him to snap, "Well, it ain't like being the pro." We reminisced for a little while longer about Green Valley and people we knew from those days, and then I explained I had to go. We shook hands, and Aubrey plugged his stogie back into its socket and slouched back into his cart.

It was already getting dark. I went to a movie, though I don't remember its name or what the film was about. The night was unusually warm, with a hint of early spring in the air. Afterward, I drove to Green Valley Parkway and parked Old Blue on the shoulder. I got out and looked around. In the moonlight, you could still see the remains of the old golf course. I was standing in the middle of the third fairway, my favorite hole. I walked up the knoll where I always aimed my tee shot and stood awhile. A car pulled up behind Old Blue, a white security cruiser. A rent-a-cop, hitching up his pants, walked slowly up the hill. He said good evening and asked what I was doing.

I said I was looking for something I'd lost.

"What's that?" He wiggled a toothpick in his teeth.

"You'll laugh," I said. "A golf course."

He laughed as if he didn't believe me and said I would have to move along because I was loitering on private property.

"A couple times I got home from here in two," I said, indicating the land falling away toward the far trees, where the green used to be tucked.

"You *what?*"

"I reached the green in two. You have no idea what a thrill that was."

His voice grew sterner. "Look. I'm going to have to insist you move along, or I'll have to call the Greensboro police."

"No problem," I said, and left.

The next day I drove out of town to do a bit of work. It had been three weeks since I last worked on anything, and I was relieved to steer Old Blue four hours to the east to Wilmington, where I sat down with Ike Grainger, the famous USGA rules official. Grainger had just turned one hundred years old and my piece on him—a man who had made some of the most critical rulings in many of the biggest matches in the history of the game—was for the centennial edition program of the U.S. Open, which was to be held at Shinnecock Hills in June.

Later that night, as Dad and I sat watching the conference semifinals of a basketball tournament from some arena out West, I told him some of what Grainger and I had discussed—how the rule of equity is the heart and soul of golf, how whenever there's no formal rule to cover a situation or dispute, you must try and do what's most *fair*—and said how much Grainger's love of the game had reminded me of his. I also told my father I wished he could accompany me to Shinnecock.

"Maybe I'll get out of this contraption and we'll go," he said quietly, thumping the arm of the wheelchair. I said I'd be pleased to arrange the passes.

"I'm sorry for so much trouble," he added, coughing dryly, shifting uneasily in his chair.

"It's no trouble, Dad."

"You'll just never know how much I loved you all."

"We love you, too." My mother had quietly appeared in the kitchen doorway, dressed in her quilted bathrobe, the overhead light shining behind her, fingers to her throat. She was helpless to do anything but wait. My father didn't see her. She was crying. She turned and went back to bed.

A little while later, Dad said, "You know what I'd really like, Jim? I'd like to crawl in bed with your mother."

"You got it."

I woke up my mother and carried my father to their bed. Switching off the light, I heard my mother planting soft kisses on her husband's face. Her voice had a girlish cant. "You scoot over here, hon, and let's snuggle, just you and me. *There* now. Warm enough?" His reply possessed more strength than I had heard or seen for days. "Yes. Thanks. Delighted to be in bed with you."

"My goodness, sweetie, you need a shave."

The next day, he asked me to give him a shave.

I shaved my father with his own safety razor, slipping glances at his eyes. His pale gray eyes were even paler, farther away. They made me think of Gorky's description of the dying Tolstoy: *He listens attentively as though recalling something which he has forgotten, or as though for something new and unknown.*

Afterward, while he slept, I went out to see a man who gave hot-air balloon rides for weddings, anniversaries, and other "special occasions," it turned out, except dying. He couldn't believe I wanted to take my dying father up in a hot-air balloon. There were insurance considerations.

"I'll pay you twice your normal fee, sign a waiver, whatever's necessary," I pressed him. "Just a few minutes up in the air. You, my father, my mother, and a little bottle of good French wine." *Something new and unknown.*

He thought about it, chewing his lip. Then he consulted a schedule log, shrugged, and said he was booked until April. He smiled apologetically. He said he might be able to do something for me in April.

. . .

Buddhists and Native American people believe the way a person dies tells the story of how he lived. To them, dying is a living art, the beginning of further passage to something new and unknown.

For a change, I tried not to think too much about the future, what was going to happen to my mother after my father was gone, how our lives would change, how I would feel. As a child, my greatest unspoken fear was that my father would somehow just *disappear*. I don't know where this illogical terror came from. He never gave me the slightest reason to believe it might happen. As I grew from boy to man and then to middle-aged man with children of his own, he was always *there*.

Now, as my father slipped away, I simply could not imagine a world without him in it. As long as your father is alive, someone said, you will always be a son.

My father's younger brothers arrived. First Jim, then Bob, then Ben. They sat with my aging aunts on the den couch and talked about the trials of their own grown families while my mother, alternately smiling and hiding out in the kitchen, went slowly out of her mind. The television played throughout, a mindless electronic treacle of Regis and Kathie Lee, soaps, Jenny Jones, weight-loss infomercials, Murphy Brown retreads. As more people arrived and the conversation swelled to a dull roar, the local noon news came on, reporting that a local high school star quarterback had been arrested for participating in a drive-by shooting. There was a chance of sleet in the forecast. The ACC tournament, just getting under way, had brought record crowds to town.

My uncle Jim glanced at me. He and I were the only two in the room watching the news, wondering about the outside world. Jim was my favorite uncle, perhaps because he favored my father, his older brother, in so many ways. They were closest in age and eerily similar in worldview and temperament. I thought of Jim as Opti, Jr.

He had been the best man at my parents' wedding. He came over and sat beside me on the couch. News of the gangbanger quarterback reminded him that he and Dad had played on the same high school football team and even dated some of the same girls and had fallen in love with flying at about the same time as teenagers. "The thing about your dad," he said, smiling wistfully, "was he was always so interested in everything around him . . ." and then Jim's words simply stopped. His eyes filled with emotion. He couldn't finish the sentence.

I patted his knee. He patted mine and then got up and disappeared into my old bedroom to sit and talk with his sleeping brother. He came back a while later, wiping his eyes.

My uncle Bob was of sterner stuff, a devout Southern Baptist, a forest ranger who believed in original sin. He was a good and kind man, though very different from my father in the way he looked at the world and considered his frail fellow creatures. Pulling me aside, with his arm around my shoulders, Bob asked me in all seriousness if I thought my father "had a right relationship with Jesus."

His unexpected question made me think of Dad on our trip to Scotland, burrowed into his Bible and doggedly searching for some perfect nugget of Scripture for his men's Bible class. I smiled at Bob, slipped my arm around his back, and replied that I thought Dad and Jesus would get along just fine, but Jesus had better steer clear of the putting green with Opti the Mystic if he knew what was good for him. Otherwise, I said, Jesus would be buying supper.

Bob laughed nervously at my little irreverence. He said I had a "sly sense of humor" just like my father.

I thanked him.

My uncle Ben, the family baby, was standing nearby listening. He laughed at this exchange, looking a little like an aging Robert Kennedy, all big front teeth and curly thin hair. He and my aunt Bernice were childless. Their dog Goldie was waiting in the car.

Though Ben had once taken me flying over Miami in his plane, he was the uncle I really didn't know.

They meant so well—the waiting uncles and the visiting neighbors who came by with thoughtful casseroles no one had the appetite to touch and sat for an eternity and made friendly chitchat and asked if I still played the guitar and wanted to know the details of my career and my own growing family and what it was like to live in Maine in the winter. One plump elderly friend of my mother's who had blue-rinsed hair and a voice like a Portland harbor foghorn sat talking about all the PGA Tour stars she'd met at the GGO over the years. As she rambled on, my mind slipped back to the tranquil golden glade at Compiègne. At that moment I wished like the dickens my father could have been with me there—and then realized he had been.

"So what's he *really* like?" the woman demanded, batting her lushly overpainted eyelashes at me.

"Who?" I asked from the edge of *La Forêt de l'Amour*.

"Jack Nicklaus."

"I haven't a clue," I said, adding: "I sell coffins."

"*What?*" She gave me a horrified look.

"I'm sorry," I said. "That was just an old joke. It seems to work for a friend of mine." I told her Jack Nicklaus was great. Everything you expect the oft-called player of the century to be—even if I personally ranked him somewhere after Bobby Jones and Sam Snead. I smiled at her, hoping she would just go away like the fog.

The truth was, with all due respect, I wanted them all to go away and leave us alone. Death is so exhausting. I began to look forward to the lonely overnight *cable* vigils with my father and brother. Next to the daytime crowd, the nighttime crowd—with their miracle car-wax finishes and mail-order prosthetic limb discounts—seemed almost tolerable.

We watched an old Jeff Chandler western together, followed by an infomercial for Hollywood psychics, followed by Notre Dame coach Lou Holtz peddling a video golf instruction series, followed by mud wrestling *live* from a Houston bar! By then, my brother Dick was asleep in the other easy chair. I knew this was hitting him very hard. He had just gone through a difficult divorce and was working hard to keep my father's business together.

My father finally dozed off, too. I carried him to bed, and he opened his eyes. "What are you doing here?" he asked, surprised.

"Putting you in your bed."

"I don't want to be in this bed."

"I know. But you need to rest, and I'm supposed to make sure you get some."

He asked me why I was being so mean to him.

"I'm not being mean," I said. "I love you."

"Why don't you go paint the house," he suggested.

"Okay. What color shall I paint it?"

"Carolina blue."

I smiled. "Are you sure?"

"Yes." A loyal Tar Heel to the end. I sat on the edge of the bed until he was asleep, mulling it over.

The next day, a Friday, Carolina got knocked out in the ACC basketball tournament. I decided not to break the news to Opti. Besides, his mind was already somewhere new and unknown. Certain mystics believe that a calm meditative state as death approaches is the closest a human being can get to true enlightenment. When my father asked me where we were, I explained we were still inside our house on Dogwood Drive.

"No," he said with great conviction, "There's Uncle Jimmy's gate." He was smiling at the wall but seeing a gate in his grandfather's pasture.

I looked at the wall and said, "Oh, yeah. How 'bout that?" He asked me for some water, and I brought it. Taking a sip, he said, "That's good spring water. We have an excellent well, don't we?"

"The best," I agreed.

That night the heavy rain turned to sleet, glass shards bouncing off the mullioned windows. Around midnight, Dad sat up and pulled out his catheter. I replaced it, and he yanked it out again. "Stop that, please," I said. "Did you paint the house yet?" he asked, giving the line another tug. His strength surprised me. My brother arrived, and we more or less held him in place until the hospice technician arrived with a strong sedative.

"I don't think it's the physical pain that's bothering him," Dick observed. "I think he just wants to get up and roam around a final time."

He was right, of course. Dad's indefatigable will was putting up a final heroic struggle even as his physical strength ebbed away.

I sat with a finger plugged into a hole in my father's abdomen, waiting for the suppository pain-killer to melt, listening to the sleet ricochet off the windows. I noticed his lips were making little pursing movements. He was finally calm again. "What are you doing?" I asked, not really expecting an answer. He replied with a peaceful whisper: "Kissing the babies."

Other people arrived, pastors, neighbors bringing more covered dishes, people I recognized from my childhood, and a steady procession of people I'd never met before who acted as if my father had been their best friend. A woman smelling intensely of Giorgio explained my father had once fixed her flat tire right in the parking lot of the Harris Teeter supermarket and they'd become "grocery store buddies" after that. "Him and me had a regular little thing going," she said, giving me a wink.

The Tracy kids came, all grown up now—Mimi, Pam, Bobby, and his wife Claire. We talked about good times at Sedgefield and

remembered how we'd tagged after Palmer and Snead and how
Mimi's boyfriends had seemed to all drive littered sports cars and
how Pam had once drunk paint. I told them how vast their house
had seemed to me as a child, but how modest as a man—almost as if
time had shrunk it. Mimi, a senior flight attendant for Delta, explained that she'd recently gone up to the house and knocked on the
door and been given a tour by the nice man who lived there now.
"Afterward," she said, "I just bawled my eyes out."

Bill Mims and Bob Tilden, Dad's oldest golf pals, dropped by.
They seemed pleased to hear that Dad had thought of them one
day at Turnberry. Bob confirmed the funny story about nearly killing himself with a driver, then went in to say good-bye to my
father.

"Are you aware," Mims said to me, leaning close as he waited,
"that your dad invented a famous golf shot? It's true. It's called the
Oh Shit shot. Unfortunately, he could only do it when I was his
playing partner." Bill squeezed my shoulder and smiled at me and
stepped into Dad's bedroom. He came out blinking and wiping his
eyes.

That night, a rainswept Sunday, Dad opened his eyes and
looked at me. I was surprised by his sudden alertness.

"Hey, Opti," I said.

"I was just thinking about something. You should take Jack and
Maggie to Shinnecock instead of me. They would love that."

"We'll see."

"Good." He nodded, closed his eyes, and then opened them
again as if he'd remembered something.

"Is that rain?" he said.

"Yes."

"Don't worry. It'll be fine in the morning. Go kiss your wife."

I assured him I wasn't worried. I said I would kiss my wife.
These were the last words I heard my father say.

. . .

Several hours later, on a sunny March morning after days of soaking rain, I saw Mr. Andy, my father's gardener, who was from Cambodia, park his little truck out front. I walked out to tell him my father had died overnight.

Mr. Andy's English was no better than my French, but with tears welling above his tanned angular cheeks, he began telling me how my father and mother had given his family clothes and other things when they first resettled in America. He hugged me, then marched off to speak to my mother before running the aerator over the front yard.

Cars began pulling up on the street again, uncles were coming back, more casseroles and strangers arriving. My mother, after weeks of almost dazed inactivity, now sprang into management overdrive mode, bustling about the house with renewed Germanic energy. I was glad to see it—but I was nearly flayed.

I simply got in Old Blue and left. It was, as Dad had said it would be, a fine day in Carolina. I drove to a golf discount shop on Battleground Avenue and carried my father's old Wilson irons inside and asked the clerk if he could regrip them for me. He said he could have them for me by noon. Then I called my oldest friend, Pat McDaid. I'd avoided seeing Pat the entire time I'd been home, but I wanted to see him now.

Moreover, I wanted to play him in a golf match.

He picked me up, and we drove to a public course called Longview. It was not a good course—basically what we used to call a "goat farm," with fairways full of wild onions and roundtop greens you could practice your chipping on. But thanks to the crowds in town for the ACC tournament, all the better courses were booked solid. Longview could have been Augusta National for all I noticed or cared.

Pat's an excellent player who thrives on trying to beat me in any game. Our sports rivalry spanned thirty years. It started on the basketball court behind his father's house (a block from mine) when we were ten, spread to touch football games in the street, and somehow wound up on the golf course. For years I thrashed his brains out in golf. Then he started practicing and getting better. One day a few years ago he sank a miraculous ninety-foot downhill left-to-right breaker to beat me, à la Opti the Mystic, and fell to the ground laughing insanely. After that, our matches were forever too close to call. He was a brilliant Irishman full of blarney, and I dearly loved him.

I don't have a clue who won our match the day my father died. Pat swears he doesn't either. His own father was dying, and we talked about that and other things, I guess, though neither of us can recall what was said. The sun was warm, the grass was new, spring had come. It was a tolerable day, and Pat was a tolerable opponent, and that, under the circumstances, supplied all that I could reasonably have desired in the way of entertainment.

Dust to Dust

Thinking of his father, Curtis Strange broke down and wept when he won the U.S. Open.

On summer evenings as a child, Larry Mize used to practice chip shots in the front yard with his father, aiming to hit a narrow spot on the grass—eerily presaging the low chip shot he struck from an impossible lie many years later, to snatch a playoff victory in the Masters from Greg Norman.

Tom Watson sometimes heard his father's voice urging him to keep his head still during putts, while Nicklaus's father, an Ohio pharmacist, drilled into his son the importance of relentlessly practicing. Payne Stewart has two majors under his belt, but the tournament that means the most to him, he'll tell you, is his first win at Quad Cities in 1982—because his father Bill, who died of cancer a short time later, was there to witness it. Mark O'Meara is on record as saying his happiest moment on a golf course came when he won Pebble Beach with his father as an amateur playing partner. With Peter Jacobsen, golf was a family afffair. "Everybody played and competed with everybody else," he recalls. "Gosh, it was fun." Guy Boros's late father Julius put the club in his son's hand at about age ten, telling him simply "to always have fun." Guy was leading a tournament in Texas when he learned his father had collapsed and died of a heart attack. Guy played on, as his father would have wanted, holding back tears. He failed to win the tournament but made a lot of admirers.

Ben Crenshaw's father Charlie, an Austin lawyer, took Ben to see Harvey Penick when Ben was six. Penick told Ben to "go knock the ball around just to see if you like it." He did. "I regard that time as the nicest time of my life," Crenshaw once told me.

It is surprising, over the years, how often the mention of a parent has worked its way into my interviews with the world's greatest players. Every player's story was different, but somewhere in the narrative a parent seemed to play the critical role of bringing the child to the game. The stories of sons and daughters who followed their fathers into the game are as commonplace and compelling as the game itself—the Palmers, the Nicklauses, the Watsons, the Floyds, the Stocktons, the Loves.

Glenna Vare followed her dad to the golf course one summer morning in Providence, picking up an old spoon and giving it a swing. Her first drive, at age eleven, flew a hundred yards. Her father saw something and encouraged it. LPGA Hall of Famer Joanne Carner's father did odd jobs around a country club just so his daughter could follow her dream of being a great amateur player; she became a legend in the process. Ditto Patty Berg, Louise Suggs, Betsy Rawls—a supportive parent brought them to the golf course and said just *play*. Nancy Lopez, Betsy King, and Beth Daniel tell similar tales. Patty Sheehan's papa Bobo used to help lay out a makeshift course for his sons and daughter to play on around the family house in Vermont, and all these years later he can still be seen tagging faithfully after his daughter's large, admiring galleries.

One night in Tampa several years ago I was having dinner with Paul Azinger and his father Ralph. Azinger was finishing a year in which he'd won his first three tournaments. His star seemed so bright. When Ralph excused himself and left the table for a moment, Azinger leaned across the table and said to me: "That man is the reason I'm here. The way he thinks. The way he lives. We haven't always seen eye to eye, but you know what? Someday I hope I can show the world I'm half as courageous as he is."

Eight years later, when Azinger's cancer blew a hole in his life, he did. He withdrew from the tour for months, underwent aggressive treatment, and came back with a deeper appreciation of his gift in his life.

On my first working interview for *Golf Magazine,* I stood on the practice range at Sea Island Golf Club watching Davis Love III hit moon shots to the back of the range. I'd never seen a more powerful swing, a swing he learned from his father Davis Love, Jr., a protégé of Harvey Penick and one of the most respected teachers of the game. Perhaps no modern rookie had a finer pedigree or more promise than Davis Three. Two days before he was born in 1964, his father nearly won the Masters.

"When I was about eight or nine," Davis explained later, as we walked together back from the range, "I went to my father and told him I wanted to be a professional golfer. The thing is, he never pushed the game on me. I wanted to do it because of *him.* He said if I really wanted to do that, he would help me do it. We started out. He would show me things and write it all down. He would give me these yellow-legal-pad notes with his thoughts about what I should do. It drove me kind of crazy at times, all those notes, but there's no question in my mind that my father's love and faith brought me here."

Life separates us too soon. That's what my father had said on the road to Scotland.

In the days following Opti's funeral, as I got back to the busy routines of my own work and family life, I thought perhaps my father and I had luckily escaped this fate. Perhaps we hadn't been separated *too soon*. After all, we'd had forty years to be together, two and a half decades to play as golf pals, and the golf trip of a lifetime to finish up the day. As far back as I could remember, there wasn't a moment when I doubted my father's love, a moment when he failed to express his love or help me when I asked for it.

This was far more than most men get, I told myself. We'd gone the full distance, finished the round, and said what needed saying. After a life rich with memories—just the kind of life Aunt Augusta would have admired—my father had died a peaceful death at the same age as Buddha, seeing in the afterlife, perhaps, a beloved pasture from his childhood or—who knows?—a beautiful golf course waiting with an open first tee.

For a while, these things sustained me and gave me strength. Life got back to normal. In many respects it even got better. For our tenth anniversary my wife gave me a beautiful concert-quality classical guitar, and I played my first recital in twenty years for my daughter's first-grade class—Bach. Lennon and McCartney. All the big guys. Near the end, one small-fry with Coke-bottle spectacles looked up and asked if I "knew anything really good." I played a few Barney tunes and brought down the house.

For that same anniversary, I sent my overworked working wife to one of the most exclusive health spas in the world. You could have made two trips around Scotland for what it cost her to be fed gerbil-sized portions of inedible vegetarian goo for five straight days, force-marched into the hills by an aerobics lunatic, water-cannoned on the bum, and therapeutically pounded upon by muscular people with suspicious foreign accents. It was her idea of heaven.

The spring that tentatively showed itself in Carolina finally crept north to Maine. My club traditionally opens around the time of the Masters golf tournament. After the long layoff, I went out with my regular pals, the hockey coach and the college sports director, and shot 75 in my very first outing, as if I could do it any day in my sleep. They haggled about what they saw new in my game. But then, Terry and Sid use any excuse to haggle with each other on the golf course.

Sid essayed that I was striking the ball better. Terry was sure it was my putting. As usual, I opted to stay out of the debate.

My game *was* slightly different. I had a new set of clubs and I'd gone back to a traditional heel-shafted blade putter like the one I'd used as a kid—and I was also trying once again to lead with the left hand and putt like a kid. It seemed to be making more balls mysteriously roll into the hole. I explained this to Sid and Terry. Terry said he thought I was also more relaxed on the golf course than he'd seen me in quite a while. Ever the coach, he said my "game head" was "really where it should be. You don't seem to be rushing the shots as much."

"You're crazy, Terry," Sid snapped happily at him. "It's his new irons. Anybody can see that."

We toddled off down the fairway of a brand-new season with them arguing like old times. It felt good.

The truth is, you love *and* hate to see a regular golf pal start to play a whole lot better, and if you're the player who's striking the ball better, you never want to examine these things too closely. My scores began to inch down scarily. I began to regularly shoot in the mid-to-high 70s and made a quick trip to England in which I fired rounds 73, 72, 71 on three pretty good tracks and scored eagles on consecutive days. Like Bobby Jones, I considered walking away from the game while I was hot.

Back home, a couple of the old stags up on the club's grill deck predicted I might actually be a factor in the club championship, come summer. Winning the club championship would have been a great way to say good-bye to Opti, I told myself, and then I realized we'd already said good-bye in the best way possible and I really had nothing more to prove.

Writer Peter Dobereiner once described golf as life's greatest pretend drama. Had I really found some missing element of my game, or was it just one of those mysterious things that happen only in a pretend drama like golf?

I was still trying to figure that out on Masters Sunday, when my daughter and son surprised me by asking to go play golf. I wanted to stay home and watch the Masters finish because (a) it's my job and I get paid princely sums to do it, and (b) two players I greatly admire, Davis Love and Ben Crenshaw, were neck and neck coming down the stretch.

Instead, I took my kids to the golf course. It was late afternoon when we got there, but the air was unseasonably warm and inviting for early April in Maine. Not surprisingly, not many players were about. Jack saw the gas carts sitting by the clubhouse and begged to take one, and Maggie quickly joined the beggar's chorus. They politely endured my Sophoclean lecture on "The Virtues of Walking in Golf," then pleaded shamelessly again for a riding cart. Dickie, the assistant pro, agreed to let us take one but demanded we stick to the back nine, which was drier.

We drove to the tenth tee. I love the back nine at my club. It's the original nine of the club, which was laid out the same year as Murdo Macpherson's magnificent Machrie.

I struck a decent drive off ten and agreed to let Jack drive the cart for the first hole. He popped onto the seat, jammed down the accelerator, and nearly tossed both his sister and me out onto the ground. We careened wildly for a moment or two until I could get a hand clamped safely onto the steering wheel. Jack grinned at me. "I love golf," he declared. And then, a few yards farther along, he added: "When does hockey begin again, Dad?"

For years I'd hoped I might raise the next Tom Watson or Johnny Miller. Perhaps the next Bobby Orr was really more like it.

If only to humor his old man, though, Jack took his "inside club" up onto the tenth green and putted out the first hole, then picked up his ball and scampered back to preserve his driver's rights behind the wheel. Maggie made a nice little chip shot from off the fringe that rolled to within ten feet of the cup. I congratulated her. She picked up her putter and walked over to her ball, looked once at the hole, then rapped a ball that nearly went into the cup. I congratulated her again. We high-fived and went to the next hole.

As we played, a couple things kept crowding into my head, distracting me from the pleasure of the moment. I was naturally wondering about the Masters, a tournament everybody in the golf world expected Davis Love to win someday. A few days before, Harvey Penick, Ben Crenshaw's longtime teacher and Love's own father's mentor, had passed away in Austin. I knew emotions were running very high down in Augusta, Georgia, that afternoon. I only hoped my video recorder was properly running, too.

I was also troubled by a dream I'd just had. In it, I'd forgotten the sound of my own father's voice. I woke up in a fierce sweat and realized I'd been weeping. Unable to go back to sleep, I sat in a chair by the window, struck by the powerful reality that I would never again be able simply to pick up the phone and call my father and hear him laugh and say he was going to pin my ears back. I remem-

ber sitting in that chair thinking I was no longer a *son*. Bob had lost
Bing.

It was grief pouring forth, though it took me a while to fully
recognize and accept that. Sometime after the dream, at the suggestion of a friend, I actually went and sat in a quiet upstairs room with
a friendly family sociologist named Herman, a fellow southerner
who shared my passion for the frozen North. We talked for several
weeks about childhood, marriage, and fathers. We talked about Kristin and golf, guitars and politics, death and St. Andrews. We talked
about how mothers give us life and fathers help define us. He helped
me see that a man is never finished being a son—and he never leaves
the influence of his father's life behind. In some ways, he helped me
see that it is more difficult to say good-bye to a great father than a
poor one.

During our last session he said, "Before we wind this up, I'd like
to come back to your father."

"Really?" I said. "Wasn't that the point of all this exercise—to
neatly dispose of him forever?"

Herman smiled. "He probably would have preferred it that way.
It strikes me that he gave you something very useful, but you may
not even be aware of it yet."

"What's that?"

"A gift for letting go. He showed you the value of accepting life
and the importance of letting it go. When it's time, you'll do it.
You'll hear his voice again."

Somewhere a couple blocks away, the Congregational church bell
was tolling the noon hour. We stood and shook hands. Herman
suggested I think of making some final act of closure that Opti
would have appreciated.

I thanked Herman for his help. I still couldn't hear my father's
voice, but I walked out feeling better.

·   ·   ·

None of this was apparent to me on that unnaturally warm Masters Sunday with my kids, though. The pain of the dream was still too fresh. And yet something happened that had Opti's invisible hands all over it.

We played a couple holes and skipped a couple holes. Jack seemed to be confusing golf with formula car racing. Maggie, on the other hand, dropped several lengthy putts that had her glowing and me beaming. I told her she reminded me of her grandfather, "the putting machine," and said she might be the next Glenna Vare.

"Who's *that*?" she demanded.

"I'll tell you sometime."

Something about the fine afternoon and being away from the world with my kids began to soothe me. Maybe it was the angle of the light or the riding cart and the general emptiness of the course that seemed to recall that wonderful day at Muirfield with my father and Archie Baird.

Something amazing, at any rate, happened, when Maggie and I walked off the sixteenth green to where Jack the chauffeur sat impatiently with his lead foot poised over the accelerator. We climbed aboard, and he nudged me gently in the ribs. He smiled up at me and suggested that I scoot over. I asked him why, thinking maybe I was cramping his driving style.

"For Granddaddy," he answered matter-of-factly.

I looked at him.

"What?"

"For Granddaddy," he repeated calmly. "He's riding with us."

I stared at my five-year-old son, unable to speak for a moment. Then his sister let out one of her infectious belly laughs, and I laughed, too.

"Jack's such a goof," she said.

"Do you believe Granddaddy's riding with us?" I asked her.

She looked at Jack and then at me and then grinned. A child's belief is so strong, you can almost feel it. She was missing four teeth.

"Sure," she replied, as if that much should be obvious even to a dolt like me. "And you know what else?"

"What?"

"You sound like Granddaddy. Especially when you sneeze."

"*Really?*" I said.

"Uh-huh."

Slipping my arms around both my children, I felt a powerful stinging in my eyes. I couldn't yet hear my father's voice, but I could hear his words. Long ago on a golf course that was no longer there, he'd told me to open my eyes and see the glory of the world. *The way to heaven,* he said, *is heaven.*

At that same moment about twelve hundred miles away, Ben Crenshaw was doubling over as his tears of joy flowed. He'd won his second Masters, beating Davis Love by two strokes in a finish that, under the circumstances, seemed heaven-sent. Love's effort had been nothing short of heroic, too. Only three players in history had played better than his 275 total. Their names were Hogan, Nicklaus, and Floyd.

I confess I wasn't thinking about the powerful events happening down in Georgia, though. I was thinking about . . . . well, finally, nothing but *this.* It felt wonderful.

"Okay, pal," I said. "Let 'er rip."

And with that, we careened wildly down the fairway.

Life, Thoreau said, is a great circle sailing.

Three months after my father's death, I found myself once again hurrying down from the Scores to the Old Course with my golf bag slung on my back. I was back in the Old Grey Toon to gather material for an essay about the upcoming Open championship, talking with people like Fred Lockhart and the Links Trust Management about the passions and politics of locals in the birthplace of the game.

I decided to go out late so I could loiter on the course, and the starter was kind enough to match me up with the final group of the day, an unlikely trio of lively Australians. One of them was dressed like Crocodile Dundee, complete with rolled-up jeans and working boots. Another was a budding golf writer named Paul. The third was a physician on vacation with his wife. Amazingly, none of the Aussies had ever met until arriving at the Old Course. Golf makes us members of the same big nation.

As we teed up under the starter's watchful eye, Crocodile Dundee leaned over and admitted to me that he hadn't been on a golf course in ten years; he'd lied about his handicap to get on the Old Course. "Hope I don't top the bloody thing," he said.

I assured him if he did, it would be okay. Topping a ball on the first tee of the Old Course was one of golf's greatest traditions. It was the widest fairway and toughest opening shot in all of golf. Ex-presidents routinely topped balls here. So did pros. Ditto us mortals. There was something special in the air here, I said, that made topping your drive a rewarding experience. Also, the hole is mercifully short.

"Right," Crocodile said. "But what if I miss it completely, mate?"

He didn't. We both played an amusingly erratic round, firing shots all over the place. Paul the golf writer played best, going out to the Eden estuary in 41 before blistering the home march with a succession of brilliant birdies and pars. I settled in to play my usual humdrum Old Course game, a par here, a triple bogey there, trying not to think too much about what was coming up. Snead's 75 would have to fall another day.

As we approached the Road Hole bunker on the seventeenth

hole, I pulled a small blue velvet satchel out of my golf bag and began undoing the silken cords. The others watched solemnly. I'd warned them what was coming—my real reason for playing in the final group of the day. "You guys look like the three other horsemen of the Apocalypse," I said to them. "Please show a little proper disrespect." I told them my old man had said golf is a game that made you smile. "So please smile, *damnit.*"

As they smiled, I slowly scattered my father's cremated ashes around the Road Hole bunker and dumped some into the sand itself.

Lacking Opti's gift of prophecy, I couldn't have known then that in a few weeks' time Arnold Palmer would pause on the little stone bridge over Swilcan Burn and wave good-bye to his faithful army, marking his final appearance at the British Open. Likewise, nobody could have fathomed that big John Daly would make a miraculous shot from the depths of that same Road Hole bunker that was even more remarkable than my old man's—allowing Wild Thing to win the 124th British Open and burying a number of his own ghosts in the process. I would think of Freddie Jupp and imagine her glee.

No, I couldn't have known of these wondrous things to come. Nor even guessed at them.

All I knew was that a circle in my life had finally been completed, and perhaps, as I felt that day with my kids on Masters Sunday, another larger one began.

My new Aussie mates and I finished the Road Hole with bogeys and walked to the eighteenth tee. I don't remember a lot of talking. The darkness had caught up to us. We teed up and finished the hole and shook hands. I can't for the life of me remember what I scored on the hole because I either decided not to or forgot to write it down. In any case, I was definitely in NATO.

I walked slowly up the Scores, with a mind that was remarkably at ease for the first time in a very long time. Then I decided to walk back and just look at the Old Course in the darkness.

Halfway down the hill, a boy passed headed the other way, a fellow late finisher. He was maybe eleven or twelve, hurrying home to dinner with his head bent and his bag on his back. He looked up as we passed, his clubs softly clicking. I thought of myself headed home from Green Valley. I thought of Jack maybe someday playing here with his old man.

"Did you shoot a good one?" I asked.

"Not so good, sir," he admitted. "Me driver's a wee bit off."

"That's okay," I said. "Enjoy it. The game ends too soon, you know."

"Right. Thanks."

He walked on and I walked, and then I stopped. That's when I realized I'd heard it—my father's voice.

I smiled. Opti was back.

James Dodson is a contributing editor and award-winning columnist for *Golf Magazine*. He is also the golf correspondent for *Departures Magazine*. His work has appeared in many national publications including *Gentlemen's Quarterly*, *Travel and Leisure*, *Outside Magazine*, *Reader's Digest*, and *Town and Country*. A former senior writer for the *Atlanta Journal-Constitution Sunday Magazine* and *Yankee Magazine*, he is a past winner of the William Allen White Award for Public Affairs, reporting from the University of Kansas Journalism School. He also won the Golf Writers of America Award for his columns in 1995. He lives in Maine.